THE NOTION OF AN IDEAL AUDIENCE IN LEGAL ARGUMENT

Law and Philosophy Library

VOLUME 45

THE NOTION
OF AN
IDEAL AUDIENCE
IN
LEGAL ARGUMENT

by

GEORGE C. CHRISTIE

Duke University,
Durham,
North Carolina, U.S.A.

KLUWER ACADEMIC PUBLISHERS
DORDRECHT / BOSTON / LONDON

Library of Congress Cataloging-in-Publication Data

Christie, George C.
  The notion of an ideal audience in legal argument / by George C. Christie.
    p. cm. -- (Law and philosophy library ; v. 45)
  Includes bibliographical references and index.
  ISBN 0-7923-6283-7 (HB : alk. paper)
  1. Law--Methodology. 2. Reasoning. I. Title. II. Series.

  K213 .C487 2000
  340'.11--dc21

00-035745

ISBN 0-7923-6283-7

Published by Kluwer Academic Publishers,
P.O. Box 17, 3300 AA Dordrecht, The Netherlands.

Sold and distributed in North, Central and South America
by Kluwer Academic Publishers,
101 Philip Drive, Norwell, MA 02061, U.S.A.

In all other countries, sold and distributed
by Kluwer Academic Publishers,
P.O. Box 322, 3300 AH Dordrecht, The Netherlands.

Printed on acid-free paper

Printed in the Netherlands.

To the memory
of
Chaïm Perelman

TABLE OF CONTENTS

PREFACE

As the dedication of this book suggests, the genesis of this book arises from my association with Chaïm Perelman. Because I was one of the few Americans to comment on his *Traité de l'argumentation: la nouvelle rhétorique*, before it was translated into English, I was invited to a conference celebrating the translation of that monumental work into English that was held in August 1970 in Santa Barbara, California at the Center for the Study of Democratic Institutions, which was then under the directorship of the late Robert M. Hutchins. From that beginning, Professor Perelman and I developed a strong and warm friendship which was cemented when Professor Perelman and his wife, Fela, came to North Carolina in 1979 as a fellow at the National Humanities Center. I enjoyed the occasions on which I was able to participate in the activities of the *Centre National de Recherches de Logique* which had been established, under Professor Perelman's aegis, in Belgium. A trip to Brussels was always something to which I looked forward. Since Professor Perelman's sudden and untimely death in January 1984, shortly after he had been singularly honored by being made a baron by King Baudouin, I have benefited greatly from my participation in the programs of the Perelman Foundation which was established through the generosity and efforts of Baronne Fela Perelman; a remarkable woman in her own right who has now sadly also passed away.

One of the aspects of Professor Perelman's work that I found most intriguing was his frequent references to the "universal audience." It is a source of great regret that Professor Perelman did not develop this notion further during his life time, particularly in the context of legal argumentation. For me, the notion of a universal audience has proved to be a very fruitful one. As will be seen in Chapter 2 of this book, it helped me to see how the predictive theories of law of the legal realists were much less incompatible with the positivist theories of people such as H. L. A. Hart than has been commonly thought. Over the course of my academic career, I have devoted myself to the study of subjects such as the nature of legal reasoning, the place of principle in the doctrinal study and development of the law, the scope of the defense of necessity, and that most difficult subject, the scope of the discretion to be allowed to inferior judicial decisionmakers. I came to see that these and other perennial topics of legal theory, which otherwise often seemed to be fairly discreet subjects of inquiry, could be seen to have much in common if one were prepared to recognize that legal argument, like all argument, is addressed to an audience, and like all serious argument, ultimately addressed to a universal or ideal audience. The task to which this book is devoted is to flesh out the notion of a universal or ideal audience into something more concrete and explore how different conceptions of this universal or ideal audience influence legal argument and underlie many basic disagreements at both the theoretical and practical levels.

In the preparation of this book, I have profited from the generous help of many people. I should like to acknowledge expressly the outstanding assistance of the reference librarians of the Duke University Law School Library and of my two student research assistants, Neal Gordon and Adam Hoffman. To my two former students, Erika King and Michael Mirande, who, despite the heavy demands of their professional lives, read and commented on the entire manuscript in draft, I owe a special debt of gratitude. Finally, I should like to thank Ms. Peggy House, of the Duke Law School staff, without whose assistance in preparing and formatting the text, this book would never have seen the light of day.

George C. Christie
Durham, NC USA
January 2000

CHAPTER 1

INTRODUCTION

The late Chaïm Perelman reminded us that all speech is directed towards an audience.[1] Perelman, of course, was primarily concerned with the techniques of argumentation used in a public arena, but it does no injustice to his basic thesis to take the notion of "speech" in its broadest sense so as to include within it any mental activity which is carried on in something like a verbal form. This would, of course, include what Perelman called "self-deliberation" or indeed anything that we would be prepared to call thinking. It is hard to imagine how we could think without some sort of language that would serve as the medium of our thinking.[2] The language could be purely symbolic, such as would be the case if we were thinking in a mathematical idiom or in a musical notation. If we are sane our thinking follows the same patterns and logical structures as does our conscious verbal speech. We are all familiar with thinking out loud, and nobody thinks that thinking out loud is somehow different from just thinking. Certainly when we try to describe our thoughts, we can only do so in a verbal form. Indeed, there is the even more basic point captured by Charles Taylor's observation that "[t]o study human beings is to study beings who only exist in, or are partly constituted by, a certain language."[3] Obviously then, if all speech is directed towards an audience and if thinking is a type of speech act, even our thoughts are audience directed. But who is the audience to whom our thoughts are addressed and is there more than one such audience? Is this audience or are these audiences the same as those we address when we are actually speaking to other people?

Let us begin trying to answer these questions by first discussing who is the audience of a person's ordinary speech. At one level the answer seems obvious. The audience consists of the person or persons we are

---

[1] C. Perelman and L. Olbrechts-Tyteca, THE NEW RHETORIC: A TREATISE OF ARGUMENTATION §§ 2-11 (pp. 13-47) (J. Wilkinson and P. Weaver transl. 1969), originally published as *Traité de l'argumentation* (1958) and hereinafter cited as THE NEW RHETORIC. The section references are the same in the English and French versions; the page references are to the English translation.

[2] *See* B. Aune, KNOWLEDGE, MIND, AND NATURE 177-223 (1967).

[3] C. Taylor, SOURCES OF THE SELF 34-35 (1989).

trying to persuade or inform or amuse or impress or mislead, etc. But a moments reflection shows that the problem is more complicated than that because we are often mistaken as to the nature or our audience. Even if we know our audience very well, say we are speaking to our spouse of twenty years, there are limits to the extent to which we can completely assimilate ourselves to the audience. To some extent there will always be some element of construction in our notion of an audience, and we are sometimes dimly aware of this even in our most intimate relationships. We may for example be appealing to what we think or hope is the "finer" side of our spouse or to our conception of what, based on our previous conversations or arguments, is likely to appeal to or infuriate our spouse in the present circumstances.

As our audience extends to more and more people, and as this wider audience consists of more and more people with whom we have no personal relations, it becomes more and more obvious that our notion of the audience whom we are addressing is in large part a construct. It is a construct that, to be sure, has a rational foundation, but nonetheless is still in large part a construct. How many times have we felt that we had "misjudged our audience," even an audience that we felt that we knew quite well? To the extent that we have succeeded in our objective of persuading or impressing or misleading or amusing our audience, the concept of an audience that we have constructed has proved adequate to our task.[4] That is the most that we can hope for.

In our everyday life we adjust to our audience instinctively, particularly if we are functioning in our native environment. As George Herbert Mead long ago pointed out, we develop our sense of self out of our interactions with others.[5] We take the attitudes of other human beings towards society at large and towards each other into account in organizing our experience

---

[4] As Perelman put it, "The essential consideration for the speaker who has set himself the task of persuading concrete individuals is that his construction of the audience should be adequate to the occasion." THE NEW RHETORIC at § 4 (p. 19).

[5] G. Mead, MIND SELF, & SOCIETY 135-236 (1934). The point was well expressed more recently by Charles Taylor. "One is a self only among other selves. A self can never be described without reference to those who surround it." C. Taylor, *op. cit. supra*, note 3, at 35.

and in dealing with the world around us.[6] As we become socialized in a particular society we come to internalize the social practices and attitudes of that society, which becomes for us, in Mead's words, " the generalized other;" and "it is in this form that the social process or community enters as a determining factor into the individual's thinking" and controls the conduct of its members.[7]

Sometimes we are particularly conscious that we are addressing an audience, as when we are making a presentation or when we are speaking to a large number of people, even if only informally. Nevertheless, even in these situations, if we are merely trying to inform our audience of some matter of fact, rather than using factual statements as part of an attempt to persuade it or to inspire it or to mislead it, the need to focus on the nature of the audience at hand does not seem to be a pressing concern. Normally all we need is the assurance that we share a common language with our audience and that our audience can understand our accent. Our audience is more impersonal and abstract than it would be if we were trying to persuade. But sometimes, even when we have not set out to persuade our audience but only to describe some state of affairs, it will become apparent that our audience has doubts about our credibility. We have informed our audience in the sense of having imparted information to it, but in another sense we have not succeeded in informing it. When this is the case informing becomes another form of persuasion in which our concept of our audience, although still a construct, will become less abstract and impersonal.

The reason that the notion of an audience is more abstract and thus less present in our minds when we are relating a matter of fact and have no reason to believe that we are being misunderstood by our listeners or that our credibility is in dispute is that we are "telling the truth" and truth, after all, is truth. As Bernard Williams has said "what anyone truly believes must be consistent with what others truly believe, and anyone deliberating about the truth is committed, by the nature of the process, to the aim of a

---

[6] In reliance on Mead's work, this point is well developed in C. Taylor, THE ETHICS OF AUTHENTICITY 32-34 (1992).

[7] G. Mead, *op. cit. supra* note 5, at 155.

consistent set of beliefs, one's own and others'."[8] Here we have the nub of what Perelman called the "universal audience."[9] It is the audience of what George Herbert Mead called "universal discourse," that is discourse directed at what Mead variously called "rational society" or the "rational world."[10] Truth is what we and the ideal audience that we have constructed, an audience that consists of ourselves and all other seekers of truth, are prepared to accept. And when we think, we are addressing this same audience. No sane person sets out to lie to himself. Indeed to lie, whether to oneself or to others, presupposes that one is aware of the true state of affairs.

Admittedly, self-interest or passion can lead us to believe some strange things but, if we are to continue to hold these beliefs and at the same time preserve our sanity, we must persuade ourselves that these beliefs are true in the sense that they would be accepted as true by anyone similarly situated as we are. The fact that our views may be mistaken, and even our explicit recognition that our attempts to arrive at the truth may be unsuccessful, does not mean either that there is no such thing as truth or, more to the point of this book, that a belief that there is such a thing as truth, which should be the object of our endeavors, is not a material part of our human experience.

It is of course fashionable, in some circles, to assert that all knowledge is socially constructed and that the belief in objectivity in any form of discourse merely serves to hide from ourselves the fact that our view of even the physical world is not only something we arrive at in a social context but is actually nothing more than a reflection of the social power structures in which we live. The short answer to this argument is that, in their own lives, these people act as if they accept the findings of science. They have no hesitation in trusting their lives to air transportation or in relying on the word processing capabilities of computers for producing their articles and books. More to the point, in their daily lives they also seem to rely on universal concepts that are clearly surrogates for the sorts of universal notion with which this book is concerned. The work of people who maintain that truth is merely a construct and that there is no objective

---

[8] B. Williams, ETHICS AND THE LIMITS OF PHILOSOPHY 68 (1985).

[9] THE NEW RHETORIC at § 4 (pp. 19-23).

[10] G. Mead, *op. cit. supra* note 5, at 195.

knowledge is shot full of notions like "correct," or "valid," or "accurate," and of talk about "evidence" and "the probable results" of social action.[11]

This is a book on how the notion of an ideal audience influences practical reasoning and ultimately behavior, and particularly on how it influences both the style and substance of legal reasoning and even actually constrains the behavior of judges and other officials. The notion of an ideal audience, however, has more than a practical importance. It is also an important analytical tool that can help us make sense of certain philosophical and legal puzzles that are not otherwise easily explainable. I shall, in the next chapter, discuss two such instances—the first more general and philosophical, the second somewhat more narrow and legal—in which recognition of the fact that we all ultimately address an ideal or universal audience can lead us to a major increase in our theoretical understanding of important philosophical and legal issues. The remainder of the book will then be devoted to a discussion of how, on both a theoretical and practical level, the notion of an ideal audience figures in the day-to-day operation of legal systems. The nature of the ideal audiences that we construct will, for example, influence our views regarding the proper way to interpret constitutions, statutes, and treatises and whether we believe that the law in general, or at least particular portions of the law, must be organized around certain overriding general principles rather than simply recognized as the socially and politically acceptable result of a long historical process. As might be expected, and as we shall see in the course of our discussion, different legal systems will have different notions of what sorts of arguments would be acceptable to an ideal audience. It should also not be surprising, as shall be amply illustrated in the course of our discussion, that, even within a given legal system, the notion of an ideal audience that the participants in that legal system construct for themselves is not a static one. It will always, to some degree at least, be subject to change.

---

[11] This is the thrust of the criticism leveled by Jenny Teichman against Barbara Herrnstein Smith. *See* J. Teichman, *Substitutes for Truth*, THE NEW CRITERION, Dec. 1997, at 71, review of B. Herrnstein Smith, BELIEF AND RESISTANCE: DYNAMICS OF CONTEMPORARY INTELLECTUAL CONTROVERSY (1997).

CHAPTER 2

THE NOTION OF AN IDEAL AUDIENCE
AS AN ANALYTICAL TOOL

A. A General Philosophical Example—Illuminating the Power of Rhetoric

There is a passage towards the end of the monumental *Treatise of Human Nature*, in which Hume addressed himself to the question of how good government and human progress are at all possible. Hume started from two important premises: first, that men were naturally endowed with only limited altruism; and second, that they had a natural tendency to prefer short-run advantages, even at the expense of what was in their long-term interest. Given these assumptions, how was the material and social betterment of the human condition possible? To answer that question in the affirmative, Hume resorted to an ingenious expedient. He suggested that an affirmative answer was possible because in a well-functioning society, such as the Great Britain of his day, one could create a class of leaders and load them down with economic and social advantages, thereby creating a ruling class which had a short-term interest in maintaining the stability and proper functioning of society. Moreover, through this arrangement, one could do more than maintain the *status quo*. In Hume's own words:

But government extends farther its beneficial influence; and not contented to protect men in those conventions they make for their mutual interest, it often obliges them to make such conventions, and forces them to seek their own advantage, by a concurrence in some common end or purpose. There is no quality in human nature, which causes more fatal errors in our conduct, than that which leads us to prefer whatever is present to the distant and remote, and makes us desire objects more according to their situation than their intrinsic value. Two neighbors may agree to drain a meadow, which they possess in common; because 'tis easy for them to know each others mind; and each must perceive, that the immediate consequence of his failing in his part, is the abandoning the whole project. But 'tis very difficult, and indeed impossible, that a thousand persons shou'd agree in any such action; it being difficult for them to concert so complicated a design and still more difficult for them to execute it; while each seeks a pretext to free himself of the trouble and expence, and wou'd lay the whole burden on others. Political society easily remedies both these inconveniences. Magistrates find an immediate interest in the interest of any considerable part of their subjects. They need consult no body but themselves to form any scheme for the promoting of that interest. And as the failure of any one piece in the execution is connected, tho' not immediately, with the failure of the whole, they prevent that failure, because they find no interest in it, either immediate or remote. Thus bridges are built; harbours open'd; ramparts rais'd; canals form'd; fleets equip'd; and armies disciplin'd; every where, by the care of the government, which, tho' compos'd of men subject to all human infirmities, becomes, by one of the finest and most subtle inventions imaginable, a composition, which is, in some measure, exempted from all these infirmities.[1]

Hume makes a noble effort, but it is fairly clear that his solution to the question he has posed is unsatisfactory. For one thing, Hume has not told us how to identify the long-term interests of society. The most he has done is to show how the perceived short-term and intermediate-term interests of a substantial portion of the population can be translated into community goals. But what if the satisfaction of these interests is not in the long-term interest of society? More importantly, what if the short-term interest of the governing elite--such as, for example, their interest in retaining their offices and privileges--conflicts with the long-term interest of society? Every society, for example, has had its Watergate. And, if situations like Watergate are extreme instances, it would nevertheless be naive not to recognize that, if the prize is great enough, there are few indeed who would be above pandering, to some extent, to the short-term interest of substantial segments of the populace in order to win the prize.

Does this mean that, if we accept Hume's premises about human nature and the human condition, there is no room for optimism about the future of humanity? That whatever progress occurs is just a matter of chance? One can concede that what might be considered human progress is not altogether free from controversy, but most people would accept that the dramatic improvements in life expectancy in the Western world in the last century represent progress, and, more importantly for our purposes, not many people would refuse to acknowledge that a society in which slavery has been abolished and in which there is a positive commitment to social and legal equality regardless of race, sex or religion is a better society than one which has not committed itself to these goals. But, if Hume is right that we are naturally drawn to pursue our immediate, short-term interests, how was such improvement in the social condition possible?

Here is where a recognition of the powerful role played by notions of an ideal audience provides an important insight. I would submit that the

---

[1] D. Hume, A TREATISE OF HUMAN NATURE, BK. III, § vii at 538-39 (L. Selby-Biggs ed. 1888).

possibility of human progress, particularly in the area of social arrangements, lies in large part in man's power of speech, in the fact that man has a tendency to become trapped by his own rhetoric. Human beings are naturally given to pontification, that is to framing speech that is directed to an ideal or universal audience. It seems to be a function of human nature. Talk, of course, is easy when no significant practical interests are at stake. Sooner or later, however, we are confronted with factual situations which test our pontifications. To put the matter as concisely as possible, and in Human terms: For some of us more frequently than for others, but for almost all of us some of the time, the short-term interest in not appearing ridiculous by behaving inconsistently forces us, however reluctantly, to practice what we preach. I would suggest that the ending of slavery, and now of racial segregation and the inferior status of women, are instances where exactly this has happened. If we claim that human beings are created equal and purport to act on that basis in dealing with some groups of people, sooner or later the requirement of consistency will force us to behave accordingly in our dealings with other groups of people. Otherwise, we will have to admit openly that we are either irrational or, what on a moral level is an analogous notion, insincere.

This was the dilemma faced by Thomas Jefferson, who wrote those magnificent lines in the American Declaration of Independence:

We hold these truths to self evident: that all men are created equal; that they are endowed by their Creator with certain inalienable rights; that among these are life, liberty, and the pursuit of happiness.[2]

---

[2] As Jefferson actually drafted the Declaration the phrase "with certain inalienable rights" read instead "with inherent and inalienable rights," a form of expression which seems even more inconsistent with the recognition of slavery. THE LIFE AND SELECTED WRITINGS OF THOMAS JEFFERSON 22 (Mod. Lib. ed. A. Koch & W. Peden 1944) [hereinafter cited as LIFE AND SELECTED WRITINGS]. Indeed, in a portion of his draft completely excised by the Continental Congress, Jefferson berated George III because:

> He has waged cruel war against human nature itself, violating its most sacred rights of life and liberty in the persons of a distant people who never offended him, captivating and carrying them into slavery in another hemisphere, or to incur miserable death in their transportation hither. This piratical warfare, the opprobrium of **INFIDEL** powers, is the warfare of the **CHRISTIAN** king of Great Britain. Determined to

It would be hard to maintain that Jefferson did not believe in what he was saying. He was clearly speaking to an ideal audience that was as close as one could come to Perelman's "universal audience." But Jefferson, of course, owned a substantial number of slaves throughout his entire adult life. He was well aware of the contradiction between the ringing words of the Declaration and the social practice of his time, particularly in his beloved Virginia. It was a constant source of intellectual embarrassment for him, which he sought to alleviate by accepting the justice and inevitability of the eventual abolition of slavery,[3] by recognizing how impractical it would be to abolish slavery immediately in a society where the ownership of slaves represented such a substantial portion of the total wealth of the community,[4] and by convincing himself that, in some important characteristics, black people were inferior to whites, such as in a capacity for poetry or in the appreciation of painting and sculpture.[5]   The discomforting embarrassment felt by Jefferson was felt by others and the rationalizations grew less and less convincing. It is hard to believe that, even without a civil war, slavery would not have been abolished in the United States before the end of the nineteenth century, as it had been earlier

---

keep open a market where **MEN** should be bought and sold, he has prostituted his negative for suppressing every legislative attempt to prohibit or to restrain this execrable commerce.   And that this assemblage of horrors might want no fact of distinguished die, he is now exciting those very people to rise in arms among us, and to purchase that liberty of which he has deprived them, by murdering the people on whom he also obtruded them: thus paying off former crimes committed against the **LIBERTIES** of one people, with crimes which he urges them to commit against the **LIVES** of another.

Id. At 25-26.

[3] *See id.* at 278-79, 698-99.

[4] *See* F. Brodie, AN INTIMATE HISTORY 466 (1974); D. Malone, JEFFERSON AND THE ORDEAL OF LIBERTY 208-09 (1962) (this is volume III of Malone's JEFFERSON AND HIS TIME). A much cited statement by Captain Edmund Bacon, Jefferson's overseer for over 20 years, is contained in H. Pierson, JEFFERSON AT MONTICELLO: THE PRIVATE LIFE OF THOMAS JEFFERSON 110-11 (1862).

[5] LIFE AND SELECTED WRITINGS at 258-62. For this reason Jefferson believed that, after emancipation, the former Negro slaves should be transported to a distant place where they could live among themselves and not come in contact with white society. *Id.* at 262.

in the century in the British Empire and as it was well before the end of the century by all the other European nations and their former colonies in the new world.[6]

The current rapid change in the status of women provides an excellent contemporary illustration of the power of broad rhetorical expressions—obviously appeals to an ideal audience—to serve as the engine for social changes whose possible ultimate ramifications were clearly not envisaged at the outset. A brief description of how the status of women changed in one prominent American institution of higher education is very instructive. When Yale University first seriously considered admitting women undergraduates in 1966 and explored the possibility of a merger with Vassar College, a proposal which was ultimately rejected by the Vassar trustees, the thinking at Yale was that women undergraduates should be assigned to a coordinate college with its own faculty and curriculum but with cross-registration with Yale.[7] This was the tack that planning took even after the failure to reach agreement with Vassar. In the words of the *Yale Alumni Magazine* in December 1967 (quoting President Kingman Brewster): "[t]he value of the coordinate relationship as opposed to admitting women to Yale is that it allows a university to 'educate women not as a direct by-product of educating men.' Because most women 'do not plan to go on to advanced study after receiving their baccalaureates,' their curriculum could be 'less departmental, more problem oriented and more divisional.'"[8] Within a year, however, Yale adopted a plan to admit 250 freshmen and 250 upper-classmen, a total of 500 women, as full members of Yale College.[9] Having passed that hurdle, the next question was the percentage of women. At first 20 percent was suggested, then 40 percent.[10] The outcome, of course, was a commitment to a sex-blind institution, even

---

[6] Some of the nineteenth century process of abolishing slavery, particularly in the Western Hemisphere, including the colonies of European powers, is described in H. Thomas, THE SLAVE TRADE: THE HISTORY OF THE ATLANTIC SLAVE TRADE 1440-1870 (1997), at 786-90.

[7] YALE ALUMNI MAGAZINE, Dec. 1967, at 18; N.Y. Times. Nov. 21, 1967, at 1, col. 5.

[8] YALE ALUMNI MAGAZINE, Dec. 1967, at 18. *See also* N.Y. Times, Nov. 21, 1967, at 1, col. 5.

[9] *See* N.Y. Times, Nov. 15, 1968, at 1, col. 1.

[10] *See id.*, Dec. 11, 1972, at 43, col. 1.

if that meant breaking what many Yale alumni understood to be a commitment that, however many women were admitted, there would be no decrease in the number of male undergraduates at Yale.[11] Given the appeals to universal values with which college presidents and other educators addressed the "concerned" students of the sixties, could there have been any doubt as to the eventual result even if the individual speech makers did not clearly appreciate what they were committing themselves to?

As these examples illustrate, the power of rhetoric lies in the circumstance that we cannot escape the fact that the ideal audiences we are addressing, when we are talking about truth or justice, are characterized by demands for universality and consistency. That our concept of rationality, as well as even the possibility of human communication and of purposeful human activity, depends on a belief in and a commitment to consistency is self-evident. This is not of course to denigrate the value of creativity and innovation but, however serendipitous a creative insight or discovery might be, it achieves its true value by being integrated into the existing body of thought or by forcing us to construct a new intellectual framework with which to organize our world.[12]

Of course we are also all familiar with the abuses that have resulted from the confluence of the human tendency to pontificate and the human need at least to appear consistent. These abuses are typically the result of focusing on a spurious semantic consistency at the expense of all substantive considerations; that is at the expense of what one might loosely call the underlying logic of the situation. For example, there will always be arguments made that, since the United States Congress can make no laws

---

[11] *See id.,* June 3, 1973, § 1, at 39, col. 1. The Harvard Faculty of Arts and Sciences subsequently adopted a plan to unify Harvard and Radcliffe and the implementation of a sex-blind admissions policy to begin with the Class of 1980 (which entered Harvard in the Fall of 1976). 1975 HARVARD ALMANAC, at 7. Since 1972, of course, all American public institutions of higher education, receiving federal assistance, and all such private institutions, *except* private undergraduate institutions, are obliged to institute sex-blind admissions policies. 20 U.S.C. § 1681(a).

[12] If any citation is necessary, *see* T. Kuhn, THE STRUCTURE OF SCIENTIFIC REVOLUTIONS (1962). In the process of reconstructing his intellectual framework, it is of course also sometimes the case that one ends up by having a different view of what his "world" really is, but that is a different matter.

restricting speech or the press, it cannot tax the profits of newspapers.[13] And then there is the boy in *Tristram Shandy* who argued with his father that he was entitled to sleep with his grandmother. "'You lay, Sir, with my mother' . . . 'why may not I lie with yours.'"[14] But as Emerson said, it is not consistency but a foolish consistency which is the hobgoblin of little minds.[15] Nonetheless, we must not forget that sometimes people who argue in good faith may be so overwhelmed by the need to be consistent that, in order to avoid cognitive dissonance, they come to believe as true some pretty strange things, and these odd beliefs may even ultimately affect how their concept of the ideal audience becomes instantiated in practice. This is a point which will occasionally resurface as our discussion proceeds.

Historically, the commitment to consistency as a practical concept has been shown nowhere more clearly than in the law. Consistency is a quality expected by the audiences, both real and ideal, that are addressed by judges. Even dishonest judges are obliged to take these expectations into consideration. All these are again matters to which we shall have occasion to return as the discussion proceeds.

---

[13] In Associated Press v. NLRB, 301 U.S. 103 (1937), it was argued that the National Labor Relations Act could not constitutionally be applied to cover editorial personnel of the AP. The Court summarily rejected the argument. The petitioner relied on Grosjean v. American Press Co., 297 U.S. 233 (1936), where the Court struck down a Louisiana tax on newspapers with a circulation of over 20,000, but the Court in *Grosjean* specifically declared that "[t]he tax here involved is bad not because it takes money from the pockets of appellees." *Id.* at 250. Rather, it was because it was specifically aimed at newspaper circulation. *See also* Mabee v. White Plains Publishing Co., 327 U.S. 178 (1946) (Fair Labor Standards Act may be applied to newspapers). In 1971, Senator Cranston suggested that wage and price controls could not be applied to newspapers, broadcasters, and other media. Senators Hart and Packwood, among others, disputed his contention. *See* 117 CONG. REC. 43,510-20 (1971). An amendment proposed by Senator Cranston to incorporate his views in the pending legislation eventually failed. *Id.* at 43,519-20. For the unsuccessful argument that a prosecution for violation of the Mann Act was unconstitutional because the purpose of the transportation was to make a pornographic movie, *see* United States v. Roeder, 526 F.2d 736, 739 (10th Cir. 1975).

[14] L. Sterne, THE LIFE AND OPINIONS OF TRISTAM SHANDY, Bk. IV, ch. 29, at 300 (World Classics ed. 1951).

[15] R. Emerson, *Self Reliance*, in ESSAYS: FIRST SERIES 27, 35 (Random House ed. 1944).

B. An Example from Legal Theory—Is a Predictive Theory of Law Logically Possible?

It is time now to provide an example of how an adequate appreciation of the role that notions of an ideal audience play in practical reasoning can help resolve one of the significant theoretical controversies of modern jurisprudence.

The controversy involves the question of whether a predictive theory of law is a logical possibility from the perspective of a person who is a judge. As we shall see, following the lead of H.L.A. Hart, the predominant position in England and America is that it is not a logical possibility. To appreciate the full dimension of the controversy, some background discussion is necessary. In 1958 *On Law and Justice* by Alf Ross was published in England and a year later in the United States.[16] This work was an English translation of a book that had been published in Denmark in 1953. It was this book that, as we shall soon see, Hart used as the focus of his attack on predictive theories of law.

On Law and Justice is an ambitious work in which Ross attempted to synthesize three strands of prior thought. The first was American legal realism, which attacked traditional legal scholarship for presenting legal decisionmaking as the discovery of the pre-existing legal principles and rules from which the results in particular cases were derived by a process of logical deduction.[17] According to the American legal realists, this was a false picture that hid, even from judges and lawyers themselves, the true nature of the judicial process. Judges like other people were influenced by

---

[16] A. Ross, ON LAW AND JUSTICE (1959) [hereinafter LAW AND JUSTICE].

[17] A good but necessarily only a partial history of American legal realism is L. Kalman, LEGAL REALISM at YALE, 1927-1960 (1986). Some feel for the intellectual threads of American legal realism can also be obtained from the editorial notes and readings in G. Christie, JURISPRUDENCE: TEXT AND READINGS ON THE PHILOSOPHY OF LAW 640-751 (1973). Many of the major themes of American legal realism were of course anticipated in the work of European scholars. *See e.g.* R. von Jhering, LAW AS A MEANS TO AN END (I. Husik transl. 1924). (This was a translation of the first part, published in 1877, of *Der Zweck im Recht*); F. Gény, MÉTHODE D'INTERPRÉTATION ET SOURCES EN DROIT PRIVÉ POSITIF (1899), the second revised and enlarged edition of which was translated into English by J. Mayo in 1954.

their passions and prejudices. At its best, judicial decisionmaking should reflect the empirically determined needs of a society and the best available judgments as to the social arrangements that will meet these social needs. If one wanted to study legal decisionmaking, one should devote one's energies to judges' behavioral responses to the cases brought before them. Unless one was a legal historian interested in history for its own sake, what one was interested in was the ability to predict how judges would react to future cases. What judges said in their opinions was just one piece of evidence and often by no means the most helpful evidence on the basis of which to make useful predictions. Some of the American legal realists, such as Jerome Frank,[18] emphasized that perhaps the most relevant bit of information on the basis of which to predict a judge's future decisional behavior was the judge's psychological make-up.

The second strand of thought that Ross was attempting to include in his synthesis is generally called "Scandinavian legal realism," a school of thought of which Ross himself would be considered a latter-day member.[19] This group was very much influenced by the policy-driven behavioral approach of the American legal realists but believed that, as enunciated by American scholars, it failed to take into account that law, although ultimately dependent on coercion, does not, on an every day basis, seem so much something that people somehow *must* obey or simply *do* obey but rather appears to them as something that they *should* obey. These emotive features of law were not simply a perhaps regrettable by-product of human nature but were rather one of law's essential components. Thinkers, like the Swedes Axel Hägerström and his disciple, Karl Olivecrona, were concerned with how the members of a given society came to internalize its norms. Hägerström emphasized how the imperative nature of legal language and the hierarchical organization of a state's legal system influenced this process of internalization,[20] while Olivecrona was concerned with the mechanics of how this process of internalization actually took place in the

---

[18] See J. Frank, LAW AND THE MODERN MIND (1930).
[19] For an overview of Scandinavian legal realism, *see* G. Christie, *op. cit. supra,* note 17, at 751-85.
[20] *See* A. Hägerström, INQUIRIES INTO THE NATURE OF LAW AND MORALS (C. D. Broad transl. 1953).

individual citizen.[21] For Olivecrona, the felt binding nature of law arose from the individual's internalizing a system of norms as a means of making it possible for him to live in society without fear. This is the way that, as a small child, the individual confronted his family environment and adjusted to it. As the individual grows up, the larger society seems as overwhelming, as structured, and as all powerful as his family milieu was to him as a child, when he was totally dependent on his parents, and particularly, as a very small child, on his mother, for food, warmth and shelter.

The third strand of Ross's synthesis came from the work of Hans Kelsen.[22] In order to be comprehensible as a legal system, a set of norms must exhibit a certain logical structure in which the subsidiary norms of the system can be shown to be derivable from the higher norms of the system and ultimately from the system's basic norm (or "grandnorm"). This basic norm could be the basis either of what Kelsen called a "dynamic" system of norms or of what he called a "static" system of norms. In a static system, such as for example a system of natural law, the content of the subsidiary norms would be derivable from the basic norm, of which they might be considered instantiations. In a dynamic system of norms, the basic norm was a power-conferring one, namely one that simply authorized someone or some entity to make law. To avoid an infinite regress, the validity of the basic norm itself had to be either self-evident, as would be the case if the basic norm in question were that of a static system, or simply assumed, if the basic norm in question were that of a dynamic system. Kelsen took it for granted that the basic norms of modern legal systems were dynamic in nature.

In bringing these separate strands together, Ross took from the American legal realists the insistence that law, as an academic discipline, was a social science concerned with the observation, analysis, and

---

[21] *See* K. Olivecrona, LAW AS FACT (1939), and LAW AS FACT (2d ed. 1971). Despite the common title and a common underlying theme, these are really two different books.

[22] Of the many works of Kelsen, it suffices to cite his two major works available in English translations. H. Kelsen, GENERAL THEORY OF LAW AND STATE (A. Wedberg transl. 1945) and H. Kelsen, THE PURE THEORY OF LAW (2d ed. M. Knight transl. 1987), first published in German in 1960.

systematization of observable behavior. Like most of the American legal realists, Ross took it for granted that the behavior of the judge was the principal focal point of legal studies. The behavior of legislators was of course a worthy subject of study for the social scientist, but that was more a subject for the specialist in legal sociology rather than for the traditional legal scholar, i.e. the specialist in jurisprudence. From his Scandinavian predecessors, Ross took the insistence that law—although ultimately based on coercion in the sense that unenforced law would eventually lose its quality of being felt as binding—exerted an emotive force on those who were governed by a particular legal regime that inclined them to obey its directives. Law was not force writ large. A national legal order was rather a set of norms. Finally, from Kelsen, Ross took the point that law was more than just a set of norms, it was a *system* of norms, and the further point that it was the function of the legal scholar to construct the conceptual framework which would organize a particular set of norms into a comprehensible system of norms.

In addition to drawing on these three strands of thought, Ross also fully accepted the conclusions of the prevailing predominant school of linguistic philosophy that only statements that were capable of being true or false were possible subjects of scientific discourse.[23] Laws were prescriptions and, as such, incapable of truth value. But, following Kelsen's usage, he was prepared to accept that laws were either valid or invalid, and it was Ross's position that a statement that some particular prescription was valid law was capable of being true or false. Accordingly, he concluded that statements about what the law is, i.e. statements as to what might be a valid proposition of law, should be interpreted as *predictions* that, should a situation arise that would bring into play the legal proposition in question, the judge would behave in a certain way because he felt *bound* to do so.[24] Ross did not want to maintain that the behavior of the judge would necessarily have to consist in applying the legal norm in question, because he recognized that even a realist might not want to abandon his descriptive statements of the legal norms of a system any time a judge behaved in a contrary manner. Ross's final formulation of his predictive theory of law

---

[23] *See* LAW AND JUSTICE at 6-9.
[24] *See id.* at 38-46.

therefore took a narrower form. A statement by a scholar as to what is a valid legal norm of a legal system is a prediction that, should the appropriate circumstances arise, the norm in question "will form an integral part of the reasoning underlying the judgment" rendered in the case.[25] Ross wished to accommodate his theory to the fact that not only might the facts be such as to bring into operation superseding legal norms but also that, in reaching his actual decision, "the ideas which the judge holds as to what is valid law do not constitute the only factor by which he is motivated."[26] Thus a scholar confronted with seemingly unexplainable (or irrational or inconsistent) behavior is not necessarily always obliged to reformulate his doctrinal statements.

Shortly after Ross's book appeared in its English language version in 1958, H. L. A. Hart published a critical review of it,[27] and there are indeed many aspects of Ross's definition of law that are troublesome. I, for example, would want to ask what it might be for a supposed norm to form an "integral part" of the judge's reasoning processes? Moreover, in order to do so, must it have the same verbal form and intentional meaning for observer-predictor and judge-decider? One can avoid these problems by treating the norms as maxims, in which case it is also easier to see how they could form an "integral part of the reasoning underlying" a decision, even if that decision were contrary to one's expectations formulated on the basis of those maxims. But then these maxims would hardly be functioning as "norms." These are obviously important problems. The problem of identifying what are in point of fact the actual norms of a legal system that judges consider binding is certainly a very difficult endeavor. The problem exists under any theory that makes the identification of the actual rules or norms of law its central feature. One might, as I have argued at length elsewhere, consider even dropping the insistence that law must be considered as essentially a set of rules or norms that theoretically could all be described in some authoritative verbal formulation.[28] But, so long as one

---

[25] *Id.* at 42.

[26] *Id.* at 43.

[27] H. Hart, *Scandinavian Realism*, [1959] CAMB. L. J. 233.

[28] *See* G. Christie, LAW, NORMS AND AUTHORITY (1982). Predictive theories are particularly confronted by the difficulty of actually describing the so-called rules of law

insists on the potential identifiability of legal norms, the problems of identification will remain, whether one is considering a theory like that of Hart himself, that insists that law must be viewed as a collection of rules,[29] or a theory like Ronald Dworkin's, that considers law an amalgam of legal rules, legal principles, and moral rights,[30] or finally a predictive theory like that of Ross.

Since Hart himself subscribed to the view that the law consists of a set of potentially identifiable legal norms, these aspects of Ross's work did not trouble him. The main thrust of Hart's criticism was focused rather on the logic underlying Ross' thesis. As is well known, Hart in his own work always insisted on the distinction between the so-called internal position of a judge and the external position of an outside observer, such as that of a scholar or even that of a lawyer advising a client.[31] In his review of Ross's book, Hart contended that, from the internal position of the judge, it was logically impossible to consider the law as a set of predictions,[32] and he repeated these criticisms in *The Concept of Law* a few years later.[33] A judge after all was engaged in the enterprise of deciding particular cases and not of predicting how he would decide these cases. The judge was therefore concerned with ascertaining what rules of law were binding upon him and what other factors, if any, he should take into account in making his decision. In other words, deciding is different from predicting, particularly in a normative context where the judge is concerned with determining what he *should* do, that is in finding a reason to decide a case in one way or another.

Hart's criticism was never challenged, and in the English-speaking world, it has become, almost by default, the definitive criticism of the realist definition of law in terms of the set of predictions of official

---

because there are a potentially infinite number of predictions of varying degrees of probability that can be made about the future behavior of legal decision makers. *See* G. Christie, *The Notion of Validity in Modern Jurisprudence*, 48 MINN. L. REV. 1049 (1964).

[29] H. Hart, THE CONCEPT OF LAW (1961) [hereinafter THE CONCEPT OF LAW].

[30] There will be some more detailed discussions of Dworkin's work in later chapters.

[31] *See* THE CONCEPT OF LAW at 55-60.

[32] *See* Hart, *supra* note 27, at 236-40.

[33] *See* THE CONCEPT OF LAW at 79-88.

behavior.[34] This was so despite the fact that, if Hart's criticism has any validity, it is only valid with regard to final appellate courts. When lower courts decide cases they are obviously engaged in a process that requires them to predict the potential reaction of higher courts. It does not stretch either language or common sense to say that, in stating the law applicable to cases before them, such courts are typically in effect predicting that the higher court will approve their statement of the law. Indeed, lower courts state the law in a certain way precisely because they are predicting that that is what the appellate courts would declare the law to be.

If one wanted to ignore a court's statement of the law and focus instead on something more narrow like "the decision" in the instant case, it still makes sense to say that the lower court's decision is typically one that the lower court believes will either be approved by, or at least be left undisturbed by, the higher court. Moreover, there are cases in which a judge, even a judge on a highest appellate court, is even more obviously engaged in a predictive exercise, as when he attempts to decide a case governed by the law of another jurisdiction. This is of course what the United States federal courts are doing all the time in cases arising under their diversity jurisdiction. With the increasing mobility of people and the expansion of trade beyond not only state or provincial boundaries but also national borders, courts in all nations are increasingly confronting situations in which they feel obliged to decide cases in the way that they imagine (i.e., predict) the cases would be decided by the highest court of some other jurisdiction. Final appellate courts, moreover, cannot ignore possible nonjudicial reaction to their decisions. Legislators can and sometimes do very quickly override judicial decisions.[35] Nor, even in the United States,

---

[34] This can be clearly seen in assertions such as:
> Predictivism provides the judge with few justificatory resources. The deciding judge is not trying to predict anything. He is trying to decide, and doing so in light of any relevant reasons of authority and reasons of substance.

R. Summers, INSTRUMENTALISM AND AMERICAN LEGAL THEORY 132 (1982).

[35] In the Portal to Portal Act of 1947, 61 Stat. 84, 29 U.S.C. § 251, Congress retroactively overruled, and withdrew federal court jurisdiction over, cases seeking to implement Anderson v. Mt. Clemens Pottery Co., 328 U.S. 680 (1946); Jewell Ridge Corp. v. Local

can the possibility of constitutional or other structural changes as reactions to their decisions be completely overlooked by final appellate courts in agonizing over their decisions. In other words, legislators and the public at large are members of the audience that final appellate courts are addressing.[36]

Legislators and the public at large are, however, only part of the audience addressed by judges sitting on final appellate courts. Of greater significance is the fact that judges are part of an elite profession and as such very conscious of the expectations of their co-professionals. How a judge conceives of his profession and of his role within that profession will figure very prominently in the vision he has of the audience he is addressing. Beyond these particular sorts of audiences, if the judge accepts, as most judges unquestionably do, that the role they fill places unique responsibilities upon them to ground their decisions in reason, then the judge will also be addressing some kind of ideal or, to use Perelman's term, a "universal audience."

I submit that this application of Perelman's fundamental insights shows that it is a mistake to dismiss summarily Ross's work as based upon a logical mistake, for Ross has come close to an important insight. As we have seen, according to Ross, a statement purporting to state a valid norm (or rule of law) is a prediction that, should a set of facts arise to which the norm is applicable, the norm in question "will form an integral part of the

---

No. 617, 325 U.S. 161 (1945); Tennessee Coal, Iron & R.R. Co. v. Muscoda Local No. 123, 321 U.S. 590 (1944). Those cases construed the Fair Labor Standards Act of 1938 in a manner to impose huge potential liabilities upon employers. Between July 1, 1946 and January 1, 1947, almost six billion dollars worth of claims were filed. The constitutionality of the 1947 act was upheld in a host of lower federal courts. *See, e.g.,* Battaglia v. General Motors Corp., 169 F.2d 254, *cert. denied,* 335 U.S. 887 (1948); Sesse v. Bethlehem Steel Co., 168 F.2d 58 (1948). For a British example, see the War Damage Act of 1965 (1965, c.18), overruling Burmah Oil Corp. v. Lord Advocate, [1965] A.C. 75, [1965] 2 W.L.R. 1231. 2 All E.R. 348 (Sc. 1964).
[36] "'But there's wan thing I'm sure about.'
   'What's that?' asked Mr. Hennessy.
   'That is,' said Mr. Dooley, 'no matter whether th' constitution follows th' flag or not, th' supreme court follows th' illiction returns.'"
F. Dunne, MR. DOOLEY'S OPINIONS 26 (1901).

reasoning of the judgment" rendered in that case. As I have already noted, I do not wish to consider here the problems involved in determining when or how a purported norm forms an integral part of the reasoning behind a judgment or whether law can fruitfully be considered as a set of norms or rules. I merely address the criticism that Ross and the other realists must be wrong because they adopt a predictive approach to the question what is law. In defense of Ross, I wish to assert that, when someone states a supposed rule of law, such a person, even if he is a judge on a highest appellate court, can usefully be considered as expressing his present belief that the requirements of consistency in the application of law and a commitment to the fundamental postulates of a legal system, such as the primacy of the constitution and the validly enacted statutes of that system, will require a judge to decide cases as if the purported norm were binding upon him.

If the person making a statement as to what is a valid norm is a judge, he can be considered to be doing one or both of two things. First, he is stating his present belief that the requirements of consistency and the fundamental postulates of the legal system require him to decide the case before him in accordance with the purported norm he has enunciated; and/or second, he is stating his present belief as to what these same factors will require a future judge to consider as binding in a future case. Insofar as a judge is stating his present belief as to what the factors present in the case before him will require a future judge to do, the predictive element is too clear to require discussion. Insofar as a judge is stating his present belief that the requirements of consistency and the fundamental postulates of the legal system require him to decide the case in a particular way, the judge is addressing an ideal or universal audience and he is asserting, predicting if you will, that that audience accepts now and will accept in the future the soundness of his decision. Under either of these interpretations of what a judge is doing, there are important predictive elements.

The validity of these conclusions is clearly illustrated when one looks at some famous dissenting opinions. In 1972, in *Furman v. Georgia*,[37] the Supreme Court of the United States struck down the imposition of a

---

[37] 408 U.S. 238 (1972).

sentence of death under the then current Georgia statute because the statute did not permit a sufficiently individualized decision on whether the death penalty should be enforced in any particular case. Georgia was one of a number of American states that redrafted its statutory provisions concerning the death penalty to meet the objections voiced in *Furman*. In 1976, in *Gregg v. Georgia*,[38] the Court, in a seven to two decision, upheld a sentence of death imposed under the revised statutory provisions. No more than three members of the Court joined in any of the opinions written by a member of the majority. Justices Brennan and Marshall dissented. While it is impossible to reprint much from their opinions, a few excerpts will give the reader a feel for the nature and tone of their argument. In his dissent, Justice Brennan asserted:

This Court inescapably has the duty, as the ultimate arbiter of the meaning of our Constitution, to say whether, when individuals condemned to death stand before our Bar, "moral concepts" require us to hold that the law has progressed to the point where we should declare that the punishment of death, like punishments on the rack, the screw, and the wheel, is no longer tolerable in our civilized society . . . I emphasize only that foremost among the "moral concepts" recognized in our cases and inherent in the Clause is the primary moral principle that the State, even as it punishes, must treat its citizens in a manner consistent with their intrinsic worth as human beings . . .[39]

Justice Marshall's dissenting opinion has somewhat the same fervor and appeal to universal values:

Since the decision in *Furman* the legislatures of 35 States have enacted new statutes authorizing the imposition of the death sentence for certain crimes, and Congress has enacted a law providing the death penalty for air piracy resulting in death. I would be less than candid if I did not acknowledge that these developments have a significant bearing on a realistic assessment of the moral acceptability of the death penalty to the American people. But if the death penalty turns, as I have urged, on the opinion of an informed citizenry, then even the enactment of new death statutes cannot be viewed as conclusive. In *Furman* I observed that the American people are largely unaware of the information critical to a judgment on the morality of the death penalty, and concluded that if they were better informed they would consider it shocking, unjust, and unacceptable . . . .

---

[38]   428 U.S. 153 (1976).
[39]   *Id.* at 229.

Even assuming, however, that the post-*Furman* enactment of statutes authorizing the death penalty renders the prediction of the views of an informed citizenry an uncertain basis for a constitutional decision, the enactment of these statutes has no bearing whatsoever on the conclusion that the death penalty is unconstitutional because it is excessive. An excessive penalty is invalid under the Cruel and Unusual Punishments Clause "even though popular sentiment may favor" it.[40]

If these are not appeals to the universal audience and an appeal to the judgment of history and more specifically to future judges who, if they are fair, rational, and committed to moral principle, Justices Brennan and Marshall are certain, will overturn the Court's decision in *Gregg,* I do not know what is.[41] One is reminded of Thucydides' declaration in book one of his history of the Peloponnesian war that he feared that the absence of romance in his work would detract from its interest for some of his contemporaries. Nevertheless, he would be content if his work were judged useful by those who desired an exact knowledge of the past to aid them in understanding the future. Thucydides concludes, "I have written my work, not as an essay which is to win the applause of the moment, but as a possession for all time."[42]

There are two possible objections to the foregoing analysis that might appear at first glance to have some plausibility but that in fact are untenable. The first objection is that a judge deciding a case is typically, in actual practice, simply not addressing an audience. A moment's reflection, however, reveals that this assertion cannot be maintained. Under Hart's idealized view of the judicial role, the judge, who must decide the case, is searching for the rule of law that covers the case, that is, he is searching for the binding rule of law.[43] If the case is one at the fringe of the penumbra of

---

[40] *Id.* at 232-33.

[41] Habermas captures this point very well when he declares, "the dissenting opinion attached to the justification of a Supreme Court ruling, for example, is meant to record arguments that in similar cases might convince the majority of a future panel of judges." J. Habermas, BETWEEN FACTS AND NORMS 179 (W. Rehg transl. 1996). The context makes clear that Habermas is referring generally to any supreme court and not to the Supreme Court of the United States.

[42] Thucydides, THE PELOPONNESIAN WAR, Bk. I (1.22), THE LANDMARK THUCYDIDES 16 (1996). (This is an annotated edition utilizing the classic R. Crawley translation.)

[43] *See* THE CONCEPT OF LAW, at 119-20 and *passim.*

a rule of law or even beyond the penumbra, the judge is presumably groping for the best decision he can reach keeping in mind the demands of public policy and the judge's institutional role. In any event, whatever the nature of the case before him, the objection to my thesis is that the judge is engaged in a process of discovery, not of prediction. The contention that the judge in this process of search is not consciously attuned to an audience is, however, preposterous. Certainly the judge's opinion (his judgment in the English sense) is addressed to the parties and their counsel and to the broader professional and even lay audience. Furthermore, insofar as the judge in his opinion is claiming that his decision was "correct," he is also addressing and trying to persuade an ideal or universal audience committed to rational discourse that he has in fact reached the right decision. If he were not, why would he be trying so hard to justify it?

But what about the judge's actual conclusion before he sets about to justify it? Assuming it is plausible to distinguish the decisionmaking process from the process of justification—and like many I am skeptical of the plausibility of such a move—it seems clear that the decisionmaking process under this hypothesis is an individual psychological event. The decision could be reached by the judge's gauging the reactions of others to various possible decisions, or by just a feeling in his bones, or by the judge's convincing himself to abide by the toss of a coin. This is a fruitless inquiry. Focusing upon the public statements of the judge and the judge's process of deciding that these public statements are the appropriate ones in the context in which he finds himself—and this after all is what Hart is talking about—it clearly is the case that these public statements are addressed to an audience and that they have been composed with this contemplated audience in mind.

The second objection accepts that judicial opinions are addressed to an audience. The objection asserts that, when all is said and done, the fact remains that the judge's opinion is not cast in the form of a prediction. That is of course in one sense a valid, but not very helpful, point. In the first place, how an oral utterance is to be taken cannot really be determined by formal criteria. It is a question of context and depends on the construction put on it by the listener. "You will shut the door?" is ostensibly in the form of a question but in many contexts would be interpreted as a request or an order.[44] In the second place, we are talking about whether a judge's opinion can usefully be interpreted as a form of prediction. Hart, for example, is perfectly prepared to concede that counsel's statement to a client "the law is X" can profitably be interpreted as a prediction, a prediction of future judicial behavior.[45] Hart's point was that, in contrast, a judge's opinion (or statement) cannot logically be so interpreted. In so concluding, I hope to have shown that he was wrong.

---

[44] A person who argues that judicial pronouncements as to what the law is cannot be considered to be predictions because they are not expressed as predictions would have to agree that law cannot profitably be considered as consisting of rules. Most so-called rules of law are not stated in rule form in the judicial pronouncement from which they are derived.

[45] Hart, *supra* note 27, at 237. Hart expresses skepticism as to whether such statements can *always* be considered as predictions.

CHAPTER 3

WHAT ARE THE CONSTRAINTS THAT CAN BE IMPOSED ON ARGUMENTS ADDRESSED TO AN IDEAL AUDIENCE?

In the previous chapter we discussed the inevitability of human appeals to an ideal or universal audience and, more importantly, how recognizing the existence of these appeals can help solve certain important philosophical and legal puzzles. Our inquiry into the notion of an ideal audience in legal argumentation will require us to examine a host of other questions. These include: What is the nature of such an ideal audience, particularly in a legal context? Is the ideal audience different in different legal systems and, if so, what are some of the factors that account for this difference? Before beginning to answer these questions, which will be discussed in future chapters, it will be useful to consider an important preliminary question: Can any constraints be imposed on the type of arguments that can be addressed to an ideal or universal audience or on the ability of some members of a society to address this audience? The constraints that some have suggested are not merely philosophical or theoretical but rather constraints that are to be imposed by serious social and sometimes even legal pressure.

It is of course undoubtedly true that each person has his own ideal audience. The question is whether each person's notion of an ideal audience is something completely unique to that individual. If it were, the matters with which this chapter will be concerned would be of minimal interest. But, since human beings exist in a social context—indeed they are partly constituted by the social context in which they live—there is obviously, in each society, a notion of an ideal audience that is widely shared. To deny this is to deny that there is any shared social morality in a society, but any such denial flies in the face of all the empirical evidence. Indeed one could hardly even talk of a society if there were not some shared customs and moral sentiments among the members of that society. It is because arguments addressed to an ideal audience take place in a social context that the question of possible restraints on that argument takes on any important practical significance.

Most observers would appear to accept that, in anything approaching Habermas' ideal speech[1] situation—the sort of speech situation which, Habermas accepts, serves as the background to our attempts to communicate with an ideal audience—there can be no constraint on who can speak and what can be said. In such an ideal speech situation, speech must be free and unencumbered because, to quote Habermas, the "proceduralized reason," in a democratic society, "refuses to concede that a consensus is free of coercion . . . unless the consensus has come about . . . on the basis of an anarchic, unfettered communicative freedom."[2] The problem is whether this same freedom in communication is to be recognized in non-ideal speech situations, such as, of course, in the usual circumstance of actual social life. For example, Habermas asserts that, in legal reasoning, the "practice of argumentation is characterized by the intention of winning the assent of a universal audience to a problematic proposition in a non-coercive but regulated contest for the better arguments based on the best information and reasons."[3] But, in order to engage in this type of argumentation with an ideal or universal audience, we "always already intuitively rely on a practice in which we presume that we sufficiently approximate the ideal conditions of a speech situation specially immunized against repression and inequality."[4] Obviously, as Habermas himself maintains, there will have to be procedural rules regulating the actual conducting of the argument—what, as we have just seen, Habermas calls a "proceduralized reason"—but is this enough to make a speech situation "immune from repression and inequality," and what is to be done if it is not enough? Habermas does not address either of these questions. Others, however, have. Since the problem arises in all forms of argumentation and not just in legal argument, it is worth examining what these people have said about the problem both in legal and non-legal contexts and, more

---

[1] For a good discussion in English of Habermas' earlier German writing on this subject, see R. Geuss, THE IDEA OF A CRITICAL THEORY 65-70, 72-73 (1981). See also J. Habermas, THEORY AND PRACTICE 16-17 (J. Viertel transl. 1973); J. Habermas, MORAL CONSCIOUSNESS AND COMMUNICATIVE ACTION 201-03 (C. Lenhardt and S. Nicholson transl. 1990).

[2] J. Habermas, BETWEEN FACTS AND NORMS 186 (W. Rehg transl. 1996).

[3] Id. at 228.

[4] Ibid.

importantly, what they suggest the legal system can do, by regulating public speech and imposing some constraints on the arguments that can be considered by the universal audience to which legal and political arguments are made, to remedy what they foresee as the shortcomings of unconstrained speech.

John Rawls, for example, asserts that "political speech . . . must be regulated to insure the fair value of the political liberties."[5] He criticizes the Supreme Court of the United States, in its campaign finance decisions,[6] for failing to recognize that, to insure the "fair value" of political liberties, "it is necessary to prevent those with greater property and wealth, and the greater skills of organization which accompany them, from controlling the electoral process to their advantage."[7] Citizens must not only have a full but also an "equally effective voice in a fair scheme of representation . . . . Formal equality is not enough."[8] He concludes that "[t]he First Amendment no more enjoins a system of representation according to influence effectively exerted in free political rivalry between unequals than the Fourteenth Amendment enjoins a system of liberty of contract and free competition between unequals in the economy."[9] In the name of equality, according to Rawls, access to the political forum can be legally regulated to account for the fact that people have different financial resources and organizational skills. But equality is a difficult hobby-horse to ride. Some people are more articulate and persuasive than others; some have more knowledge than others. If equality were the prime good, then restrictions on the participation of people with these particular skills in political debate

[5] J. Rawls, POLITICAL LIBERALISM 358 (1993) (hereinafter POLITICAL LIBERALISM).
[6] Buckley v. Valeo, 424 U.S. 1 (1976) and First Nat'l Bk v. Belloti, 435 U.S. 765 (1978).
[7] POLITICAL LIBERALISM at 360.
[8] Id. at 361.
[9] Id. at 362. To support his conclusions on the legitimacy of imposing some restrictions on the ability of some people to participate in political debate in order to facilitate effective equality of access, Rawls places much reliance on the United States Supreme Court's reapportionment decisions (id. at 361-62) which are often described as premised on the ideal of "one man, one vote." See, e.g. one of the cases cited by Rawls, Wesbury v. Sanders, 376 U.S. 1, 11 (1964) ("every man's vote to count alike"). Rawls does not pause to note that the Senate of the United States is organized in direct opposition to any such principle; the approximately 30,000,000 inhabitants of California elect only two Senators, as do both Alaska and Wyoming, each of which has less than 500,000 inhabitants.

should also be restricted, subject, perhaps, to a Rawlsian proviso that efficiency concerns, such as the ability to increase the value of political liberty for the least politically advantaged, might justify some deviation from the absolute equality of the fair value of each citizen's political liberties, of which, for Rawls, freedom of speech is just one component.[10]

Cass Sunstein takes a similar tack. In the absence of economic equality, limiting a person's ability to enter into political debate by, for example, limiting campaign expenditures, should not be considered impermissible.[11] Like Rawls, he takes issue with the Supreme Court's holding that Congress can place no limits on how much a person can spend to further his own campaign for public office, or to construct a forum for the expression of his own personal political views. Sunstein notes that the market system, which has given some people a greater ability than others to influence political debate, has in itself been made possible by the existence of the legal system.[12] The clear implication of Sunstein's argument is that this legal regulatory structure, which has allowed the presently existing distributions and accumulations of wealth to arise, could be altered in a way that furthers "the good of political equality." Query, would he and Rawls impose limits on the amount of money a person can expend in legal representation to defend himself from criminal accusations? Sunstein eschews, at least in this context, any attempt to impose constraints on the points of view that may be expressed in political debate, although, to someone whose point of view is that the Government should have no power to limit political debate in any manner, this eschewal may offer scant consolation.

For all his paeans to the notion of equality, however, Sunstein writes from a perspective that is suspicious of popular culture. He is at once elitist and yet in favor of equality. This inconsistency leads him to the ambivalent declaration "that government should be cautious about spurring on its own the use of new technologies to promote immediate, massive public reactions to popular issues. Government by referendum is at best a mixed blessing,

---

[10] *See* POLITICAL LIBERALISM at 358.
[11] *See* C. Sunstein, FREE MARKETS AND SOCIAL JUSTICE 228-30 (1997).
[12] *See id.* at 230.

with possible unfortunate consequences where it is tried."[13] His premise is that "[r]egulatory efforts to facilitate communication need not be transformed into an effort to abandon republican goals."[14] He fears that "[a] system of individually designed communications options could, by contrast, result in a high degree of balkanization, in which people are not presented with new or contrary perspectives. Such a nation could not easily satisfy democratic and deliberative goals."[15] In such a political society not only might communication between people with different perspectives be difficult or even impossible, but, he fears that "[i]n such a nation, there may be little commonality among people with diverse commitments, as one group caricatures another or understands it by means of simple slogans that debase reality and eliminate mutual understanding."[16] It is obvious then that, if Sunstein is not prepared to countenance regulation of content—although, in the passages quoted, he seems to suggest that some such restrictions might be a good thing—he is certainly in favor of a system in which certain enlightened members of society, i.e. government officials, guide the course of political discussion by regulating the structural framework of that discussion and deciding which techniques of public communication shall be accessible to all members of the public and which shall not.

Owen Fiss is less diffident than either Rawls or Sunstein about the occasional desirability of regulating public speech, even political speech. He shares their belief in the desirability of campaign finance regulation that limits the amounts of money that a person may spend to support a political position.[17] He goes beyond them, however, in stating that "the key to fulfilling ultimate purposes of the First Amendment" and of the freedom of speech which it enshrines is not the promotion of autonomy but the ability of speech "to enrich public debate."[18] The "actual effect" of speech is the prime consideration. He bluntly declares "[s]peech is protected when (and only when) it does [enrich public debate], and precisely because it does, not

---

[13] *Id.* at 187.
[14] *Ibid.*
[15] *Ibid.*
[16] *Ibid.*
[17] O. Fiss, LIBERALISM DIVIDED 5-6, 26-30 (1996).
[18] *Id.* at 15.

because it is an exercise in autonomy."[19] At times, he asserts, autonomy might have to be sacrificed to insure that public debate is sufficiently rich to permit "true collective self-determination."[20] According to Fiss, "the phrase 'the freedom of speech' in the First Amendment refers to . . . a social state of affairs, not the action of an individual or institution."[21] Starting from this perspective, he has no difficulty supporting attempts to prohibit pornographic speech[22] and to censor the speech of some persons in circumstances in which he would not censor the speech of racial minorities.[23] Without such legal restrictions on speech, minorities, he claims, "feel less entitled and less inclined to voice their views in the public square, and withdraw into themselves. They are silenced almost as effectively as if the state intervened to silence them."[24] He accepts similar claims about the effects of pornography, namely that it leads to the silencing of women.[25] To support some type of content regulation on this ground is, in his view, to be true to the demands of democracy because democracy requires that "everyone have an equal chance to speak and be heard."[26] Finally, in a paper addressed to the newly emerging states in Eastern Europe after the fall of the Berlin Wall, he cautioned them about believing that "the newly privatized media will give the public all that it wishes."[27] Echoing the elitism of Sunstein, he distinguishes between "democratically determined speech" and "robust public debate." Suppose, he asks, that people decide that they are sick and tired of robust public debate and that they are exhausted by discussions of economic policy or of the treatment of ethnic minorities and that they "are only interested in mind-dulling entertainment, tabloid newspapers, or television programs that give expression to their sexual fantasies."[28] In such circumstances, he asks,

---

[19] *Ibid.*
[20] *Id.* at 16.
[21] *Id.* at 15.
[22] *See id.* at 69-87.
[23] *See id.* at 111-20.
[24] *Id.* at 117.
[25] *See id.* at 83-87.
[26] *Id.* at 87.
[27] *Id.* at 145.
[28] *Id.* at 146.

would "a democracy require us to respect that choice?" Fiss' short answer is "I think not."[29]

The argument for using the law to restrict the speech of some to further the interests of others is not confined to the argument that the restricted speech would otherwise silence the speech of minorities or, in the case of pornography, silence the speech of women. For example, such speech needs to be restricted, it is urged, because it positively harms members of the affected groups. Many of the arguments for restricting pornography rely, for example, on the (unproven) assertion that it reinforces an image of women as subservient and submissive, which may also come to be an image that women have of themselves and not merely a male fantasy. These are similar to arguments that have been made for using the law to restrict racially offensive speech. Such speech, it is said, not only silences the speech of members of minority groups but has more far-reaching effects. Michael Sandel, for example, asserts that such speech "may fail to respect persons as members of the particular communities to which they belong, and on whose status their social esteem may largely depend," and that the argument "that speech only advocates and never constitutes social practices fails to acknowledge the injuries that speech can inflict independent of the physical harm it may cause."[30]

As developed by the writers whose work we have just described, the notion of an ideal or universal audience seems inevitably in practice to require one to move towards restrictions on speech that, to many people, smack of totalitarianism. This seems rather odd. How can speech be free and not free at the same time? The notion that public speech is "half free" does not seem very satisfactory. One can accept that there usually must be some procedural regulation of speech situations but, even here, one must be cautious. In the courts of law, where the fairness of the process can be as important as the outcome of the process, one can accept that there must be rules for determining the order in which people can speak and, for the sake of economy of effort, rules restricting the interjection of irrelevant material and, sometimes, even time limits on the duration of the argument. But, even in legal argumentation, interruptions are tolerated, such as in the

[29] *Ibid.*
[30] M. Sandel, DEMOCRACY'S DISCONTENT 89 (1996).

objections raised by counsel to the questions asked by opposing counsel and in the often disruptive questions posed by judges in the course of counsel's argument.

In most contexts, the speakers engage in a process of self-regulation. They tolerate a considerable amount of interruptions and even heckling. Indeed, heckling is not only tolerated but also accepted as legitimate in parliamentary debate which, in certain respects, is subject to regulation with regard to relevancy and time limitations that resemble the regulation of legal argumentation. As anyone who has observed debates in the British House of Commons can attest, heckling in that august body sometimes resembles an art form. In ordinary speech about public events, some people are more strident than others; some are more persistent and patient, able to wait out their opponents until they can have their say. No one can possibly claim that there is any empirical support for the proposition that where speech is free and robust there is less speech than in an environment in which the content of speech is regulated or in which the ability of speakers to participate in the debate is limited. There may, at times, be a cacophony but, so long as there is no physical intimidation, all points of view will eventually be expressed.

Certainly where speech is used to incite violence there are grounds for restricting it but, even here, the courts, at least in the United States, have come to insist that the incitement must be direct and immediate.[31] Fear of future violence is not enough. Likewise, false speech can be punished but, again even here, traditional common-law doctrine has favored speech by premising liability on proof of actual financial harm, as in the torts of misrepresentation and unfair competition, or on the presumption that injury to reputation will have an economic impact upon an individual, as in defamation. Moreover, in the case of defamation, certain types of public speech have always received varying degrees of privilege;[32] and, at least in

---

[31] *See* Brandenburg v. Ohio, 395 U.S. 444 (1969).

[32] The absolute immunity of legislators from liability for anything said in the performance of their legislative duties is of long-standing in English-speaking countries. Judges, prosecutors, and witnesses are likewise immune from liability for what they say in the course of official proceedings although, of course, witnesses can be prosecuted for perjury. Moreover, in the United States, federal officials and, at least high-ranking, state officials enjoy absolute immunity from actions for defamation for statements made in the course

the United States, the ability of public officials and public figures to recover for defamation has been further circumscribed.[33]

The fact that speech that incites to immediate violence is legitimately subject to regulation or that many forms of false speech are subject to punishment is no ground for restricting speech that is either true or, because it expresses merely an opinion, is not capable of being either true or false. There is of course the problematic category of obscene speech which is prohibited on the grounds of the "harm" it does to the public. Perhaps because obscenity is often, like beauty, in the eyes of the beholder, the courts, at least in the United States, have been quick to allow artistic and redeeming social value as defenses in prosecutions for obscenity[34] and, in most jurisdictions, prosecuting authorities have allowed obscenity statutes to suffer from benign neglect. Moreover, the Supreme Court of the United States has made clear that, if people want to "enjoy" obscenity in the privacy of their own homes, they are free to do so.[35]

The argument of people like Fiss, Rawls, and Sunstein is of course not that restricting the content of public speech or the access of certain people to the public forum actually leads to more speech but rather that the restrictions they wish to impose will lead to 'better' speech, even if it is less speech. They never really tell us, however, who in a democracy is authorized to determine what is better speech. The only possible candidate, the people themselves, they positively believe is unfitted to the task. The disdain for popular opinion is perhaps nowhere more starkly expressed than in Rawls' strident attack on advertising in what he calls "imperfect and oligopolistic markets."[36] Under these conditions, according to Rawls, the aim of a firm's advertising expenditures is to expand or defend its market share. Rawls boldly asserts that "[m]uch of this kind of advertising is socially wasteful, and a well-ordered society that tries to preserve competition and to remove imperfections would seek reasonable ways to limit it," such as by using tax incentives or enforcing agreements by

---

of performing their official functions. *See* Barr v. Matteo, 360 U.S. 564 (1959).

[33] *See* New York Times Co. v. Sullivan, 376 U.S. 254 (1964); Gertz v. Robert Welch, Inc., 418 U.S. 323 (1974).

[34] *See* Miller v. California, 413 U.S. 15 (1973).

[35] *See* Stanley v. Georgia, 394 U.S. 557 (1969).

[36] POLITICAL LIBERALISM, at 364.

competitors to restrict such advertising, presumably by exempting such agreements from the anti-trust laws.[37]

If the writers, who have advocated in one way or another restrictions on either the content of public speech or on the access of certain people to the public forum, had given more thought to the history of constitutional protections of free speech, such as the historical purpose of the First Amendment to the Constitution of the United States, they might have been more hesitant in suggesting that some regulations of speech beyond that which is currently accepted might not only be desirable but compatible with that historical tradition. Fiss, Rawls, and Sunstein take an instrumental view of the First Amendment. The purpose of freedom of speech is to further democracy, in Fiss' sense of what democracy is all about, or republican values in the sense of what Sunstein thinks republican values are all about, or in order to insure what Rawls calls the "fair value" of political liberties. These are, in some ways, extrapolations from Alexander Meikeljohn's notion that the core value expressed in the First Amendment is the protection of robust political debate,[38] although I wish to make it clear that I am not suggesting that he would have endorsed any of the restrictions that have been proposed by the writers to whom I have referred.

Obviously, some kind of protection of political speech—even if it is only a limited protection—is an essential precondition of a democratic society. But I would submit that the historical record fairly clearly reveals that the purpose of the First Amendment was to forestall the Federal Government's ever getting into the business of regulating speech, whether it was religious speech—a major source of disaffection in seventeenth and eighteenth century England—or political speech.[39] That is, as I will develop in a more general context in the next chapter, the core idea is not so much that speech is a right which the state is now promising to respect, but rather that regulation of speech, however desirable or useful or whatever, is beyond the competence of the National Government. It is the gradual extension of the First Amendment to cover the more comprehensive

---

[37] *Id.* at 365.

[38] A. Meikeljohn, FREE SPEECH AND ITS RELATION TO SELF-GOVERNMENT (1948).

[39] *See* W. Van Alstyne, *Congressional Power and Free Speech: Levy's Legacy Revisited* 99 HARV. L. REV. 1089 (1986).

regulatory activities of the States' governments by the Twentieth Century incorporation of its provisions into the Fourteenth Amendment that undoubtedly increases the pressure for a First Amendment with a less sweeping vision. It may well be, as these writers maintain, although I very much doubt it, that the restrictions they propose would enhance "democracy" or "republican values" or the fair value of political liberty but, from the perspective of the framer of the First Amendment, that was irrelevant.

We have been exploring the attempt to create something approaching an ideal speech situation in the real world by active government intervention. We have suggested that public speech must be left largely free from state regulation because attempts to restrict its content or to restrict the access of some, in the often chimerical hope of improving the access of others, contradict the whole purpose of a public forum, which is to provide a venue for free and open discussion. Imposing the world view of an intellectual elite upon the rest of society and limiting the freedom of some to participate as fully as they might wish in public debate hardly seem to be the way to encourage free and open discussion. Certainly the notion of an ideal or universal audience does not require the imposition of such restrictions.

More subtle and supposedly more neutral restrictions on what people can say in public debate have proceeded on the premise that public debate must be confined to those who advance arguments that could be accepted by persons who do not share the basic religious or moral commitments of the speaker. That is to say, so-called religious fundamentalists can engage in political debate but only if they refrain from making arguments whose validity would require acceptance of the world view of the speaker. This is a view that has been espoused by Amy Gutmann and Dennis Thompson, in their co-authored *Democracy and Disagreement*, as well as by John Rawls in his *Political Liberalism*. Rawls is quite explicit that conceptions of justice that can be included within the content of what he calls "public reason" must be "presented independently of any wider comprehensive religious or philosophical doctrine."[40] If taken seriously, most of the people who are arguing about the constitutionality of restrictions on

---

[40] POLITICAL LIBERALISM, at 223.

abortion would be barred from the debate because their arguments are of course indeed based on such "wider comprehensive religious or philosophical doctrine."

It is undoubtedly to meet this particular objection that Rawls amplified his position in a subsequent article. He restated his position that, in a just democratic society, the "fair terms of cooperation" among the citizens require "an idea of reciprocity," that is that citizens offer one another and accept "fair terms" of cooperation which they are prepared to accept as the basis of action, "even at the cost of their own interests in particular situations, provided that other citizens also accept those terms."[41] For Rawls this means that, when social arrangements "are proposed as the most reasonable terms of fair cooperation, those proposing them must also think it at least reasonable for others to accept them," even if they do not share the same comprehensive religious or moral beliefs.[42] Rawls thus now makes clear that he recognizes—how could he not—that people, in presenting their argument, may be motivated by their basic beliefs and values and even express them in debate, but he insists that we must "in due course . . . give properly public reasons to support the principles and policies our comprehensive doctrine is said to support."[43] One cannot rely merely on statements of one's basic beliefs and values. This restriction is imposed not only on judges, whose framework of decision we might all accept as narrowly confined, but on all public officials and legislators. More importantly, if the "*ideal* of public reason" is to be achieved, private citizens, when they vote or discuss public issues, are enjoined to "think of themselves as if they were legislators following public reason."[44] Similar assertions as to the limitations that must be placed on public reason are made by Gutmann and Thompson. For them the requirement of reciprocity necessitates that the claims that citizens make on one another regarding public goods must be "on terms that . . . [others] can accept in principle."[45] That is, "in the face of moral disagreement in politics, the principle of

---

[41] J. Rawls, *The Idea of Public Reason Revisited,* 64 U. CHI. L. REV. 765, 770 (1997).
[42] *Ibid.*
[43] *Id.* at 776.
[44] *Id.* at 768-69.
[45] A. Gutmann and D. Thompson, DEMOCRACY AND DISAGREEMENT 55 (1996).

reciprocity tells citizens to appeal to reasons that are recognizably moral in form and mutually acceptable in content."[46]

To my mind these are not very plausible positions if we ignore for a moment the state as coercive regulator and focus instead on the individuals who wish to engage in a public debate in which, to quote Habermas, they are intent on "winning the assent of a universal audience" to some particular proposition. This is a debate which is antecedent to the state and which would continue to take place even if the state as benign or oppressive regulator were to fade away. What commitments must those who wish to engage in this debate make to their fellow participants in the debate? Rawls, as well as Gutmann and Thompson, have suggested that public debate about basic social arrangements and issues requires that the arguments which the participants address to each other must, at the very least, be such as could be accepted by all the other participants, taking as a given the basic values and beliefs they actually hold at any given time. Under this view, in a secular society, it would be out of order for a religious person to use religious reasons to support a position with regard to the public toleration or proscription of abortion or of assisted suicide.[47] His basic beliefs can only be brought into the debate if the positions these beliefs support can also be supported by public reasons, that is by reasons that all other members of the public could, in theory, reasonably accept whatever the nature of their basic beliefs. Conversely, in a religious society, secular reasons would presumably be inappropriate in arguing about the same issues. But this is not only an unnecessary restriction on the freedom of people to engage in political debate; it is also at variance with actual social practice. No less a figure than St. Thomas Aquinas readily acknowledged that even law, itself, let alone discussions of public policy, must be framed with the material conditions and the moral sentiments of a society in mind, even if that sometimes meant tolerating practices and

---

[46] *Id.* at 58.

[47] *See* M. Golding, *Liberal Theory and Jewish Politics*, in TIKKUN OLAM: SOCIAL RESPONSIBILITY IN JEWISH THOUGHT AND LAW (D. Shatz ed. 1997), at 201-14, who questions whether there is any place for orthodox Jews in a society governed by "public reason," as envisaged by Rawls.

customs which were at variance with the dictates even of a widely shared religion.[48]

There is no reason why purely religious beliefs cannot be brought forth in public debate in a totally secular society. Admittedly the more narrowly held a particular belief or value judgment is the less likely it is to persuade those who do not share this belief, but even idiosyncratic beliefs and sentiments can influence others. People can be influenced, and quite properly so, by the intensity with which a belief is held as well as by their intellectual acceptance of that belief. Besides, to restrict the type of reasons, as would Rawls and Gutmann and Thompson, assumes a static universe of beliefs and values and that is a clearly false assumption. People do change their beliefs not only individually but collectively. Societies in which particular religious beliefs were dominant have become secular societies and societies that were secular in orientation have turned towards a religious orientation. In some contemporary societies, such as Israel and many Moslem countries, there is a continuing struggle between those who subscribe to an outlook dominated by religious concerns and values and those whose outlook is dominated by secular concerns and values. The dogmatism of Rawls and Gutmann and Thompson seems to require that not only must people be able to agree on a particular policy or law but that they must agree on the policy or law for the same reasons.

This is surely too strong a condition and contradicts common experience, even in a completely secular society. One person may support farm subsidies for a particular crop because he thinks it makes fewer demands on the environment, say it requires less fertilizer and subjects the land to less erosion. Another person might support the same legislation because it lends itself to production on small farms and he is committed to preserving a social structure that features family farms. Another person might favor the legislation because he is concerned with the balance of payments and the crop in question is largely exported. Not only might these people support the legislation for different reasons but they each might not accept the legitimacy of the values underlying the position of the others. For example, the environmentalist might not accept the relevance of balance of payment concerns when it is a question of possible adverse

---

[48] St. Thomas Aquinas, SUMMA THEOLOGIAE, Part One of the Second Part, Q.96, 2d Art.

environmental impact. In Rawls' terms, balance of payment concerns would not seem to be a legitimate part of public reason in such a society if most or a sufficiently large part of society reject it as a public reason when environmental concerns are at issue.

I would submit that the commitments the participants in public debate must share, if they are trying to convince their fellow participants by arguments that would win the assent of an ideal audience, are very few. The first is that whatever assertions they make must be ones in which they believe. This is not to say that humor or sarcasm has no place in public debate, but when a statement is made that the speaker wants others to accept as true, he warrants his own belief in the truth of his statement. This is almost a truism. Every writer, who has considered the question, has taken it as a given that inter-subjective communication is impossible if the norm of truthfulness, in the sense of an honest belief in the truth of what is asserted, were not universally accepted as a precondition of human discourse. And while people often, for whatever reason, deviate in practice from the observance of the moral norms that they purportedly unconditionally accept, it makes no sense to dissemble one's beliefs to a universal audience or ideal audience. More than in any other discourse, discourse with an ideal audience presupposes truthfulness. Second they must, at some point, be prepared to pause and listen to the arguments of others. The third and final commitment that the participants in public debate must share is the rejection of force as the means of winning the debate. While a society must act and therefore must enact legislation requiring its members to do certain acts or to refrain from doing certain acts, it can not require them to be persuaded by the discussion or to refrain from trying to reopen the debate. The most that a society may demand is that the dissenters not oppose the decision of the majority by a resort to force.[49]

---

[49] *Cf.* T. Hobbes, LEVIATHAN, *A Review and Conclusion* 388 (Everyman ed. 1914). "Therefore I put down for one of the most effectual seeds of the Death of any State, that the Conquerors require not only a Submission of men's actions to them for the future, but also an approbation of all their actions past."

CHAPTER 4

SOME UNIVERSAL FEATURES OF
IDEAL AUDIENCES IN LEGAL CONTEXTS

It is time now to turn in a more focused way to the consideration of how the notion of an ideal or universal audience—we have used the terms interchangeably—actually operates in legal argumentation. Some aspects of the ideal audience that manifest themselves in legal argumentation seem to have truly universal acceptance; others, although thought of as universal, seem more closely tied to particular cultures. Let us begin by examining those attributes of legal argumentation that seem to be universally accepted in actual fact. These tend to concern the structure of the legal process and to focus on the role of the judge. A judge is expected to be impartial. He should have no interest in the outcome of the case or ties of affection with any of the litigants. He must have the patience to listen to all the parties before him, a notion encapsuled in the old Latin maxim, *audi alteram partem*. The judge is furthermore expected to base his decision on the proofs and arguments presented to him. In the event he feels obliged to decide the case on a basis not discussed by the parties, ideally the judge should give the parties an opportunity to be heard on these new issues before final judgment is rendered. Above all the judge should be situated in a governmental structure that guarantees his independence from either the executive or the legislature and he must be protected from the wrath of private parties who might react negatively to his decisions. All this is encapsuled under the concept of the "rule of law," a concept whose achievement in practice has been one of the greatest achievements of Western civilization and whose importance for social and economic development is now universally accepted. It took a long time to achieve in the Western world and it is becoming readily apparent that its achievement in much of the rest of the world will come only as the result of an arduous effort.

Some of these features of the judicial process that are imposed by our idealized conception of how the judicial process should operate focus on the other participants in that process. There are codes of ethics governing the conduct of counsel ranging from the requirement that he preserve the confidence of his client and avoid having any conflict of interest with his client to the way counsel conducts himself in court and deals with opposing counsel. Other features of the accepted idealized view of the judicial process concern the litigants themselves. They have, for example, the right to be represented by counsel. In criminal cases, it is generally accepted that a defendant may not be forced to testify against himself, even if there is not universal agreement on what should be the consequence of his refusal to testify. In no event, however, can he be subjected to torture. Most importantly, a criminal defendant is generally conceded to have the right to confront his accusers, a right that has traditionally been particularly fiercely defended by the common law. Most of these features of our idealized notion of what the judicial forum should look like, however, directly concern the structure of that process and the forms that legal argumentation should take. They only indirectly concern the content of that argumentation.

There are, however, other broadly accepted features of the ideal audience's view of what the judicial process should look like that do more directly concern the content of legal argumentation. This can be seen nowhere more clearly than in the expectations we have for someone who fulfils the role of a judge. It is expected that a judge will not merely decide a case but will explain and justify his decision. Not all legal systems use the elaborate discursive model of justification that characterizes the Anglo-American legal systems but in all legal systems some explanation and justification is considered necessary. It is moreover expected that the explanations and justifications put forth by the judge are such as would be capable, to use Habermas' words, of winning the assent of a universal audience. That this expectation exerts a powerful influence on a judge can be clearly demonstrated if we consider the question from the perspective of a "dishonest judge." Such a judge rejects the normative force of all the presuppositions of legal argumentation that we have mentioned. He uses his position as a judge to further only what might be called his own interests. He may be interested, for example, in bribes, in advancing his own political career, or in promoting the fortunes of a particular political party, or whatever.

As unprincipled and dishonest as a judge might be, he nevertheless functions in a world in which there are obvious limitations on what he can do that operate to constrain him as much as they do an honest judge. Many of these limitations are a direct consequence of the basic nature of legal argumentation. While a dishonest judge would have no compunctions about setting forth reasons in which he does not believe, nonetheless, if he is to be effective, his reasoning must be capable of meeting the expectations of his many audiences. The audiences that such a judge is obliged to address include the general public, the other branches of government, and, in the case of lower courts, the courts of appeal that have the power to review his judgments. There will also, of course, be the professional audience of lawyers and legal scholars. Many of its members, as of the other audiences as well, will be operating under the assumption that the judge is, and indeed should be, addressing the universal audience. To persuade the members of the audiences which he is addressing, a dishonest judge will therefore have to render decisions for which justifications can be given which will be considered as plausibly acceptable to the universal audience. That is not to say that judges cannot disregard these audiences. The point has been well put by Karl Lewellyn. Lewellyn was not considering a venal judge but one who wished to reach the decision which he thought was the correct decision in some broader sense of the word but which was not the legally correct decision. Lewellyn accepted that a judge could, and in some situations perhaps should, reach the decision that he thought was correct even if it could not be legally justified. He pointed out, however, that, if even well-meaning judges should do this too often, "we should have to get rid of the guilty judges; we might in the process and for a while get rid even of the Courts."[1]

The key point is that judges do not render decisions in a vacuum. They exist in a universe in which people have expectations. No one in the long run is successful in the performance of any social role unless he fulfils to some minimal degree those expectations. As we have noted, the expectations to which a judge must respond are not only the expectations of other political actors and of the general public but also the expectations of his professional peers, that is, of legal practitioners and legal scholars. A judge who failed to meet these expectations would destroy his legitimacy. One may say of course that this would depend upon the level of expectation of his audience and, particularly, of his professional audience. If the professional audience is cynical and if the society is one in which either by

---

[1] K. Lewellyn, THE COMMON LAW TRADITION 220 (1960).

law or custom severe criticism of judicial decisions is either not permitted or frowned upon as undignified or impolite, then a valuable constraint on dishonest judges will be lost. But this is not surprising. Experience teaches us that a free society requires free discussion. So does a society committed to the pursuit of reason and justice.

That is not to say that a society in which there is free discussion is necessarily just or acts reasonably, just as it is not the case that, if scientists have freedom of inquiry, they will necessarily discover scientific truths. The point is merely that, without a robust discussion, they are much more unlikely to reach any of these goals. As we saw in Chapter 2, the fear of ridicule, the fear of being made to look absurd, is a powerful human emotion. A judge may know that his decisions will neither be reversed by a higher court nor overruled by legislation because the legislature is too busy or because a sufficient number of legislators are in complicity with the judge. But he may fear being made to look like a fool or a charlatan and thus to forfeit the respect of his peers and, in the long run, of posterity as well. In short, the requirement that a judge must justify his decision substantially restricts the ability of dishonest judges to abuse their trust because, in justifying their decisions, even dishonest judges must take into account audiences whose expectations can include, and indeed in western civilization do include, the expectations of an idealized audience. How great a restraint the force of professional opinion will be will depend in large part upon the vigor of public criticism in the society in question.

One must recognize, of course, that even honest judges are sometimes put in a position where they feel that the conventional method of deciding a case leads to unsatisfactory results, as in the situations mentioned by Lewellyn in which the judge can reach only the desirable result more or less by fiat. This recognition forces us to recognize that, when a judge appeals to an ideal audience, he is in the last analysis making the argument that, if the members of the ideal audience were in his position, they would decide as he did or, in the limiting case, at least sympathetically understand why he decided the case as he did. One such type of case, which need not detain us for long, concerns the formal aspects of legal reasoning. Sometimes, for some judges, a case can be so complicated that a judge might realize that his own processes of reasoning are simply not up to the task. Since he is obliged to decide the case before him, the best he can do is to muddle through and hope that he can convince a universal audience that he has done the best that he could. After all we cannot all always be up to the tasks that we are obliged to perform. More germane to our discussion is the type of extreme case in which an accused drug baron has made it clear that, if the judge convicts him, the judge's spouse and children will be killed, and the executive power is unable to offer sufficient guarantees of their safety. In this type of case, a judge who decides in favor of a drug dealer might still be making an appeal to the universal audience. His appeal to that audience would be of the form, "I am only a human being and, as such, can only be expected to behave as a human being. I cannot be expected to have the courage of a god."

In the United States, and many other countries as well, the drug baron case seems an unlikely scenario. But less extreme cases have arisen. In those situations to insist that a judge is trying to persuade the universal audience that, if it were in his position, it would reach the same decision as he did is not necessarily to say that the honest and conscientious judge must also always believe that he has been able to convince the universal audience that the decision he has reached is the legally correct decision. It is enough if the judge honestly appeals to the universal audience to accept that his decision is an appropriate one, under the circumstances, even if in a technical sense it would be impossible to argue that it is the legally correct decision. For example, consider the pre-Civil War cases in the United States in which judges were confronted with the problem of enforcing the federal fugitive slave laws.[2] Some judges accepted the legal validity of this legislation but nevertheless found reasons to refuse to enforce that legislation in the cases before them, reasons which the judges in question realized were legally suspect. Other judges confronted with the same problem enforced the laws but not merely or perhaps even primarily because they felt the fugitive slave laws were legally valid but because they felt that preserving the integrity of the federal union, which was threatened with secession by the slave states, was the greater good. In situations such

---

[2] On this complex subject, *see* R. Cover, JUSTICE ACCUSED (1975); R. K. Newmyer, SUPREME COURT JUSTICE JOSEPH STORY: STATESMAN OF THE OLD REPUBLIC 208-09, 344-58, 365-79 (1985). For a good overview of the arguments, *see* Comment, *Justice Story, Slavery, and the Natural Law Foundations of American Constitutionalism*, 55 U. CHI. L. REV. 273 (1988).

as these, the conscientious judge can again be considered to be appealing to the sympathy of the universal audience. The universal audience is in good faith being asked not only to understand the position of the judge but also, unlike the drug dealer case, to consider whether, if it were to step into his shoes, it would not reach the same decision regardless of the legal niceties of the situation.

Even in a society with a long and stable legal tradition, such as the United States, there are still occasionally cases with such important and disruptive political implications that a judge might strain to find a justification for avoiding having to rule on the merits of an issue because he reasonably believes that, were he to decide the merits of the question, the political consequences would be disastrous. For example, in 1956, when the United States Supreme Court was starting to engage in the process of enforcing its school desegregation decision,[3] it refused to hear on the merits a case in which state anti-miscegenation laws were being challenged.[4] These laws, which prohibited inter-racial marriage, were rarely enforced and many of the states which had such legislation were in the process of repealing them.[5] Whatever else might be said about the Supreme Court's disposition of the case,[6] there were strong prudential reasons for avoiding the necessity of making a ruling that would only have further inflamed public opinion and made it that much harder actually to implement the Court's decisions requiring the integration of public schools and other public facilities.[7]

---

[3] Brown v. Board of Education, 347 U.S. 483 (1954).

[4] Naim v. Naim, 350 U.S. 985 (1956).

[5] Professor Wechsler, in a famous article, characterized the Court's disposition of the case as "wholly without basis in law." H. Wechsler, *Toward Neutral Principles of Constitutional Law*, 73 HARV. L. REV. 1, 34 (1959).

[6] In Loving v. Virginia, 388 U.S. 1 (1967) which as noted below, did eventually strike down the Virginia anti-miscegenation statute, the Court noted "Maryland repealed its prohibitions against interracial marriage" earlier in 1967, "leaving Virginia and 15 other states with statues outlawing interracial marriage"; 388 U.S. at 6, n. 5. This indicates that in 1958, when the *Naim* case was summarily disposed of, there were at least 17 states with such statutes.

[7] In a manner of speaking this was Professor Bickel's argument. In responding to Professor Wechsler, *supra*, note 5, he readily agreed that a decision upholding the statute would have been totally unprincipled. On the other hand, he recognized that, for the

It should never be forgotten that the ideal or universal audiences, which are presupposed in legal argument, have expectations that go beyond the roles of the judges and the litigants and concern the legislature and all other ultimate law makers, such as the drafters of constitutions. This is a point that was very well put by Lon Fuller when he spoke of the "inner morality of the law."[8] Fuller began by emphasizing the almost universal agreement that law should strive for generality.[9] Under the constitutions of many American states, the ability of the state legislature to enact special or private laws, i.e., laws that concern only one person or entity, are severely limited.[10] Second, to continue presenting Fuller's thesis, it is universally accepted

---

reasons I have already mentioned in the text, the Court might not at that time have wanted to squander its capital, so to speak, on such an emotionally charged issue with little practical import. Professor Bickel argued that the Court was not obliged to be principled in deciding when to exercise its procedural discretion to hear a case on the merits. On such procedural matters, the Court could exercise the political prudence that was forbidden to it when it heard cases on the merits. A. Bickel, THE LEAST DANGEROUS BRANCH 70 (1962). For Bickel's response to Wechsler's more general arguments *see id.* at 49-65, 70-72.

[8] L. Fuller, THE MORALITY OF LAW 42-43 (1964), (hereinafter cited as THE MORALITY OF LAW).

[9] *See id.* at 46-49. Perhaps the most famous insistence on the generality of law in the English language is that of John Austin. *See* 1 J. Austin, LECTURES ON JURISPRUDENCE 92-96 (R. Campbell ed. 1885). The reference is to Lecture 1 which is often printed separately, together with what are now called the rest of Austin's first six lectures, as *The Province of Jurisprudence Determined.*

[10] For example, under Article II, § 24 of the Constitution of North Carolina, the General Assembly, the legislature of North Carolina, is "prohibited" from enacting "any local, private, or special act or resolution" on a variety of subjects, fourteen in all, including "granting of a divorce" or "altering the name of any person" or "restoring to the right of citizenship any person convicted of a felony," or, on a less personal level, "regulating labor, trade, mining, or manufacturing." Taking a less particularized approach, Article 4, § 29 of the Michigan Constitution provides that "[t]he legislature shall pass no local or special act in any case where a general act can be made applicable"and providing where such local or special acts are permitted such acts cannot take effect until approved by two-thirds of the entire membership of each house of the Michigan legislature and a majority of the electors voting in the district affected. There are of course ways of avoiding some of these prohibitions. For example, MICH. COMP. L. § 117.5i gives certain snow removal powers to any "city with a population of over 1,000,000." The only Michigan city which could possibly have a population over 1,000,000 is of course Detroit.

that, in a civilized society, laws must be promulgated.[11] Third, as Fuller points out, it is almost as equally universally accepted as a desideratum that laws should not operate retroactively.[12] In the criminal law, this is often expressed as a prohibition of *ex post facto* laws. It is furthermore accepted that law should strive for clarity, that it should not be contradictory, and that it should not require the impossible.[13] Fuller also noted that it is desirable that laws should be consistent over time, i.e., that they "should not be changed too frequently."[14] This of course has been a recognized desideratum of law at least since the time of Aristotle.[15] Finally, Fuller noted that it is certainly an aspirational goal of all legal systems, even if often honored in the breach, that there should be a "congruence between official action and the law."[16] In a sense this last requirement is a way of describing what the rule of law is all about.

We may of course agree with H.L.A. Hart that the legal systems of some quite iniquitous regimes could certainly in theory, and quite possibly also in practice, do a fairly good job of complying with what Fuller called the "inner morality of the law."[17] We may also accept, as Fuller himself did, that the so-called "inner morality of the law" is a morality of aspiration because even a just regime cannot always comply with all of these requirements if it is actually to achieve justice. Still the need to try to comply with these requirements does impose some constraints on what law-making authorities can do and therefore on the form that legal argumentation takes. The ideal or universal audience to which legal argument is ultimately addressed expects these constraints to be taken seriously.

---

[11] *See* THE MORALITY OF LAW at 49-51.

[12] *See id.* at 51-62.

[13] *See id.* at 63-79.

[14] *Id.* at 79.

[15] *See* Aristotle, THE POLITICS, Bk.II c.8 (1269a). *See also* St. Thomas Aquinas, THE SUMMA THEOLOGIAE, Part One of the Second Part, Q.97, Art. 2.

[16] THE MORALITY OF LAW at 81.

[17] *See* H. Hart, *Book Review*, 78 HARV. L. REV. 1281, 1288 (1965). *See also* H. Hart, THE CONCEPT OF LAW 202 (1961), in which Hart had made the same point a few years before Fuller published his book, and to which Fuller, taking the point as aimed at him, responded. *See* THE MORALITY OF LAW at 153-55. As just described at the beginning of this note, Hart reiterated his criticism in his review of Fuller's book.

CHAPTER 5

DIFFERENT CONCEPTIONS OF THE IDEAL AUDIENCE—A FIRST LOOK

As noted in the previous chapter, there are many universal features of law that reflect broadly accepted notions of the roles of judges and other participants in the legal process and of the forms that legal regulation must take—features that clearly influence and constrain our notions of the ideal form of legal argument. It is nevertheless indisputable that there are also differences in the way different cultures envision the ideal form of argument. That different cultures, even within the Western legal tradition, should have somewhat different conceptions of the ideal or universal audiences to which legal arguments are made is of course not surprising. It merely reflects the fact that our notion of an ideal or universal audience is basically a construct, even if it is a construct that we constantly presuppose and could not do without. Moreover, the existence of these differences certainly does not detract from the fact that these more particularized conceptions of an ideal audience and of the arguments that will appeal to those audiences serve as additional constraints on the form and nature of legal argument for those who are part of a subculture of a particular civilization.

Although most people would be prepared to accept as a fact needing no demonstration that there are important subcultural differences within any dominant legal tradition, say the Western legal tradition, it may be helpful to give some actual examples and then try to explain what accounts for these differences. The first few examples concern statutory interpretation and the interpretation of treaties, as to which, in the United States, the same interpretive techniques are used. The use of an example involving a treaty also facilitates comparative analysis, since the same treaty provisions will often have been considered by different national courts. The remaining examples will concern constitutional interpretation.

One of the crucial questions of modern legal theory is the relationship between the legislature and the judiciary, particularly as the theoretical underpinnings of that relationship find expression in the judicial interpretation of statutes. We may take it as given that, in the Western world, the primacy of the legislature to the other branches of government is universally accepted. In some countries, such as the United States, there may be judicially enforceable constitutional limits to legislative authority. And in some countries, such as again the United States, there may be some powers of the executive over such matters as foreign affairs, the command of the armed forces, and the exercise of clemency through the granting of pardons, that are beyond direct legislative control. But, within its sphere of competence the legislative branch is supreme. The question is how this acknowledged supremacy manifests itself in the judicial performance of the task of statutory interpretation.

That the task of statutory interpretation is performed differently in common-law countries than in civil-law countries is recognized by practically every commentator. Admittedly, the hostility towards legislative intervention into matters handled by customary law persisted longer in the common-law countries than it did on the continent. This hostility found expression in the old maxim: "Statutes in derogation of the common law are to be strictly construed." But, even in the United States, statutory change in the law is being accepted as a normal, not exceptional development. Nevertheless, differences in approach to the interpretation of statutes and similar instruments persist. There are of course important differences even among common-law countries in the approach taken to the interpretation of statutes and analogous written instruments, but, on the whole, in the English-speaking world, such interpretation can be said to be more literal, cramped, and, in the eyes of some, unimaginative than the approach taken elsewhere.[1] The relatively general and abstract nature of regulation that has been noted as characterizing continental codes is undoubtedly a factor influencing the differing styles of statutory interpretation,[2] as is the related factor that, when inclusive statutory legal regulation is attempted in "common law countries," it is "usually too detailed and insufficiently systematized from the perspective of logical legalists."[3]

---

[1] For a discussion of this point see R. David and J. Brierley, MAJOR LEGAL SYSTEMS IN THE WORLD TODAY 117-46, 383-86 (3d Eng. Ed. 1985). *See also* K. Zweigert and Kötz, H., INTRODUCTION TO COMPARATIVE LAW 265-71 (3d rev. ed., T. Weir transl., 1998).

[2] *See* M. Damaška, *On Circumstances Favoring Codification*, 52 REVISTA JURIDICA DE LA UNIVERSIDAD DE PUERTO RICO 355, 356-59 (1983). He notes the continental preference for what he calls "logical legalism." *Id.* at 358.

[3] *Id.* at 359.

We are of course witnessing the increasing economic integration of the Western world, a feature of modern life that will inevitably have an impact on legal developments. There are nevertheless important cultural values that, at least in the United States, militate against adoption of continental techniques of statutory interpretation. A few examples may be helpful. These examples will also provide concrete illustrations of the type of rationality that a particular culture would attribute to the ideal legislature, that is the rationality that the universal audience being addressed by the judge would expect of such a legislature.

Article 17 of the Warsaw Convention of 1929, in the English translation supplied to the United States Senate when it ratified the United States accession to that treaty, provides that an air carrier "shall be liable for damage sustained in the event of the death or wounding of a passenger or any other bodily injury suffered by a passenger."[4] In *Eastern Airlines v. Floyd*,[5] decided in April 1991, the United States Supreme Court was faced with the question of whether this language permitted recovery for psychic injuries unaccompanied by "physical injury or physical manifestation of injury." The plaintiffs had been passengers on an aircraft bound from Miami to the Bahamas, all three of whose engines lost power. The aircraft rapidly lost altitude while the passengers were informed that the aircraft "would be ditched in the ocean." Fortunately, the pilots were eventually able to restart one of the engines and the aircraft was able to return safely to Miami. Because the authoritative text of the Warsaw Convention is the French one, the case turned on whether the term "lésion corporelle," translated into English as "bodily injury," covered the plaintiffs alleged injuries. Since the negotiating history of the Warsaw Convention was silent on the issue, the United States Supreme Court embarked on an extended examination of domestic French law so as to determine how the expression "lésion corporelle" would have been construed by French lawyers in 1929. It concluded that French lawyers of that period would have construed the term to refer only to physical injuries. The Court also inquired whether any French case prior to 1929 had recognized a right to recover for the type of injuries involved in the case before it under any provision of the French

---

[4] 49 Stat. 3018 (1934).
[5] 499 U.S. 530 (1991).

civil code and found that none had done so. The Court then noted that no such recovery would have been permitted at that time under the domestic law of many of the signatories to the Warsaw Convention, including the United States. Since the Court conceived of its role as giving the words of the treaty a meaning consistent with the shared expectations of the contracting parties, it ruled unanimously that the plaintiffs could not recover for their psychic injuries under the Convention.[6]

In marked contrast to the approach taken by the United States Supreme Court, the Israeli Supreme Court,[7] in a decision considered and rejected by the United States Supreme Court,[8] had allowed recovery for purely psychic injuries. The Israeli case involved the hijacking of an Air France flight to Entebbe, Uganda, in 1976. In allowing recovery, the Israeli court declared that "desirable jurisprudential policy" favored an expansive reading of Article 17. It noted how both Anglo-American and Israeli law had evolved since 1929 to allow such recovery. For the Israeli Supreme Court, the idealized universal audience being addressed by the treaty was not one whose development had stopped in 1929.[9]

Another example of the restrictive approach to statutory interpretation taken by American courts may also prove helpful. Although I am unable to give an analogous case from a noncommon-law jurisdiction, I would hazard the guess that most continental jurists would have no trouble

---

[6] A Scottish case, Hammond v. Bristow Helicopters, Ltd., [1999] Scot. L. Times 919 (Ct. Sess. 1998), and an Australian case Kotsambasis v. Singapore Airlines, Ltd., 42 N.S.W.Rep. 110 (C.A. 1997) also both took the position that the treaty should be interpreted in the light of the contemporary understanding in 1926 and thus, not surprisingly, reached the same conclusion as did the United States Supreme Court in the *Floyd* case. Since neither of these other courts is a national court of final appeal, these decisions cannot of course be taken as a definitive statement of what the law is either in Australia or in the United Kingdom. *Cf.* Sidhu v. British Airways PLC and Abnett v. British Airways PLC, [1997] A.C. 430 (1996).

[7] Cie. Air France v. Teichner (1984), 39 REV. FRANÇAISE DE DROIT ARIEN 232, 243 (1985), 23 EUROP. TRANSP. L. 87, 102 (1988). These are French translations. The only English translation, which however was not called to the attention of the United States Supreme Court, is apparently [1984] 1 S&B Av. Rep. VII/141.

[8] 499 U.S. at 551-52.

[9] Israel follows a mixed common-law and civil-law tradition. *See* R. David and D. Brierly, *op. cit. supra* note 1, at 25-26.

concluding that the case should have been decided differently. The case is *United States v. Smith*,[10] and it was decided in March 1991, only a few weeks before *Eastern Airlines v. Floyd*. The *Smith* case involved the construction of the Federal Tort Claims Act which governs tort actions against the Federal Government. Enacted in 1946,[11] the Tort Claims Act initially merely provided a tort remedy against the United States. It did not limit the plaintiff's ability to bring an action against the offending federal employee under the common law of the several states. Only after the plaintiff had been awarded a judgement against the United States was his ability to proceed against the federal employee restricted. Over the course of time, however, Congress has made the remedy against the United States the plaintiff's exclusive remedy, first in some limited types of situations, including malpractice actions against Government doctors, and then, since 1988, for all torts committed by United States Government employees in the scope of their employment.[12]

The *Smith* case arose in 1982 and involved the alleged negligence of a U.S. Army doctor in delivering the child of the wife of an American soldier in a United States Army hospital in Vicenza, Italy. The child was born with massive brain damage. His parents, in 1987, brought a common-law action against the doctor in a federal court in California seeking relief under California and Italian law. The United States intervened and sought to have itself substituted as the defendant *in lieu* of the doctor. One might ask why would the plaintiffs care. Admittedly, they would not have a jury trial in an action against the Government, but they would also not have to worry about recovering any amounts awarded. The plaintiffs' problem arose from the fact that, in another portion of the Tort Claims Act, it is specifically stated that no action can be brought against the United States for "claims arising in a foreign country."[13] While the action was pending the Liability Reform Act of 1988, which, as already explained, made the Tort Claims Act remedy against the United States Government the exclusive remedy for *all* torts committed by Government employees in the

---

[10] 499 U.S. 160 (1991).
[11] 60 Stat. 842 (1946).
[12] 28 U.S.C. § 2679(b)(1) (1994).
[13] 28 U.S.C. § 2680(k) (1994).

scope of their employment, came into effect. The United States Supreme Court reviewed this legislation and the similar earlier legislation regarding malpractice actions and took them at face value. It held that the remedy against the United States was the only remedy available to the Smiths. Since, as we have just seen, the Tort Claims Act does not permit recovery against the United States for injuries arising in foreign countries, the Smiths' action regrettably had to be dismissed. Of the nine justices, only Justice Stevens dissented. He argued that the statutory provisions making the remedy against the United States the exclusive remedy of those injured by government employees should be interpreted so as to apply only in circumstances in which an action against the United States is possible. This is certainly a plausible argument and, given the less technical methods of statutory interpretation of continental legal systems, it would probably be persuasive to most continental lawyers. To an American lawyer, however, the Court's decision in the *Smith* case does not seem all that odd or unreasonable.[14] Indeed, I believe the Court probably reached the *legally* correct decision.

Why this difference in approach? We would probably all concede that a legal solution that left the Smiths without a legal remedy for the brain damage to their child, assuming that the damage was in fact the result of the doctor's negligence, is not the ideal solution. How then could the universal audience, to whom the members of the United States Supreme Court can be considered to be addressing their argument, accept such a conclusion as the correct one? It is too easy to say that the conclusion reached by the Court in the *Smith* case reflects a commitment to the primacy of the legislature. A continental lawyer who thinks that the Court's conclusion was wrong would strenuously deny that he is ignoring the primacy of the legislature. The continental lawyer would claim that he has a different conception of what the legislature is and of what it would want. He envisages a legislature that is more rational and humane.[15] Why would an American lawyer and, very possibly other common-law lawyers as well, have a more cramped, a less idealized, view of the legislature?

---

[14] I also do not believe that an English or other common-law lawyer would have found the Court's decision unreasonable either.
[15] *Cf.* note 24, *infra*, and accompanying text.

As I have already indicated, the answer cannot be that common-law courts and lawyers have an innate hostility to legislatures that reflects itself in a glorification of the irrational and occasional pettiness of legislative solutions. To whatever extent such attitudes ever actually prevailed, they were largely part of a legal climate that no longer exists. The answer, I would submit, lies in a different direction.

One factor that we shall discuss at greater length throughout the course of this book is the extent to which a particular legal system is concerned with achieving some kind of global rationality among its various directives and principles. Although, as we shall see in later chapters, there are those who are urging a change in approach, the common law has been notoriously prepared to settle for what, following Joseph Raz, we might call local rationality[16] rather than attempting to achieve a more ambitions and general form of legal rationality. Other important factors are differing conceptions of the functions of government in a democracy. There are finally some fundamental differences in the structure of government that might be somewhat unique to the United States that may also explain the difference in approach to statutory interpretation that we are attempting to understand.

The United States does not have a parliamentary system of government. The executive cannot control the legislative process. More often than not in recent times the same party has not controlled the executive and the two co-equal branches of the American legislature. Even when the Presidency, the House of Representatives and the Senate have been controlled by the same party, the lack of strong centralized parties, along the European model, has meant that the executive has not been able to control the legislative process to the same extent as can be done in Europe. Although there is a legislative drafting service available to help representatives and senators draft legislation, much legislation is not subjected to that professional screening. Indeed many important elements of legislation are inserted into legislation as amendments in an *ad hoc* manner. In operation, the whole American system functions as a device for

---

[16] J. Raz, *The Relevance of Coherence*, 72 BOSTON UNIV. L. REV 273 (1992). Raz contrasts "local coherence" with "global coherence." Depending on the context, I prefer to refer to the contrast as that between local and global "rationality," or as that between local and global "consistency."

forcing compromises at every step in the legislative process and the compromises are many. What the United States Supreme Court may perhaps be doing is respecting the compromise-seeking nature of the legislative process. The almost obsessive search of American courts for congressional intent as revealed in the committee reports and debates of the Congress clearly reflects an appreciation of the fact that legislation is the product of compromise and that the courts exist to make those compromises effective. In turn, the universal audience to which American courts are addressing themselves accepts that government in a democracy is government by compromise and applauds the courts' attempts to facilitate the compromises reached in the legislative forum. In short, the ideal legislature is one committed to compromise and not a legislature always seeking to give voice to the highest standards of rationality and to further the most noble aspirations of the society of which it is the legislature.[17]

Factors such as the ones I have just discussed help explain why an American court might decide the *Smith* case the way it was decided. Nevertheless, although the decisions like that in the *Smith* case are not atypical, it would be a mistake to conclude this case captures the entire essence of the American legal system. By their very nature, all comparative studies run the risk of over generalization and this feature of such studies must always be kept in mind. Moreover, if the initial judicial reaction to legislation and even to the Constitution as a type of legislation seems to a continental mind to be too literal, legalistic, and, in short, cramped, over time one often witnesses a more expansive approach. As a statute or even a constitutional provision remains on the books for a long period of time,

---

[17] I owe much to conversation with my friend and colleague Professor Paul D. Carrington for helping me appreciate how the structure of government influences judicial techniques of statutory interpretation. I wish to stress that I have been considering legislation in the United States as the culmination of a process of *political* compromise. There has been considerable discussion in recent years of a different point - and one that I am not making in this book - that the legislation that emerges in the United States is very often really the end-product of a process of *private* compromise among various interest groups. For a good discussion of the literature, see W. Popkin, *The Collaborative Model of Statutory Interpretation*, 61 SO. CAL. L. REV. 541 (1988). Popkin accepts that " [c]ompromise is an accurate description of the legislative process," *id.* at 565, but concludes, as would I, that the perspective of viewing legislation as the product of *public* deliberation, rather than of *private* bargaining, is a more satisfactory analytical tool.

the search for the specific intent of the legislature that enacted the statute in question or of the drafters of the constitutional provision under consideration sometimes starts to lose its intensity.

For example, in 1866 Congress enacted a provision that, after subsequent re-enactments and editorial revisions, is now 42 United States Code § 1982, which provides that "all citizens of the United States shall have the same right in every State . . ., as is enjoyed by white citizens to inherit purchase, sell, hold, and convey real and personal property." On the only occasion upon which the United States Supreme Court had considered the statute in the 102 years until 1968, it had indicated that the statute only applied to state action,[18] that is that it prohibited the states either by statute, common law, or custom from placing any legal disabilities on the ability of non-whites to enter into legally enforceable contracts. This certainly was a common-sense view of what the statute said. Nonetheless, in 1968, the Court held that the statute reached private conduct so that the plaintiff could bring an action against the defendants for refusing to sell them a house "for the sole reason that one of the plaintiffs was a Negro."[19] Although sympathetic to the results, Charles Fairman, the leading historian of the post Civil War period, asserted that the Court's conclusion was not legally supportable.[20]

The same process can be seen in the Court's treatment of several clauses of the constitution. The prohibitions against "bills of attainder"[21] and "cruel and unusual punishments" have been extended beyond anything that the founding fathers could possibly have intended. Nevertheless, the pattern is a mixed one. The passage of time does not always lead to a more expansive mode of interpretation. The same constitutional provision, the Eighth Amendment, that includes the prohibition of "cruel and unusual

---

[18] *See, e.g.*, Hurd v. Hodge, 334 U.S. 24 (1948).

[19] Jones v. Alfred H. Mayer Co., 392 U.S. 409 (1968).

[20] C. Fairman, RECONSTRUCTION AND REUNION 1864-88 (1971) (This is Volume VI of the *History of the Supreme Court of the United States*, a project started as the result of the Oliver Wendell Holmes Devise). Fairman noted that the Congress that enacted the statute had separate galleries for white and black spectators. *Id* at 1259.

[21] In United States v. Brown, 381 U.S. 437 (1965), the court relied on the prohibition of bills of attainder to strike down a statute making it illegal for members of the Communist Party to be officers of labor unions.

punishment," which has been given an expansive interpretation,[22] also contains a prohibition against "excessive fines." When the United States Supreme Court was required in 1989 to decide whether jury awards of punitive damages could be challenged as "excessive fines," the Court, which held that they could not, as well as the two dissenters who thought that they could, focused primarily on what had been the contemporary understanding of that language in 1791, when the Eighth Amendment was adopted, as well as in 1689, when the English Bill of Rights, from which the clause in question was taken, had been adopted.[23]

The United States Supreme Court is obviously torn between two competing visions of what the ideal or universal audience expects of it. One vision, the traditional and still the predominant one, stresses fidelity to the traditional role of common-law judges and focuses on discovering the precisely intended meaning of statutes, constitutions, and other legal instruments. This vision eschews completely the spirit behind Article 1 of the Swiss Civil Code that, when neither statutory provision nor customary law cover the case, the judge should decide "according to the rules that he

---

[22] In Trop v. Dulles, 356 U.S. 86 (1958), the Court held that the prohibition of cruel and unusual punishment prevented Congress from stripping of United States citizenship a person convicted of desertion in wartime from the armed forces of the United States. In writing for four of the five justices who constituted the majority, Chief Justice Warren declared that the clause "must draw its meaning from the evolving standards of decency that mark the progress of a maturing society." *Id.* at 101. As is well known it is this clause that has been the focus of efforts to declare the death penalty unconstitutional. *See* Gregg v. Georgia, 428 U.S. 153 (1976); Furman v. Georgia, 408 U.S. 238 (1972). *Cf.* note 25, *infra.*

[23] Browning-Ferris Industries of Vt., Inc. v. Kelco Disposal, Inc., 492 U.S. 257 (1989). The unsuccessful challenge involved a jury award of $6,000,000 in punitive damages. The jury had awarded $51,146 in compensatory damages. The Court has subsequently held that punitive damage awards can be attacked as a denial of "due process of law," but to be struck down the award would have to be excessive indeed. *See* BMW of No. Amer. Inc. v. Gore, 517 U.S. 559 (1996). In this case the Court, in a five to four decision, struck down an award of punitive damages that was 500 times larger than the award of compensatory damages. It remarked that "[w]hen the ratio is a breathtaking 500 to 1, however, the award must surely 'raise a suspicious eyebrow'." *Id.* at 583. The four dissenters felt the Court should not have gotten involved in the issue.

would lay down if he himself had to act as legislator."[24] The competing vision, which is currently less likely to influence statutory and even constitutional interpretation, stresses that the common law has always been open to evolution at the hands of creative judges and focuses on achieving congruence between a society's professed values and its actual practices.[25]

Courts in other legal cultures take a different view of their role in constitutional adjudication. In 1990, for example, the German Constitutional Court considered two cases that dealt with legislation providing for tax exemptions for dependent children and for cash benefits paid by the government to families with children.[26] The Constitutional Court found that the aggregate of the exemptions and the cash benefits in the large majority of cases amounted to less than welfare payments for dependent children. It held that the German Constitution guaranteed the right to have income free from tax in an amount necessary to satisfy a person's most basic needs and that the challenged legislation was inconsistent with this constitutional right. These are not unique cases that can be dismissed as oddities. [27]

A common-law lawyer, even in a country with constitutional review, such as the United States, would find these cases astounding. The only remotely comparable American case is *Dandridge v. Williams*[28] decided in 1970. That case involved the administration of aid to poor families with

---

[24] THE SWISS CIVIL CODE, Art. 1 (Eng. Version by I. Williams, 1912, revised and updated by S. Wyler and B. Wyler, 1976). Switzerland is not the only European country to expect a judge in cases of uncertainty to seek a solution by resort to broader moral purposes. *See* C. Baudenbacher, *Some Remarks on the Method of Civil Law*, 34 TEX. INT'L L. J. 333 (1999).

[25] This is the point of Chief Justice Warren's declaration in Trop v. Dulles, 356 U.S. 86, (1958), quoted in footnote 22, *supra*. It is also the major thrust of Justice Brennan and Marshall's dissents, particularly that of Justice Brennan, in Gregg v. Georgia, 428 U.S. 153 (1976). Excerpts from their dissents were quoted in Chapter 2, *supra*, at pp. 22-23.

[26] Bundesverfassungsgericht, Decrees of May 29 and June 12, 1990, 82 BverfGE 60, 98.

[27] More recently the German Constitutional Court has ruled, in one case, that child care allowances available to single parents must be made available to married couples and, in another case more closely analogous to the American case about to be discussed in the text, that civil servants with more than two children should have significantly increased benefits. *See Financial Times* (London ed.), Feb 6, 1999, at p. 2.

[28] 397 U.S. 471 (1970).

dependent children under a program jointly funded by the federal government and the states. The state of Maryland published regulations awarding grants based on the number of children but with a limit on the maximum any one family could receive of $250 a month. The effect of this regulation was that any family with more than six children received the same amount regardless of the number of children in the family. After deciding that the Maryland regulation did not conflict with federal law, the Court turned to the question of whether the Maryland regulations violated the equal protection clause of the Fourteenth Amendment. The Court held that it did not. Even Justices Brennan and Marshall, who dissented on constitutional grounds, did not challenge the state's professed need to limit the amount of money expended. Their point was that whatever money was appropriated for the purpose of assisting needy families with dependent children should be disbursed on a *per* child basis.

Dandridge v. Williams, it should be noted, was decided during a period when some academics were urging the Court to recognize certain welfare rights as entitlements under the United States Constitution.[29] It was the most favorable possible time to have litigated the issue of welfare rights. The Court, of course, has never recognized any such rights and it would require a revolution in the way American courts envisage their role in government for them to do so. The universal audience addressed by the German Constitutional Court obviously has different expectations. While there are of course important differences between the German and American Constitutions on the matters with which we are concerned, there are some important similarities. The German Constitution, like the American one and unlike many other modern constitutions, does not expressly recognize welfare rights.[30] Their recognition in Germany is solely

---

[29] *See* F. Michelman, *The Supreme Court 1968 Term-Foreword: On Protecting the Poor through the Fourteenth Amendment*, 83 HARV. L. REV. 7 (1969).

[30] A possible textual basis for such rights is Article 1 which imposes upon "the state authority" the obligation to "respect and protect . . . human dignity," and Article 20 which states that Germany is a "*social* federal state." (emphasis added) By contrast, for example, Article 21 of the Greek Constitution requires the state to "care for the health of citizens" and to "adopt special measures for the protection of youth, old age, disability and for the relief of the needy." Article 22 of that constitution declares that "[w]ork constitutes a right" and that "the State shall care for the social security of working people." It is unclear

the result of judicial construction as would have to be the case if such rights were ever to be recognized in the United States.

---

to what extent these provisions are judicially enforceable.

CHAPTER 6

ACCOUNTING FOR DIFFERENCES IN PERCEPTIONS OF THE IDEAL AUDIENCE—SOME PRELIMINARY OBSERVATIONS

After first noting in chapter 4 that there is a widely shared general agreement on certain features of legal argumentation, we began, in chapter 5, to focus on the differences between the ways that various sub-cultures within the Western legal tradition envision the ideal audience to which legal arguments are addressed. In chapter 5, we focused on the interpretation of statutes and other authoritative legal instruments and gave some instances of how common-law courts, in interpreting statutes and similar instruments, tend to take a cramped and particularistic view of their task when contrasted with their continental counterparts. We saw that scholars have attributed some of these differences to a continental preference for a "logical legalism" that would be hard for common-law courts to copy, even if they were inclined to do so—and as we have noted they occasionally are so inclined—because "inclusive statutory regulations in common law countries . . . are usually too detailed and insufficiently systematized"[1] as compared to comparable statutory regulation in continental countries. I suggested that there were also additional factors at work, factors relating to differing visions as to how ideally the political process works and as to how legislation should be made that would accentuate the differences in approach between American courts and those in Western countries operating under a code-based system of law.

Obviously the differences between legal systems that affect the nature and form of legal argumentation go well beyond questions of statutory interpretation. In succeeding chapters, we shall examine differences in approach to such questions as the place of discretion in the operation of a legal system and the role of general principles in legal reasoning. Furthermore, as we shall see, the differences that we shall be examining are not only differences between various legal systems, there are also differences that manifest themselves within legal systems. While legal argumentation is clearly aimed at an ideal and universal audience, it is by

---

[1] M. Damaška, *On Circumstances Favoring Codification*, 52 REVISTA JURIDICA DE LA UNIVERSIDAD DE PUERTO RICO, 355, 359 (1983) cited and discussed in chapter 5, *supra*, at 50.

no means the case that the predominant conception as to the nature of this audience is a static one. It is a constantly evolving one and the members of any given society are often torn by conflicting visions. These again are matters that will be pursued in succeeding chapters. In this chapter, I wish to concentrate on two rather more general features that undoubtedly influence any society's vision of what the ideal audience will approve as an appropriate legal argument. The first concerns our ideal concept of how the state should function, that is how the coercive machinery of the state should be organized. The second concerns our ideal concept of what is the purpose of the state, that is what are the goals that the coercive machinery of the state should seek to achieve. The two questions are of course interrelated but there is some value in trying to address the questions sequentially, even at the cost of some overlap in the discussion.

A. *Competing Visions of the Way the State Should Be Organized*

Even in societies that share a common commitment to the rule of law, the universal audiences to which the members of those societies direct their arguments will have different ideas as to the form in which the rule of law should manifest itself. Much is made of the difference between the "adversarial" structures of legal proceedings in Anglo-American jurisdictions and the "inquisitorial" approach used in continental Europe and most of the rest of the world and which also characterized the former communist legal regimes. There is much truth contained in this distinction, but Mirjan Damaška contends that this dichotomy is not rich enough to capture the range of differences between Anglo-American systems and other types of legal systems. For a deeper understanding of the differences between various legal systems Damaška believes it is necessary to ask two basic questions when examining national legal systems:[2] What is the *form* by which the state exercises authority? And what does the state conceive its *purpose* to be? For the moment, I wish to concentrate, as much as possible, primarily on the first question.

---

[2] M. Damaška, THE FACES OF JUSTICE AND STATE AUTHORITY 8-15 (1986). Damaška is of course describing "ideal" types. He is not suggesting that any particular continental or common-law jurisdiction exactly exemplifies one or the other of these ideals.

With regard to the form of state authority, Damaška distinguishes between states exercising authority through a hierarchically organized set of officials and those states in which authority is exercised through a large number of coordinate officials.[3] A hierarchically organized structure of authority will typically have a career bureaucracy; it will have higher levels of authority to which disputes will eventually be funneled; and it will ultimately have a final common authority which will resolve disputes, even disputes among officials, definitively. Such a hierarchically organized form of authority will distrust not only lay officials but lay control of legal proceedings. It will be inclined to favor a form of judicial procedure in which officials are responsible for questioning those accused of criminal offenses as well as those participating in civil litigation. A hierarchical organization of authority will prefer a complete written record of proceedings, which will then form the "file" or "dossier" that will accompany the case on its journey up through the hierarchical ladder. Since authority is hierarchically organized, it is possible for legal proceedings to be broken up into many successive stages.[4] The idea of one crucial event, such as the trial in Anglo-American law, will be absent.[5]

In contrast, the coordinate form is characterized by the use of lay officials, the lack of a career-oriented permanent corps of officials, and the lack of a common superior to whom feuding officials can refer matters for definitive resolution.[6] According to Damaška, when authority is organized along the coordinate model, it is easier to tolerate control by the parties over the proceedings with regard both to their inauguration and to the procedural steps through which litigation progresses. As already noted, the trial becomes the crucial stage of the proceedings. Testimony is presented orally and it is not essential that a complete transcript be preserved. The review of the case on appeal will not be as thorough as in the hierarchical model, and the system will be prepared to tolerate some inconsistency of results.[7]

On the other hand, Damaška believes it to be the case that, where the conduct of the factual inquiry is primarily in the hands of the professional

---

[3] See id. at 16-46.
[4] See id. at 18-23, 47-56.
[5] See id. at 53.
[6] See id. at 23-28.
[7] See id. at 57-65.

judiciary, the probing for truth, at least in civil cases, is not as exhaustive as it can be in a society in which authority is organized along coordinate lines, as in England and America.[8] Damaška contends that the need for the judge in a hierarchically organized society, with its emphasis on inquisitorial forms, to preserve the appearance of objectivity, prevents him from engaging in the probing questioning that is permitted to partisan counsel in England and America.[9] At the same time, although a hierarchical system of authority is less willing to defer to the lead of the parties than is the case in a system of authority based on the coordinate model, in those areas where hierarchical authority is prepared to recognize the autonomy of litigants and defer to the lead of the parties, Damaška contends that it is more likely to do so by rigid rules that severely restrict the authority of the judge.[10] The reason for this is undoubtedly that hierarchically organized authority structures are inclined to limit severely the discretion of such subordinate officials as trial judges.[11] Systems organized along coordinate lines, on the other hand, which generally accord the parties a great deal of freedom, are nevertheless unlikely to accord the parties substantially absolute discretion on any particular aspect of the trial process. Instead, such societies are prepared to give trial judges substantial amounts of residual discretion.[12] In succeeding chapters, we shall explore the question of discretion in some detail; not merely in the broad comparative context that characterizes Damaška's analysis but in a more detailed analysis of how the notion of discretion actually operates within particular legal cultures.

Having described the two ways in which the authority of the state can be organized, Damaška turns to the question of what over-all purpose motivates the state and of how the form in which state power is organized

---

[8] *See id.* at 121-22, 125.

[9] *See id.* at 122.

[10] *See id.* at 125, where Damaška notes that continental judges have much less authority to call witnesses on their own initiative or against the wishes of the litigants than do their common-law counterparts.

[11] Damaška suggests that the "logical legalism" exhibited in hierarchical organizations is not favorably inclined to tolerate broad grants of discretion. *See id.* at 54-56.

[12] As an example, Damaška cites the authority of American judges to call witnesses on their own initiative whether the parties agree or not. *See id.* at 124-25.

might affect the purposes which a state seeks to achieve. One type of state is simply interested in conflict resolution. This type Damaška calls the "reactive state."[13] In terms of our discussion, the universal audience to which people appeal in a reactive state has no social agenda other than trying to keep the peace. It is content to allow people to work out their own notions of the good. In contrast to the reactive state stands the "activist state."[14] The universal audience in such a state has a very clear notion of what the public good requires. In its extreme form, it is dedicated even to changing the nature of mankind. We shall examine in greater detail some competing notions of the purpose and role of the state in the next section of this chapter.

Of course, no state in practice, and certainly no modern state, will fit completely into any one category. That is to say, there is no state without some hierarchical organization of authority, and there is no state which does not embrace some notion of the common good as something more than an aggregation of individual goods. Indeed, even at the height of laissez-faire notions of government, criminal procedure was never completely devoid of a commitment to serving state purposes, even if, in some legal systems, actual criminal trials resembled the simple conflict-solving paradigm of the civil-litigation process.

Damaška notes, as he must, that the hierarchical organization of officialdom is not incompatible with a view of society that insists that the purpose of the judicial system is merely to resolve conflicts.[15] Damaška nevertheless suggests that it is very hard for a state that conceives of its purpose as one of active intervention in society to proceed through the form of coordinate officialdom. I would add, however, that it is not impossible. The post-New Deal United States is perhaps the best example of a state that has been historically organized around what Damaška would call a largely coordinate structure of authority attempting to assume a somewhat activist purpose. To many people, of course, the sight of federal judges running school systems and prisons and of private parties seeking to establish emission standards for the automobile industry in the course of private

---

[13] *Id.* at 73-80.
[14] *Id.* at 80-88.
[15] *See id.* at 97-98.

litigation would seem anarchic.[16] Anarchic or not, it is still an attempt by a state historically organized around a coordinate form of authority to take an activist social posture. Damaška believes, however, that a society truly dedicated to an interventionist stance and to the improvement of society and the betterment of mankind will almost necessarily resort to a hierarchically organized structure of authority.[17] He suggests that Mao's China was a real-life example that came very close to the theoretical paradigm of the pure activist state.[18]

Damaška has provided us with some perceptive insights. There is no question that a society's conception of the ideal form of political organization will affect how that society goes about achieving its goals and will thus necessarily affect the nature and style of legal argumentation. Undoubtedly many of the differences between the content of, say, the American legal system and that of a continental system can thereby be explained. We shall explore some of these effects in later chapters. It is also probably true that, all other things being equal, a society committed to a market economy is more likely to adopt what Damaška calls a coordinate form of political organization. It is probably even more likely to be true that a society with a particular overriding vision of the function of the state and the role of its citizens in achieving that vision is more likely to adopt a hierarchically organized political and legal structure. But, as the example of the American New Deal illustrates and as we shall explore in the next section of this chapter, it does not follow that a society that adopts a coordinate form of political and legal organization will necessarily favor a vision of what constitutes the public good that focuses more on the individual. Nor does it follow that a society that adopts a hierarchically organized political and legal structure will necessarily favor a vision of the

---

[16] *See* Diamond v. General Motors Corp., 20 Cal. App.3d 374, 97 Cal. Rptr. 639(1971) (automobile emission standards). Instances of judicial supervision of school and prison systems are too numerous and well-known to require extensive citation. *See, e.g.,* M. Feeley and E. Rubin, JUDICIAL POLICY MAKING AND THE MODERN STATE (1998); L. Fischer, *When Courts Play School Board: Judicial Activism in Education,* 51 ED. LAW. REP. 693 (1989).

[17] *See* M. Damaška, *supra* note 2, at 147 *et seq.*

[18] *See id.* at 198-99.

public good that focuses more on the social and political component of that good.

B. Conflicting Views as to the Purpose of the State

It is indisputable that there is a widely shared consensus that certain substantive legal provisions are of universal validity, as is witnessed by the international convention outlawing torture and the International Covenant on Civil and Political Rights. It is nevertheless also indisputable, however, that there are important common issues that confront all advanced legal systems on which the ideal or universal audiences to which the members of these societies address their arguments would reach very different conclusions, such as for example the legitimacy of affirmative action programs or, as we have already seen, the legitimacy of restricting access to the public forum or regulating the content of public debate. Many of these differences can be traced to different notions entertained by these differently conceived ideal audiences as to the purpose of the state.

We would probably all agree with St. Thomas Aquinas that, whatever else it might also be, from the perspective of the universal audience, law is an ordinance of reason directed to the common good.[19] The reason for the differing conceptions as to what arguments the universal audience would find persuasive in discussions of the legitimacy of affirmative action or the regulation of speech is certainly not because of any disagreement with St. Thomas' statement of the purpose of law but rather because of disagreements as to what constitutes the common good. At the heart of these disagreements is a conflict between two ways of conceiving the common or public good. Is it, to quote Michael Oakeshott, "composed of the various goods that might be sought by individuals on their own account, . . . [or] an independent entity?"[20] Most people would probably reflexively answer, if asked, that their notion of the public good is an amalgam of these two conceptions. But then they would have to confront the question of

---

[19] *See* St. Thomas Aquinas, SUMMA THEOLOGIAE, Part One of the Second Part, Q. 90 Art. 4.

[20] M. Oakeshott, *The Masses in Representative Democracy*, reprinted in RATIONALISM IN POLITICS AND OTHER ESSAYS 363, 375 (1991). This is a reprint, with some additional material, of RATIONALISM IN POLITICS AND OTHER ESSAYS (1962).

which concept has primacy when the justice of particular measures would be viewed very differently from each of these two perspectives.

If the common or public good is something other than the aggregation of individual goods, then, in the limiting case, if the public interest so requires, the individual in the last analysis becomes merely an instrument for achieving that common or public good. This is clearly the premise of Rawls' notion of what constitutes a just society. Although he envisioned the ideal society as one in which people are free to choose and pursue their own notions of the good—and the ideal state a state that would facilitate that pursuit—his just society is the one that would be chosen by "representative" human beings who, because they are representative, have no individual goods or goals. Indeed his stated purpose is to create a situation in which "the deliberations of any one person are typical of all."[21]   These "homogenous" representatives, to use Rawls' term,[22] accept a social ideal in which equality and not the pursuit of individual goods is the prime value. Although liberty is lexically prior to all other goods, nevertheless the liberty of some may be curtailed if it "strengthen[s] the total system of liberty shared by all,"[23] as in Rawls' advocacy for limitations on what a person can spend to promote his political views.[24] Indeed, in *Political Liberalism*, Rawls accepts that even the priority of liberty to all other social goods may be subordinated by an even more basic principle that citizens' basic needs must be met, at least to the extent that subordination may be "necessary for citizens to understand and be able fruitfully to exercise those rights and privileges."[25]

Similarly, although "fair opportunity," which ranks just below liberty, is also prior to other forms of material well-being, Rawls suggests that the opportunities of some may be restricted to increase the opportunities of the less fortunate. He notes for example that "the most obvious injustice of the system of natural liberty is that it permits distributive shares to be

---

[21] J. Rawls, A THEORY OF JUSTICE 263 (1971), hereinafter cited as A THEORY OF JUSTICE.

[22] *Ibid.*

[23] *Id.* at 302. Rawls indicates that a less than equal liberty must be acceptable to those who are given a less than equal liberty, but, as the text indicates, one may curtail the liberty of someone without necessarily giving that person a lesser liberty than others.

[24] *See* the discussion in chapter 3, *supra* at pp. 29-30.

[25] J. Rawls, POLITICAL LIBERALISM 7 (1993).

improperly influenced . . . by factors so arbitrary from a moral point of view," such as the initial distribution of resources and the distribution of natural talents and abilities.[26] He even accepts that "the idea of equal opportunity inclines" in the direction that the family should be abolished but he shrinks from making any such suggestions.[27] Of course, insofar as the other social goods are concerned, Rawls is clear that equality of distribution is to be the norm unless an unequal distribution is to the advantage of the less favored.

The current debate on the wisdom and legitimacy of affirmative action graphically illustrates that a universal audience for whom the public good is largely an aggregation of individual goods will have a vastly different reaction to many current policy proposals than one that views the public good as something fundamentally different from the mere sum of individual goods. If one takes affirmative action in its original sense of making an extra effort to locate candidates for employment or for university admission among individuals who share certain common features, such as sex or race, with those who have in the past not been able to secure such employment or university admission,[28] no significant problem arises regardless of which view might be predominant in the audience in a question. If one takes affirmative action to mean preferences in hiring or university admissions on the basis of sex or race, problems will arise in a society which otherwise accepts that discrimination on the basis of sex or race is impermissible. Fewer problems will of course arise if preferences in hiring or admission practices are limited, as the United States Supreme Court has now indicated

---

[26] A THEORY OF JUSTICE at 72.

[27] *Id.* at 511. *See also id.* at 74, 300.

[28] This was certainly the purpose of Executive Order 11246, (Sept. 24, 1965), 3 C.F.R. 339 (1964-65), *reprinted as amended*, in 42 U.S.C. § 2000e (1994), which *inter alia* imposed such requirements on federal contractors. It expanded on the less-detailed Executive Order 10925, 26 Fed. Reg. 1977 (Mar. 6, 1961), which appears to be the first instance in which the term "affirmative action" was used with regard to civil rights. Executive Order 11246 also required federal contractors to take affirmative action to ensure that their employees were treated "during employment, without regard to their race, color, religion, sex or national origin." The whole purpose of the Executive Order was, to use its own wording, to establish a regime of "nondiscrimination." For further discussion, *see* J. Skrentny, THE IRONICS OF AFFIRMATIVE ACTION 7, 134 (1996).

they must be, to instances where the particular individual who is the beneficiary of the preference has himself been the victim of past discrimination.[29] Awarding him the preference is to recognize the harm done to his own individual good and represents an attempt to give him adequate recompense for the injury done to him. But still, even here some difficulties will arise. For an audience for whom the public good is largely a composite of individual goods, a problem is presented that might not overly concern an audience for whom the public good is something different. Normally to grant one person a preference is to deny something to another person. If the person who had to give up a position in a firm or a place at a university were in some way personally responsible for the actual discrimination against the person now receiving the preference, there is of course no problem. Each of our two hypothetical people get what they as individuals deserve.

In the real world, however, the situation is never that simple. It is almost never the case that the person disadvantaged by the granting of the preference has had any personal responsibility for the prior discrimination. For an audience for whom the public good is something other than a

---

[29] This seems to be the conclusion one would draw from the Court's three cases on preferences for minority contractions. *See* Adarand Contractors, Inc. v. Pena, 515 U.S. 200 (1995); City of Richmond v. J. A. Croson Co., 488 U.S. 469 (1989); Fullilove v. Klutznik, 448 U.S. 448 (1980). In *Fullilove* The Court upheld a federal minority set-aside on the ground that it was reasonably related to a laudable legislative goal. The Court accepted the legislative assumption that the favored class of contractors had been disadvantaged by past discrimination. In *Croson* it struck down a municipal set-aside program, subjecting it to strict scrutiny and noting that there was no evidence that there had been discrimination in the local construction industry. In *Adarand* the Court, retreating from any suggestion in *Fullilove* that a less rigorous standard might govern such cases, applied strict scrutiny to a federal minority small business set-aside program. The case was remanded for further proceedings and eventually dismissed as moot when the business enterprise that challenged the contract awarded under the set-aside program was itself certified as a disadvantaged small business entity. 169 F.3d 1292 (10th Cir. 1999). Under the program, companies controlled by members of certain minority groups were presumed to be disadvantaged. Others, like the challenger in *Adarand*, could, on application, be so designated. For the proposition that strict scrutiny is not the legally appropriate standard in such cases, see J. Rubenfeld, *Affirmative Action*, 107 YALE L. J. 427 (1997).

composite of individual goods, this lack of personal responsibility presents no great difficulty, though even such an audience might show its recognition of the importance of individual goods by claiming that the person now being disadvantaged shares some characteristic, such as sex or race, with the persons who actually did discriminate against the person who is now the beneficiary of the preference and who in some sense either benefited from that past discrimination or bears some residual moral responsibility for it. An audience that accepts this reason as a justification for disadvantaging some particular individual should, of course, be prepared to explain why sex and/or race are more important common features than class or national origin.

For an audience that accepts that the public good is primarily a composite of individual goods, however, remedial preferences present serious problems when the person now being disadvantaged is not a person who bears some personal responsibility for the discrimination now being remedied. If the preferential treatment for an actual victim of discrimination merely results in the loss of an opportunity by the other, one might say that the importance of redressing the harm to a victim of discrimination outweighs the undoubted harm to the individual who must now step aside to let the victim of past discrimination go first. It is, in a sense, like giving up one's seat in a theater or on a bus to a handicapped person or paying taxes to provide compensation to victims of a crime. As we shall have occasion shortly to discuss in greater detail, to say that the public good is largely a composite of individual goods is not to say that the good of a particular individual cannot be subordinated to some common good in some circumstances. But if, in order to give a preference to someone who has been an admitted victim of discrimination in the past, someone who already has a job and bears no personal responsibility for the past discrimination is discharged in order to create a place for the victim of the past discrimination, the matter becomes more difficult. We are now in a situation that a universal audience committed to a vision of the public good that focuses primarily on individual goods would find difficult to accept as just. We are rather entering a world of social engineering in which individual good is subordinated to the social good.

We shall have fully entered a socially engineered world when we move to the situation in which a person who is not himself a victim of past discrimination but belongs to the same sex or race as people who have been discriminated against in the past is given a preference over a person who bears no personal responsibility for past discrimination but merely belongs to the same sex or racial group as those who were responsible for the past discrimination in question. This was actually the situation presented in the *Piscataway* case, in which a local school board that needed to reduce its teaching staff chose to discharge a white teacher solely because of her race rather than draw lots to choose between her and an equally qualified black teacher.[30]   Indeed, in the sorts of scenarios that we are discussing, the person now being disadvantaged, despite sharing sexual or racial characteristics of past discriminators, might actually be less economically well off than the person now being given the preference. For an audience for whom the state exists primarily to further the individual good of each of its citizens, this situation would seem to be unacceptable. An audience for whom the public good is something that is more concerned with the social good rather than the good of discreet individuals would of course view the matter quite differently; and this difference in basic values will be reflected in the differing legal provisions of the societies which embrace one or another of these basic positions. Debates between adherents of the two basic positions may well degenerate into shouting matches in which the parties are always arguing at cross purposes. Still, in the real world, some of the most fervent advocates of preferences show their uneasiness at ignoring the good of the individual who is obliged to step aside for the public good by lamenting that we do not live in a just world where such measures would be unnecessary[31] or by agreeing that such measures must

---

[30]   Taxman v. Piscataway School District, 91 F.3d 1547 (3d Cir. 1996), *cert. granted*, 521 U.S. 1117, *cert. dismissed as moot*, 522 U.S. 1010 (1997). The white school teacher was granted summary judgment in the district court and this decision was affirmed by a divided court of appeals. The principal argument of the dissenters was that, given that releasing the black teacher would have left the school with no black teachers, retaining the black teacher was a justifiable exercise of educational discretion. While the case was pending before the Supreme Court, a civil rights group paid most of a $435,000 settlement with the white teacher, because they feared that the Supreme Court might have rendered a sweeping judgment rendering almost all affirmative action programs unlawful. *See* N. Y. Times, Sat., Dec. 6, 1997, § B, at p. 5, col. 5.

[31]   *See* C. Sunstein, AFTER THE RIGHTS REVOLUTION 201-05 (1990), who supports preferences by noting that we do not live in an ideal world but rather one in which the

only be temporary until some more just arrangement of society is achieved.[32]

The choice between a vision that sees the public good as largely a composite of individual goods and one that views the public good as something different from, although obviously influenced by, notions of individual good affects not only how one treats members of the currently disfavored category but also how one treats members of the category who are now eligible for a preference. We are talking about the situation in which the person receiving the preference has not himself been the victim of past discrimination and indeed may even be a member of an economically more privileged class than a person who will lose a position that he might have obtained but for the preference granted to the other person. Since the person being granted the preference does not derive it by virtue of anything he has suffered or done, he becomes a representative for a class of persons with whom he shows a common characteristic. In the limiting cases, which are not infrequent, in which there are many members of that class seeking positions which are quite scarce in a particular society, such as, for example, important judgeships or university professorships, determining which member of that class is an appropriate representative of the class can become a contentious issue. If the purpose of awarding a preference is to further the public good, what the preference does for the person who gets it is only a secondary consideration. The overall public good, such as a more diverse and balanced state of society, is what counts.

---

status quo is itself the result "of unjust past and present social choices." *Id.* at 204.

[32] *See* A. Gutmann and D. Thompson, DEMOCRACY AND DISAGREEMENT 341 (1996). *See also* Justice Souter's dissenting opinion in Adarand Constructors, Inc. v. Pena, 515 U.S. 200, 270 (1995).

> When the extirpation of lingering discriminatory effects is thought to require a catch-up mechanism, like the racially preferential inducement under the statutes considered here, the result may be that some members of the historically favored race are hurt by that remedial mechanism, however innocent they may be of any responsibility for any discriminatory conduct. When this price is considered reasonable, it is in part because it is a price to be paid only temporarily; if the justification for the preference is eliminating the effects of past practice, the assumption is that the effects will themselves recede into the past, becoming attenuated and finally disappearing.

It is this factor that gives coherence to former Judge A. Leon Higgenbotham's otherwise petulant and condescending public letter to Clarence Thomas after his appointment to the Supreme Court of the United States.[33] In his letter, Judge Higgenbotham made it abundantly clear that he did not think Justice Thomas was an adequate representative of the black citizens of the United States. Whether one agrees with Judge Higgenbotham's criticisms of Justice Thomas or not, the point he raises is a logically relevant one if those appointed because of their race or sex are merely viewed as representatives. Of course, there is the further question of who is to determine who is an appropriate representative of a particular group. In the absence of a separate voting register for minorities and adequate plebiscitary mechanisms, we must inevitably fall back on the elitism that, as we saw in chapter 3, is so clearly implicit in the social visions of Rawls, Sunstein, and Fiss. The choice will be made by those who present themselves as the leaders of the group in question and are accepted as such by other elites.

---

[33] A. L. Higgenbotham, Jr., *An Open Letter to Justice Clarence Thomas from a Federal Judicial Colleague*, 140 U. PA. L. REV. 1005 (1992).

CHAPTER 7

CHOOSING BETWEEN COMPETING VISIONS
OF THE GOOD—THE CASE OF NECESSITY

A. *The Need to Choose*

There are many subtle ways that the choice between competing visions of the composition of the public good will affect the arguments that we put forth to secure the assent of an ideal or universal audience. Even an audience that accepts what Jean Dabin called the "prevalence of the individual human person over every collective"[1] is forced to recognize that there are times when every society feels obliged to accept, and indeed even require, the sacrifice of some individuals for the greater good of society. Times of war and natural disaster immediately come to mind. It probably takes no greater feat of imagination than is necessary to envision a world organized around the hypothetical agreement that Rawls uses to construct his just society to assert that the members of any society who accept its legitimacy implicitly promise to preserve that society in the face of its enemies or of natural disasters. As Aristotle said, man is by nature a political animal for whom life in an organized political community is the natural condition.[2] Certainly, in most societies, most people seem to have acknowledged an obligation to preserve their society even if, unlike professional soldiers, they have made no express promise to do so. Whether one tries to explain that sense of obligation on the basis of an implied promise or of a moral duty to make some return for the benefits bestowed by society on the individuals who constitute that society, the empirical reality is that people do, in fact, by and large accept these obligations and, more importantly, they are expected by their fellow members of society to do so.[3] What justice as personified in the universal

---

[1] J. Dabin, GENERAL THEORY OF LAW § 142 (1944), reprinted in English in LEGAL PHILOSOPHIES OF LASK, RADBRUCH, AND DABIN (K. Wilk transl. 1950). The same language appears in § 196 of the second edition, *Theórie général du droit* (1967), published only in French.

[2] Aristotle, POLITICS, Bk. I, c.2 (1253a).

[3] These questions are explored in G. Christie, *On the Moral Obligation to Obey the Law*, 1990 DUKE L. J. 1311. As Ronald Dworkin has pointed out, among the benefits conferred by society on its members is simply the benefit *of* community. *See* R. Dworkin, LAW'S EMPIRE 167-216 (1986).

76

audience requires is that the individual should not be sacrificed, except in the most exigent circumstances, and that the choice of the individual to be sacrificed should be based on the most neutral criteria possible. To choose a particular military unit to be left as a hopeless rear guard, because it is the most readily available or the most able to accomplish the mission assigned to it, might be acceptable. It would not be acceptable to choose the unit to be sacrificed based on its racial composition or on the fact that it includes a large percentage of opponents of the political faction currently in control of the government. Indeed, not merely in these extreme cases, but in the allocation of all social burdens and benefits, most societies that purport to be just societies believe that benefits and burdens should not be allocated arbitrarily.

Even in day-to-day litigation between private parties some notion of a social good must inevitably intrude in order to make it possible to resolve conflicts between individuals. It is commonly understood that people are entitled to compensation when they have been injured by the intentional conduct of others or by the unreasonable conduct of others. The individual interest of the defendant in retaining full command of all his material resources pales in comparison to the claim of the plaintiff for compensation for the injuries that he has unjustly suffered. Even here, of course, sometimes important social interests will outweigh the plaintiff's claim for compensation and the corresponding social interest in ensuring that that claim is honored. In many countries, such as in the United States, there are substantial obstacles to recovery for defamation and invasion of privacy.[4] Fear of the heavy hand of the state and a desire to encourage freedom of speech and inquiry—and not primarily a concern for the defendant—are unquestionably the reasons why the plaintiff is often denied compensation in such cases. Even in less politically charged circumstances, such as in situations where bystanders bring an action for emotional distress suffered

---

[4] *See* Gertz v. Robert Welch, Inc., 418 U.S. 323 (1974) *and* New York Times Co. v. Sullivan, 376 U.S. 254 (1964), as to defamation, and Galella v. Onassis, 487 F.2d 986 (2d Cir. 1973) *and* Sidis v. F-R Publishing Co, 113 F.2d 806 (2d Cir. 1940) with regard to privacy. *See also*, with regard to privacy, The Florida Star v. B. J. F., 491 U.S. 524 (1989). Even English law which has retained much of the strict common-law liability for defamation has always recognized situations in which important social interests restricted the plaintiff's right to recovery. *See* Horrocks v. Lowe, [1975] A.C. 135 (1974).

when they have witnessed some gruesome injury tortiously inflicted upon
a third person, the courts have generally reached the conclusion that the
public good requires that there be some limitation on the categories of
possible bystanders who can recover against an admittedly negligent
defendant.[5] There are, however, some cases where the courts are called
upon to sanction the sacrifice of a person's interests that are more
problematic.

The more extreme cases of when the interests of some individuals have
to be sacrificed for some greater social good are often grouped together
under the rubric "necessity." In the discussion that follows, I wish to move
away from the cataclysmic situations that face society in times of war or
natural disaster—the cases of so-called "public necessity"—and consider
how different conceptions of the arguments that would win the assent of an
ideal or universal audience will affect how a society will react to what is
called "private" necessity, namely to situations in which an individual,
acting as an individual and not as a surrogate for the public authorities, is
confronted with emergency situations requiring the exercise of certain
painful and difficult choices.

In the law, the term private necessity is used to describe situations in
which the property, and sometimes possibly even the physical well-being
of an "innocent" person, is sacrificed in order to preserve the property or life
of one or more other persons. The term "innocent" is used to signify that
the person whose interests are to be sacrificed bears no personal
responsibility for the creation of the situation for which the sacrifice of his
interests is required, and that he himself is not presenting a threat to the
person for whose sake his interests are to be sacrificed. These situations of
so-called private necessity are thus to be distinguished from the much more
common legal case in which one party has injured another or threatened
another's safety or has assumed some sort of legally recognized relationship
with another person. Admittedly, distinctions that can be clearly described
for analytical purposes cannot always be applied in practice. Take a

---

[5] *See* White v. Chief Constable of the So. Wilts. Police, [1999] 1 All E.R. 1 (1998); Page
v. Smith [1996] A.C. 153 (1995); Thing v. La Chusa, 48 Cal.3d 644, 257 Cal. Rptr. 865
(1989); Elden v. Sheldon, 46 Cal.3d 267 (250 Cal. Rptr. 254 (1988)). The United States
Supreme Court has taken an even more restrictive position in cases governed by federal
laws. *See* Consolidated Rail Corp. v. Gottshall, 512 U.S. 532 (1994).

situation in which a woman, who is approaching the ninth month of her pregnancy, has had an outbreak of herpes and has been strongly advised by her physicians to deliver her child by Caesarean section in order to avoid subjecting the child she has been carrying to a very substantial risk of premature death or blindness. The woman refuses. Should the physicians be permitted to obtain a court order permitting them to perform the Caesarean section over the objections of the woman? This is a situation that has been presented to the courts in the United States a number of times and as to which the courts have reached different conclusions, although the predominant view has been to order the Caesarean.[6] Is this a situation in which the courts are confronted with a conflict between the goods of two people, the expectant mother and her about to be born child, who are threatening each other's physical or emotional safety; or is it a case in which the individual good of the mother, the only person then in existence, is to be sacrificed to achieve some socially determined public good? I do not propose to answer this difficult question in this book but only raise the matter to illustrate that the distinction between the category of cases classified under the rubric of necessity, in which the interests of an individual are sacrificed for some social good, and those which merely involve the resolution of a traditional conflict between the individual interests of two interacting people is not so clear cut as might at first appear.

Cases of private necessity fall into a number of categories. One broad category concerns the privilege to destroy property for some paramount social purpose. There are many situations in which this issue arises. One can begin with the privilege to destroy property to save human life. It can be compared to, and contrasted with, a possible privilege to take and consume the property of others in order to preserve human life. Then there is the further situation in which it is claimed that there is a privilege to destroy the property of others in order to save or preserve one's own

---

[6] *See* the discussion in In re A.C., 573 A.2d 1235 (D.C. Ct. App. 1990). The court ruled that the lower court's ordering of a Caesarean section over the objection of the mother was improper. The court stressed that in the case before it, in which the expectant mother was terminally ill with cancer and near death, the surgical procedure could not be said in any way to contribute to her physical welfare. On the general subject, *see* N. Rhoden, *The Judge in the Delivery Room: The Emergence of Court-Ordered Caesareans*, 74 CAL. L. REV. 1951 (1986).

property. These are all situations in which the property of some person whose property is not itself in danger and which is not posing any threat to the life or property of another is destroyed or taken and consumed to save or preserve the life or property of other persons. They are thus to be distinguished, as noted above, from cases in which someone's property is destroyed because it threatens the life or property of others, such as when an out-of-control car is about to crash into the person or property of another who is in no way responsible for the conditions that gave rise to the emergency situation. These later cases are variants of the typical situation in which the courts must resolve a conflict between the individual goods of two or more separate persons and it will be the occasion of no surprise to learn that the normal doctrines of self-defense apply. Innocent persons whose life or property is threatened by such activities of others can take reasonable measures to protect their interests and incur no obligations to pay compensation for any harm or damage that results from their reasonable efforts to defend their persons or property.

Finally, there are cases in which it is claimed by some that there is even a privilege to take the life of an innocent person if it is necessary to do so to achieve some greater social good, such as to save the lives of a greater number of innocent people. If there were to be such a privilege, one might ask if one could take the life of an innocent person in order to save some treasure of mankind, say the Parthenon or Michelangelo's *David*, from destruction. Depending on the conception of the common or public good ascribed to the universal audience to whom we imagine we are addressing our arguments in an effort to justify our actions, we shall reach different conclusions as to the existence and scope of any of these possible privileges.

In the discussion that follows, we shall first briefly discuss the privilege to destroy property before turning to a more extended discussion of the so-called privilege to take innocent life. The latter is more germane to our discussion of ideal audiences because it is less technical in scope and more directly implicates deeply held beliefs and feelings. But a discussion of the property situation is important as background because much of the legal discussion of a possible privilege to destroy innocent life relies on the more extensive legal treatment of the privilege to destroy property.

B. Choosing to Sacrifice the Property of Others

1. Destroying Property to Save Human Life

No one disputes that there is a privilege to destroy property to save human life. The only question is whether there is any obligation to compensate the owner of the property that has been destroyed. If the person whose life has been saved has not been legally at fault in creating the situation that led to his predicament, the few English and American cases directly on point make it clear, notwithstanding the contrary position taken by the American *Restatements*, that there is no obligation to compensate the owner of the property that has had to be damaged or destroyed.[7] There is indeed an express decision of the House of Lords exactly on this point.[8] This consensus among the cases in which the issue has actually needed to be decided is in accord with the law of admiralty. The people whose lives have been saved as the result of the jettison of cargo have never been required to make any general average contribution,[9] and this traditional doctrine of customary admiralty law has been codified by international conventions in 1910 and 1989.[10] Common sense would indicate that this is the only sensible solution. If a person knows that he would be liable for any damage he might cause to property, would he be as willing to come to the aid of people in distress? Would one want an airline pilot, considering where to make an emergency landing, to prefer rocky vacant ground because of the large possible liability he might incur if he lands in a softer

---

[7] The state of the law on this subject is exhaustively analyzed and discussed in G. Christie, *The Defense of Necessity Considered from the Legal and Moral Points of View*, 48 DUKE L. J. 975 (1999).

[8] Esso Petroleum Co. v. Southport Corp., [1956] A.C. 218. *See also* an earlier English decision, Mouse's Case, 12 Co. 63, 77 Eng. Rep. 1341 (K. B. 1609) cited and discussed with approval in an American case, Ploof v. Putnam 81 Vt. 471, 71 Atl. 188 (1908). For further citation to cases, see G. Christie, *supra* note 7, at 988-93.

[9] *See* G. Robinson, HANDBOOK OF ADMIRALTY LAW IN THE UNITED STATES 778-79 (1939).

[10] *See* art. 9 of the (Brussels) Convention for the Unification of Certain Rules with Respect to Assistance and Salvage at Sea, September 23, 1910, 37 Stat. 1658, 1671, and art. 16 of its successor, the (London) International Convention on Salvage, April 28, 1989, Hein's No. KAV 3169.

area which contains valuable flowers? The few American and English
cases on the subject presuppose a universal audience for whom the
preservation of life takes complete precedence over property interests. Such
an audience would approve of the statement by Devlin, J., in a judgment
denying recovery for property damaged in the course of saving life that was
upheld by the House of Lords:

The safety of human lives belongs to a different scale of values from the safety of
property. The two are beyond comparison and the necessity for saving life has at all times
been considered a proper ground for inflicting such damage as may be necessary on
another's property.[11]

What the state of the law is outside of the Anglo-American world is
difficult to determine. Even in the Anglo-American world there are not
many cases, although, as has just been noted, what cases and official
authorities there are all point in one direction. The difficulty of determining
what is the state of the law in other countries is compounded by the fact that
these are for the most part code, not common-law, jurisdictions. That
means that the law has to be ascertained from broadly-worded code
provisions and the often cursory writings of commentators on these
provisions. For example, § 228 of the German Civil Code states that
someone who " damages or destroys a thing belonging to another in order
to ward off from himself or from another a danger threatened by the thing
. . . does not act unlawfully if such injury or destruction is necessary to ward
off the danger and the damage is not out of proportion to the danger."[12]
Compensation to the owner of the property destroyed is only payable if the
person who destroys the property is responsible for creating the risk that
necessitated the destruction of the property. This seems to be in accord
with English and American law, but the provision appears by its terms only
aimed at the situation in which the property destroyed actually poses a risk
to other persons—the analogue to the self-defense situation that we
mentioned above. Section 228 would not cover the case in which, say, a
person who is about to be swept away in a storm anchors himself to the

[11] Southport Corp. v. Esso Petroleum Co., [1953] 2 All E.R. 1204, 1209-10 (Q.B.). For
the decision in the House of Lords, see note 8, *supra.*
[12] Section 228 BGB, translated in THE GERMAN CIVIL CODE § 228 (S. Goren transl. 1994).

property of another by means of which he saves himself but damages the property which he has grabbed There is, however, another provision of the German Civil Code, § 904,[13] that also bears on the subject that we have been discussing. That provision denies the owner of property the right "to prohibit interference [with his rights of ownership] . . . if the interference is necessary for the avoidance of a present danger and the damage threatened is disproportionally great compared to the damage caused to the owner by the interference." Section 904 also declares that "[t]he owner [of the property] may demand compensation for the loss suffered by him." Whether this means that one must pay compensation for property destroyed in order to save life, even if one is in no way at fault for creating the risk to life, is unclear. A comparable provision of the French penal code, Article 122-7 provides that a person who, faced with a present or imminent danger to himself or another or to property, performs an act necessary for the safety of a person or property is not subject to criminal responsibility unless there is a disproportionality between the means employed and the seriousness of the threat.[14] A standard text on French criminal law declares that the *Cour de cassation* does not appear to accept the proposition that compensation is due when property is destroyed to save life, thus favoring the position taken by the English and American cases—although it also notes that commentators continue to debate the issue.[15]

Despite the concrete evidence regarding what the courts in the United States and England have actually held on this issue, as already briefly indicated above the drafters of the *Restatement of Torts* and *Restatement (Second) of Torts* have taken the opposite position,[16] and this position has been accepted without much discussion by most commentators, although several have expressed some doubt as to the legal obligation to pay compensation if one destroys property to save the lives of third parties.[17]

---

[13] *Id.* at § 904.

[14] CODE PÉNAL art. 122-7 (author's translation).

[15] G. Stephani *et al.*, DROIT PÉNAL GÉNÉRAL 315 (15th ed. 1995).

[16] RESTATEMENT OF TORTS § 197 (1934); RESTATEMENT (SECOND) OF TORTS § 197 (1965).

[17] For example, W. Prosser, HANDBOOK OF THE LAW OF TORTS, § 24, at 126-27 (4th ed. 1971); W. P. Keeton *et al.*, PROSSER AND KEETON ON THE LAW OF TORTS, § 24, at 145-48 (5th ed. 1984), F. Harper *et al.*, 1 THE LAW OF TORTS § 1.22, at 1:84-89, § 2-43, at 2:140-

For those who accept the *Restatements'* positions, compensation must be paid whenever property is destroyed to save life. Such an assertion presupposes that the universal audience addressed in the course of legal argument values life more than property, but not so much as to absolve innocent persons from the obligation to pay compensation for property unavoidably destroyed in the process of saving lives.

The principal reliance of the two *Restatements* and the commentators has been on the ramifications of some *dicta* in *Vincent* v. *Lake Erie Transportation Co.*[18] That case involved a steamship that remained tied to its pier in Duluth, Minnesota after it had finished discharging its cargo because a storm of unprecedented severity had made it perilous for the ship to steam out to Lake Superior. The issue for the court was whether the damage that was thereby occasioned to the pier was simply storm damage, for which no one was responsible, or an instance in which one person had knowingly sacrificed someone else's property to save his own. The discussion of these issues was complicated by the fact that, in the course of the storm, the lines holding the ship to the pier periodically parted. They were immediately replaced with new lines, sometimes even with larger ones. The court ruled, over the dissents of two judges who thought the case simply represented an instance of storm damage,[19] that the ship was privileged to remain at its pier but the owners of the ship were nevertheless obliged to pay for the damage to the pier. It is this suggestion, that conduct

---

42 (3d ed. by O. Gray 1996) merely set forth the *Restatements'* position. R. Keeton, *Conditional Fault in the Law of Torts,* 72 HARV. L. REV. 401, 415-18, 427-30 (1959) generally supports the positions taken by the *Restatements* but is skeptical about whether a person who destroys property to save the lives of others has any obligation to pay compensation for the property destroyed. F. Bohlen, *Incomplete Privilege to Inflict Intentional Invasions of Interests of Property and Personality*, 39 HARV. L. REV. 307, 318-19 (1926) took the position that when property is destroyed to save the lives of others, but not one's own life, there was no obligation to pay compensation. These writers are all legal scholars. Philosophers who have considered the question seem to all have believed that compensation is owing in all circumstances when property is destroyed to save human life. *See* J. Coleman, RISKS AND WRONGS 285-302 (1992); J. Feinberg, *Voluntary Euthanasia and the Right to Life,* 7 PHIL & PUB. AFF. 93, 101-03 (1978).

[18] 109 Minn. 456, 124 N.W. 221 (1910).

[19] This certainly appears to be how English courts would have viewed the situation. *See* River Wear Comm'rs v. Adamson, [1877] 2 A.C. 743.

may be privileged, but burdened with an obligation to pay compensation for any damage done, that provides the analytical basis for concluding that, although one is privileged to damage or destroy property to save human life, nevertheless one must pay for any resulting damage.[20] It has also led to several equally questionable conclusions, such as that one is privileged to take and consume the property of others, as for example food or medicine, so long as one pays compensation, and that, following *Vincent,* one is privileged to destroy the property of others to save one's own property so long as one is prepared to pay compensation. We shall briefly examine the arguments that might be made in support of these positions in the next section.

2. Destroying the Property of Others to Preserve One's Own Property and the Taking and Consumption of the Property of Others

It would be hard to find an ideal audience that would not agree that, if one takes another's property, such as his food or his medicine to serve one's own purposes, or destroys another's property to save his own property, one has to pay compensation. But one would have to pay compensation for the property taken or destroyed whether the taking or taker was legally privileged or not. The practical importance of whether the taking was privileged lies principally, although not exclusively, in whether the person whose property is to be taken or destroyed can refuse to permit the taking or destruction and indeed even defend his property. I have explored at length in a previous work why, although the social interest in preserving life justifies destroying the property of others, there are no such privileges under Anglo-American law to destroy the property of others to save one's own property or to take and consume the property of others.[21] In this book, I merely wish to explore the nature of the arguments that might be addressed to a universal audience by a person seeking the assent of the universal audience to the existence of any of these so-called privileges.

---

[20] There is no suggestion in *Vincent* that keeping the ship tied to her berth was necessary to save human life. Indeed, the case was expressly decided on the basis that the defendants were acting "for the preservation of their property." 109 Minn. at 458, 124 N.W. at 221.

[21] *See* G. Christie, *supra* note 7, at 980-1006.

The proponent of a privilege to destroy the property of others to preserve his own property may contend that, although the owner of the property to be sacrificed may be innocent, in the sense that neither he nor his property have posed any threat to others, nevertheless when such a case reaches the courts, the judge is simply being asked to adjust the interests of two individuals and that therefore the case must be decided on the basis of which solution leads to the greatest social good. The natural response to this argument on the part of the person whose property has been taken or destroyed is to ask why is his property being singled out for sacrifice since he bears no responsibility for the creation of the situation requiring the sacrifice nor, through circumstances beyond his control, such as being the owner of a runaway car, is his property threatening to injure someone else's person or property. His property is being taken merely because it is conveniently situated. This may be an adequate reason when the public authorities decide which military unit to sacrifice or when private persons, who were not at fault, destroy property to save human life, but it is not an adequate reason in these other situations where the social good to be achieved is not as great. He would argue that it is certainly not the adjustment of a conflict between the good of two individuals but rather a taking of the property of one person as the means of furthering the welfare of others. He would certainly be entitled to ask what are the criteria to be used in deciding which property is to be taken or destroyed. Is it sheer current market value or are there other relevant considerations?

Consider the situation in which a Van Gogh painting is threatened with destruction from water escaping from a ruptured pipe. May the owner of the painting tear up a 300 year old family bible belonging to another to plug up the hole if that is the most suitable available material? And could the owner of the bible, if he acted first and the situations were reversed, use the canvas upon which the picture was painted to protect the bible that he treasures as a priceless family heirloom? The text of § 904 of the German Civil Code which has been quoted earlier[22] seems to suggest that this sort of taking might be privileged but it should be noted that George Fletcher cites a commentator on § 904 who rejects the possibility that this provision

---

[22] *See* p. 83, *supra.*

can be used to justify the seizing of someone's raincoat in order to save one's own suede coat from destruction in an unexpected rainstorm.[23]

The difficulty of the situation may be illustrated by extending our discussion to include the situation in which a private individual *takes* and *consumes* property to preserve human life. Jules Coleman, for example, poses the case in which Hal, a diabetic, loses his insulin in an accident, through no fault of his own.[24] Before he lapses into a coma, Hal rushes to the house of Carla, another diabetic. Carla is not at home but somehow Hal manages to enter her house. After first assuring himself that he has left Carla enough insulin for her daily dosage, Hal takes the insulin he needs to survive. Coleman concludes that Hal is justified in doing what he did and that he has thus not violated Carla's rights.[25] Her property rights have at most been infringed. But Carla has a right to be compensated for the insulin taken; and, if compensation is not paid, her rights would indeed be violated.[26] This is an appealing case for concluding that the social interest should prevail over the individual interest, and it would seem that a universal audience not inflexibly committed to the primacy of the individual good over the social good would surely not object. But what if Hal is in no position to pay compensation? If his need is as dire as the case posed assumes, should his poverty prevent him from being entitled to take the insulin? Is the universal audience prepared to accept the principle that only rich people can take and consume the property of others? More compellingly, what happens if Carla suddenly appears and refuses to allow Hal to take any of her insulin? She may, for example, not believe that Hal has accurately assessed how mush insulin to leave her or she may be apprehensive about her ability to replace the insulin taken or doubtful about

---

[23] G. Fletcher, RETHINKING CRIMINAL LAW § 10.2, at 777 (1978) (citing H. Jescneck, *Lehrbruch des Stafrechts: Allgemeiner Teil* (2d ed. 1972)).

[24] J. Coleman, *supra* note 17, at 282. Coleman's hypothetical is a simplified version of a hypothetical case, posed by Joel Feinberg, involving a backpacker who is suddenly caught in a blizzard and who breaks into an uninhabited cabin. The backpacker remains there until the storm abates, in the meantime consuming the food stored in the cabin and burning the furniture to keep warm. J. Feinberg, *supra* note 17, at 102.

[25] J. Coleman, *supra* note 17, at 300.

[26] The distinction that Coleman is using seems to have been developed by Judith Jarvis Thomson. *See* J. Thomson, RIGHTS, RESTITUTION, AND RISK 33 (1986).

how soon Hal will be able to pay her or perhaps just outraged that Hal wants to take *her* insulin. Would the universal audience deny her the right to refuse Hal's entreaties, even if the law would permit her to do so? May she use force to defend her possessions and, if Hal attacks her to get the insulin, use even greater force than might be considered reasonable were she merely defending her property?

These are difficult questions that have not been adequately explored in the literature. Some of the suggested legal solutions seem hardly credible. For example, the American *Restatement (Second) of Torts* gives, as an illustration of how the doctrine it enunciates should be applied, the hypothetical case in which medical personnel at the scene of an accident forcibly remove a bystander's scarf to use as a bandage.[27] Is the *Restatement (Second)* suggesting that the person whose scarf is being taken cannot legally resist? There is no decided case in English or American law, that I am aware of, that has so held or that even remotely supports that conclusion. The universal audiences to which most people appeal might be prepared to recognize that one would be under a moral obligation to volunteer one's scarf under these circumstances or that Carla should give Hal the insulin he needs, but that these audiences would approve of the taking of the scarf or the insulin by force seems highly questionable. It is instructive to note that, in our literature and our folklore, the refusal of people to discharge their moral obligations to help others is met by curses or a spate of bad luck, not by outright aggression by those in need of assistance.[28] A fuller discussion of when one can take and consume the property of another would require a discussion of whether hunger can be a defense to a prosecution for theft or whether the homeless can take over someone's building as squatters in order to find shelter from the elements.[29] This is not the place for such a discussion, which would inevitably reach a level of legal detail that would distract us from the focus of this book,

---

[27] RESTATEMENT (SECOND) OF TORTS § 263, comment e, illus. 1.

[28] A classic illustration is the fairy tale, *The Golden Goose*, in which two brothers who refuse to share their food and drink with a hungry and thirsty old man are met with bad luck and the third brother, who does share his food and drink with the old man, is blessed with extraordinary good fortune. *See* THE COMPLETE BROTHERS GRIMM FAIRY TALES 274-77 (L. Owens ed. 1981).

[29] These are among the subjects discussed in G. Christie, *supra* note 7.

namely how our notions about an ideal or universal audience affect legal argumentation. I propose instead to turn now to the more dramatic situation in which it is asserted that it is sometimes permissible for private persons to sacrifice the lives of innocent individuals to save a larger number of, we shall assume, equally innocent lives. How would a universal audience's conception of the nature of the public good affect that debate?

C. Sacrificing the Life of an Innocent Person to Save the Lives of a Greater Number of Innocent Persons

Much of the contemporary debate over the permissibility of killing an innocent person to save the lives of a greater number of people has centered around what has come to be called "The Trolley Problem." The problem was suggested in an essay by Philippa Foot[30] and has been developed and refined in the work of Judith Jarvis Thomson.[31] In Thomson's basic case, of which she discusses many variants, Bloggs, a bystander, sees an out-of-control trolley bearing down upon five helpless men who will certainly be killed if the trolley continues on its course. Bloggs can avert the catastrophe only by throwing a switch that will shunt the trolley off to a spur where it will certainly kill a different helpless man. In discussing her original version of the paradigm, which involves the driver of a runaway tram, Philippa Foot assumes "that we should say, without hesitation, that the driver of the tram should steer for the less occupied track."[32] She then explores why we would nevertheless be horrified if it were suggested that we should comply with the demands of a tyrant who threatens to torture five men if we ourselves would not torture one.[33] Foot tries to justify our

---

[30] P. Foot, *The Problem of Abortion and the Doctrine of the Double Effect*, 5 OXFORD REV. 5, 8-9 (1967), reprinted in P. Foot, VIRTUES AND VICES AND OTHER ESSAYS IN MORAL PHILOSOPHY 19, 23 (1978).

[31] J. Thomson, THE REALM OF RIGHTS 176 (1990), hereinafter cited as REALM OF RIGHTS. She also discusses the "Trolley Problem" in her earlier work, RIGHTS, RESTITUTION AND RISK (1986), hereinafter cited as RIGHTS, RESTITUTION AND RISK, *e.g.*, at pp. 78 and 94. There are minor verbal differences in the formulation of the core case as it appears in each of these discussions. For stylistic reasons, I have chosen to use one of the verbal formulations from her later book.

[32] P. Foot, *supra*, note 30, at 23.

[33] *Id.* at 25.

conflicting reactions to her version of the trolley situation and the tyrant situation by resorting to the distinction between what we do and what we allow to happen which, at a more abstract level, corresponds to the differences between our negative duties (not to harm someone) and our positive duties (to aid others).[34] All things being equal, it is more important that we not harm someone than that we help someone.[35] We must therefore not harm someone even if by so doing we fail to help the five men whom the tyrant has threatened to torture.

The problem with Foot's conclusion is not with her reliance upon the distinction between acting to bring about a result and allowing something to happen—which resembles the common law's distinction between misfeasance and nonfeasance and which, for all its limitations, has some defensible uses[36]—but with Foot's claim that the driver of the tram is faced with the choice of either breaching his negative duty not to kill five men or breaching his negative duty not to kill a single man. This is not a correct description of the driver's predicament. Since the tram is out of control, if the tram driver does not steer the tram to the other track because he does not want to kill a single workman on the other track, it would not, from the legal point of view, be correct to say that he has killed the five workmen. He has not done anything; he has merely allowed something to happen. Whereas, if he steers the tram to the other track and kills the lone workman, he has done something. Assuming that the tram driver was not responsible for his loss of control over the tram, if he allows the tram to continue on its way, nothing he did caused the death of the five workmen. From the legal perspective, the situation is much more like the tyrant/torture situation than Foot realizes. I suggest that this is the better way of viewing the situation from the moral perspective as well.

---

[34] *Id.* at 25-30.

[35] *Id.* at 28.

[36] Among the arguments that can be made in support of the distinction are the following: In the case of acting to bring about a result, one's active participation in the chain of events leading up to that result is causally essential. If one had chosen not to do anything, that result would not have occurred. When one simply allows something to happen, the result is the same as that which would have ensued if one had not existed. Merely allowing something to happen, furthermore, is not as morally salient as acting: if it were, one would be morally responsible for every unfortunate result one could have acted to prevent.

Judith Jarvis Thomson provides a different rationale for concluding that her Bloggs, in her refined version of Foot's example, would be morally justified in throwing the switch and shunting the trolley to the other track where it will kill the lone helpless man. She resiles from the stronger position that he is morally obligated to throw the switch. Of the many variants of the basic trolley case that she presents, the one as to which Thomson feels most comfortable in concluding that it is morally permissible for Bloggs, the bystander, to throw the switch is the one in which the helpless men are all workmen and part of the same crew whose tasks, on any given day, are randomly assigned.[37] Thomson envisages the possibility that, when men join this work crew, it is explained to them that their occupation is a dangerous one in which death or serious injury is a distinct possibility. They are furthermore told that, should the situation arise in which the certain death of a larger number of men can be averted by shunting a runaway trolley onto a spur and thus killing a lesser number of men, then the trolley will be shunted.[38] Thomson assumes that reasonable workmen would, *ex ante*, agree to this arrangement. Perhaps they would. Whether, if this arrangement were known and thoroughly understood, anyone would want to work on a crew with less men than another crew that was likely to be put in danger in proximity to his crew is another matter. It would probably depend on how likely the men thought the occurrence of this situation to be. If they thought that there was a reasonable likelihood of the situation's arising, one would think that they would demand a premium in pay for working on the smaller crew and, as the likelihood increased, one would expect more and more people to be reluctant to enter into any such agreement regardless of the greater pay. At any rate since, like Foot, she believes that it is morally permissible for Bloggs to throw the switch to save the five helpless men, even though by so doing another helpless man will be killed, Thomson feels obliged to explain why it is morally impermissible for a surgeon to take the organs of one person in order to transplant them into the bodies of five people who need the organs to live.[39]

---

[37] REALM OF RIGHTS at 181-87.

[38] *Id.* at 195.

[39] *Id.* at 135-43. *See also* RIGHTS, RESTITUTION AND RISK at 80-82, 89-93, 95-96.

I have discussed the legal and moral issues involved in these hypothetical situations at great length elsewhere.[40] In this work, I am only interested in exploring the presuppositions that would have to be made by a universal audience that was prepared to give its assent to the arguments either for or against the proposed solutions. I will thus refer to the legal background only to the extent that is necessary to bring out the full dimensions of the difficulties in which a person situated such as Bloggs is placed and of which a universal audience would have to be aware before it could give its assent to any of the arguments that are presented to it.

One should note at the outset that almost all of the numerous commentators who have written on the subject agree with Thomson and Foot that it is morally permissible to shunt the trolley off onto the track where it will only kill one helpless man.[41] Presumably this means that they expect that the universal audience believes that the public good requires that, if necessary, one innocent man should be sacrificed to save five other men. They are then, of course, obliged, like Foot and Thomson, to show why this principle does not justify decisions to sacrifice one innocent person to benefit five other persons in other situations; for, with one possible exception,[42] no one seems prepared to accept that one can choose to torture one innocent man to keep a tyrant from torturing five other men or that a surgeon can take the organs of one person to replace the failing organs of five other persons. Of course, if the universal audiences were to refuse to accept the arguments in favor of the permissibility of Bloggs' shunting off the trolley to avoid killing the five men, the necessity of coming up with

[40] G. Christie, *supra* note 7, at 1009-38.

[41] *See, e.g.*, L. Alexander, *Self-Defense, Justification and Excuse*, 22 PHIL. & PUB. AFF. 53, 60 (1993); M. Costa, *Another Trip on the Trolley*, 25 S. J. PHIL. 461 (1987); M. Costa, *The Trolley Problem Revisited*, 24 S. J. PHIL.437 (1986); B. Gert, *Transplants and Trolleys*, 53 PHIL. & PHENOM. RES. 173, 174 (1993); R. Hallborg, Jr., *Comparing Harms: the Lesser Evil Defense and the Trolley Problem*, 3 LEGAL THEORY 291, 295 (1997); F. Kamm, *Harming Some to Save Others*, 57 PHIL. STUD. 227, 231 (1989); M. Otsuka, *Killing the Innocent in Self Defense*, 27 PHIL. & PUB. AFF. 74, 75 (1994); E. Rakowski, *Taking and Saving Lives*, 93 COLUM. L. REV. 1063, 1065 (1993).

[42] *See* J. Harris, *The Survival Lottery*, 50 PHIL. 81, 81-87 (1975), reprinted in KILLING AND LETTING DIE, 257, 259-65 (B. Steinbock and A. Norcross eds. 1994),which discusses the transplant situation.

arguments capable of distinguishing the tyrant and surgeon cases would not arise.

Why might a universal audience refuse to accept the permissibility of Bloggs shunting off the trolley so that five men are saved at the cost of one life? A brief look at the legal and practical consequences of Bloggs' conduct, should he choose to throw the switch and shunt off the trolley, may at this point be useful. The traditional answer given by the common law to the question of whether it is permissible for private people to kill an innocent person to save the lives of a greater number of people has been no. The key cases are *The Queen v. Dudley and Stephens*[43] and *United States v. Holmes.*[44]

Dudley and Stephens, decided in 1884, involved crew members of a yacht that had sunk 1,600 miles off the Cape of Good Hope. Twenty four days after they had cast adrift from the sinking yacht in an open boat, they were picked up by a passing vessel. There were originally four men in the drifting boat. On the eighteenth day, when the men had been without food for seven days and without water for five and when their boat was probably still 1,000 miles from land, Dudley and Stephens, the two defendants, spoke to a third man, one Brooks, about the possibility of killing and eating the deceased, a seventeen year old boy, who was the fourth person aboard the drifting boat. Brooks refused to agree to this proposal as he also did to a subsequent suggestion that lots should be drawn to determine who should be killed to save the rest. Two days later, the twentieth day since they had been cast adrift, Dudley killed the boy with Stephens' consent. The three survivors fed on the body and blood of the boy until they were rescued four days later. The jury specifically found that, if the men had not fed upon the body of the boy, they would probably not have lived until they were rescued and that the boy "being in a much weaker condition, was likely to have died."[45] The jury moreover specifically found that "there was no appreciable chance of saving life except by killing some one for the others to eat." The jurors professed their ignorance of whether the killing of the boy was "felony and murder" but, if it was, Dudley and Stephens were each

---

[43] 14 Q.B.D. 273 (1884).

[44] 26 Fed. Cas. 360 (E.D.Pa. 1842) (No. 15,383).

[45] *Dudley and Stephens*, 14 Q.B.D. at 275.

guilty.[46] A panel of five judges in the Queen's Bench, to whom the issue was referred, upheld the conviction and sentenced the defendants to death, a sentence that was afterwards commuted by the Crown to six months imprisonment. The court rejected all suggestions, based upon authors such as Grotius, Pufendorf and Francis Bacon, that killing the boy in the circumstances of the case before them was justifiable.

United States v. *Holmes,* an earlier case, decided in 1842, involved some of the survivors of a ship carrying cargo, a crew of seventeen, and 65 Scotch and Irish emigrants coming to the United States that struck an iceberg. The captain, seven crew members, and one passenger got into the jolly boat. The remaining members of the crew, led by the first mate, together with 32 passengers got into the longboat, which started to leak almost immediately. The rest of the passengers were left on the ship which eventually sank. The two boats soon separated and the next day the sea began to freshen. That night, in response to an order of the first mate, Holmes and the other seaman began to throw overboard a total of fourteen male passengers who were not accompanied by wives. Two young women were also lost but it is unclear whether they were thrown out or jumped out after their brother was thrown overboard by Holmes, one of the sailors. It was for the death of this youth that Holmes was tried in an indictment for manslaughter. The next day the survivors were rescued by a passing ship.

Holmes was convicted but, in lieu of the extenuating circumstances and the fact he had spent several months in pre-trial confinement, he was sentenced to six months imprisonment and a fine of $20, although the statute authorized a penalty of imprisonment for a term of three years and a fine of $1,000. Despite the fact that the President refused to pardon Holmes, the law report indicates that "[t]he penalty was subsequently remitted."[47] In charging the jury, Justice Baldwin, serving as Circuit Justice, declared that obedience to the unlawful order of the first mate was no defense. He also told the jury that there were no circumstances in which a passenger could be sacrificed to save a sailor. Such a sacrifice could only be justified in the situation in which it was necessary to maintain a sufficient number of seamen in the longboat to man and navigate it, in which case the other passengers would be saved as well. Justice Baldwin

---

[46] *Ibid.*

[47] *Holmes,* 26 Fed. Cas. at 369.

then opined that among people "in equal positions,"[48] i.e. presumably two or more passengers or two or more seamen, such as when shipwrecked people are starving or if it is necessary that someone be jettisoned to lighten the boat, selection should be by lot. *United States v. Holmes* was called to the attention of the English judges in the *Dudley and Stephens* case. They approved of the result but, in their judgment, delivered by Lord Coleridge, they rejected the suggestion that selection by lot could supply a defense to a criminal prosecution for killing a person to feed the survivors or for throwing someone overboard to certain death by drowning in order to lighten a lifeboat.[49]

If *The Queen v. Dudley and Stephens* and *United States v. Holmes* are still good law, Bloggs could not possibly be legally entitled to throw the switch in Thomson's trolley situation. Bloggs does not even come within the *dicta* in the *Holmes* case about the possibility of drawing lots because, in the hypothetical situations envisioned in Justice Baldwin's charge to the jury, the person to be sacrificed if he "draws the short straw," is himself in equal danger of starving to death or of drowning when the overloaded lifeboat sinks. The person to be sacrificed in the trolley scenario is under no threat at all until Bloggs decides to sacrifice him. A universal audience that approved of the results of the *Dudley and Stephens* and *Holmes* cases would have to condemn Bloggs were he to throw the switch. But are these cases still good law, and do they reflect the view that would command the assent of universal audiences in the modern world?

There have not been any subsequent judicial decisions in the English-speaking world casting any doubt on the continued viability of the traditional common-law position that private parties cannot kill an innocent person in order to save the lives of a larger number of people. There have, however, been some other legal developments which might be considered to cloud the situation. The principal of these developments is the acceptance, by many jurisdictions, of what is often called "the lesser evil" defense. One of the key impetuses to this development was the project which culminated in the *Model Penal Code*. The proposed official draft was approved in 1962 and reissued, with a revised official commentary, in

---

[48] *Id.* at 367.
[49] *Dudley and Stephens*, 14 Q.B.D. at 285.

1985. The *Model Penal Code,* which uses the term "[c]hoice of [e]vils" defense, provides, in § 3.02, that (1) Conduct that the actor believes to be necessary to avoid a harm or evil to himself or to another is justifiable, provided that:

(a) the harm or evil sought to be avoided by such conduct is greater than that sought to be prevented by the law defining the offense charged; and

* * *

(c) a legislative purpose to exclude the justification claimed does not otherwise plainly appear.[50]

A companion provision, § 3.01, tells us that this privilege "does not abolish or impair any remedy for such conduct that is available in any civil action."[51] This means that, even if Bloggs could escape criminal prosecution for throwing the switch and killing the lone workman on the other track, he would still be liable in tort for substantial damages in a wrongful death action brought by the workman's next of kin. This would certainly cause Bloggs to think twice before exercising the moral discretion that Thomson is prepared to grant him.

Over twenty American states have now adopted some form of the "lesser evil" defense.[52] The actual text of § 3.02 is silent as to whether the defense is available in cases of homicide and this is true of most of the statutes and judicial decisions recognizing the defense. The statutes of two states, Missouri and Kentucky, however expressly exclude the defense in situations involving intentional homicide,[53] and in a third state, Wisconsin, in cases involving intentional homicide, the defense is limited to reducing the charge to "2nd-degree intentional homicide" (i.e. an intentional but not pre-meditated homicide).[54] Furthermore, although prompted by the *Model Penal Code,* the New York statute, which has been followed in several

---

[50]   MODEL PENAL CODE AND COMMENTARIES § 3.02 (Official Draft and Revised Comments 1985), hereinafter cited as OFFICIAL MODEL CODE.

[51]   *Id.* at § 3.01.

[52]   *See id.* at § 3.02, comment 5.

[53]   KY. REV. STAT. ANN. § 503.030 (Banks-Baldwin 1997); MO. ANN. STAT. § 563.026 (WEST 1979).

[54]   WIS. STAT. ANN. § 939.47 (West 1996).

other jurisdictions,[55] requires that the injury sought to be avoided by what would otherwise be a criminal act must "clearly outweigh" the injury that will be inflicted by the choice of the lesser evil.[56] In one of the early practice commentaries to the New York statute, it is said that the statute "is addressed to an area or kind of technically criminal behavior which virtually no one would consider improper . . . ."[57] As one of the few courts to consider this provision declared, the provision "is to be narrowly construed."[58] This would hardly seem to allow the defense to be used in a case of intentional homicide.

While the actual text of the *Model Penal Code* is silent on the issue, the official commentary makes it clear that § 3.02 is not so limited.[59] Nevertheless, the examples given in the official commentary as illustrations of § 3.02 do not cover Thomson's Bloggs.[60] The first example is of a person who, to save a town, cuts a dike with the result that a nearby farm is inundated. The illustration is unhelpful to Bloggs for two very important reasons. First, at the time of acting, the actor does not know with certainty that the occupants of the farm will be drowned. The farm may not be occupied or, if it is, the occupants may be able to escape. Second, the example presents a case of public necessity, a defense that has, in some limited circumstances, been successfully claimed by private individuals. For example, in *Harrison v. Wisdom*,[61] private persons were allowed to claim the defense of public necessity when government had collapsed, after the withdrawal of Confederate forces on the eve of the arrival of the Union Army in Clarksville, Tennessee, and private citizens destroyed merchants' stocks of whiskey and other liquors.

But public necessity is different from private necessity. Public authorities are constantly deciding what areas should be patrolled by police, where scarce fire equipment should be sent in cases of natural disaster and whether attempts to quell a riot and protect persons or property are prudent

---

[55] *See* OFFICIAL MODEL CODE, § 3.02, comment 5, note 23.
[56] N.Y. PENAL CODE § 35.05 (McKinney 1975).
[57] N.Y. PENAL CODE § 35.05, practice commentary (McKinney 1975).
[58] People v. Brown, 70 Misc.2d 224, 333 N.Y.S.2d 342 (1972).
[59] OFFICIAL MODEL CODE § 3.02, comment 3.
[60] *Ibid.*
[61] 54 Tenn. (7 Heisk.) 99 (1872).

in particular situations. This distinction between public and private necessity is neither merely verbal nor merely historic but rests, rather, upon a very fundamental feature. Public officials are charged with promoting the public or common good. They not only exercise the authority to decide that some people should be sacrificed to save a larger number of others, but also exercise a vastly more important authority, namely the authority to decide that, in some circumstances, some lives are more important than others. While they may disagree about how extreme the situation must be before public authorities are allowed to make such choices, all societies seem to allow public authorities to make such choices in some circumstances. If the war effort requires the survival of technically trained people, then these will be withdrawn from the Philippines before the Japanese Army completes its conquest, as in fact was the case.[62] Indeed, in order to provide greater safety for B-29 bomber crews, nearly 6,000 Marines and about 900 sailors lost their lives to capture Iwo Jima.[63] As we noted earlier, the question in such cases are the criteria used by the public authorities in making these choices. At the very least the decisions reflecting these choices must not be made arbitrarily. But this power of deciding that one person's life is socially more valuable than another's is forbidden to private individuals. None of the writers who think Bloggs should throw the switch seems prepared even

---

[62] W. White, THEY WERE EXPENDABLE 203-04 (1942).

[63] *See* N. Miller, WAR AT SEA 507-16 (1995). There were in addition about 25,000 wounded. *See* G. Weinberg, A WORLD AT ARMS 868 (1994). About 2,400 bombers made emergency landings on Iwo Jima which means, if each bomber had a crew of 10, that perhaps as many as 24,000 bomber crewmen benefited from the availability of Iwo Jima. *See id.* at 869; Miller, *supra,* at 516. A realistic estimate of the tradeoff in casualties is not that simple since, if Iwo Jima were not available, some of the planes undoubtedly might have made it back to their bases in the Marianas. Many more would have taken advantage of the elaborate air-sea rescue schemes that had been established, *see* Weinberg, *supra,* at 869, including the stationing of submarines at fixed points known to the air crews.

There is even some legal authority expressly recognizing the extensive authority of governmental officials to decide who shall live and who shall die. In *Chandler v. Director of Pub. Prosecutions,* [1964] A.C. 763 (1962), the court refused to allow nuclear disarmament demonstrators, who had been prosecuted for attempting to enter a Royal Air Force air station that was being used by nuclear-armed United States aircraft, to argue that Great Britain (and the world) would be safer if such aircraft were prevented from taking off. *See id.* at 774-76.

to countenance the suggestion that private persons can decide that one person's life is more valuable than another's.[64]

The second example given in the official commentary to support its conclusion that the lesser-evil defense can be raised in a prosecution for intentional homicide is of a mountain climber who falls over a precipice and who will drag his companion, to whom he is roped, with him.[65] According to the commentary, the companion "who holds on as long as possible but eventually cuts the rope, must certainly be granted the defense that he accelerated one death slightly but avoided the only alternative, the certain death of both." This case is also vastly different from Bloggs' case. It is more like a case of self-defense. Indeed, it is one of the few situations where one can imagine people agreeing in advance, "if I slip and am about to drag you with me to certain death, cut the rope to keep me from killing you." It certainly is not a case in which a person who would otherwise *not* be killed, is killed to save others. If nothing is done, both climbers will be killed, including the climber who could have been cut loose.

Somewhat the same considerations come into play in the only two other situations that I know of that might include some kind of *ex ante* agreements such as suggested in the climber case and in the scenario with which Thomson feels most comfortable in her variations of the trolley case, namely the one in which all the men are members of the same work crew. These other two situations involve seamen and underground miners. Ship captains have the authority to flood their ships' engine rooms to save their ships, even if this means certain death for the seamen manning their engine rooms.[66] Mine superintendents have an analogous authority to seal off coal

---

[64] *But cf.* L. Alexander, *supra* note 41, who argues that certain factors such as the "relative age of the parties," if these factors are generalizable *ex ante*, might be relevant.

[65] OFFICIAL MODEL CODE, § 3.02, comment 3.

[66] On May 23, 1939, in peacetime, while the United States submarine *Squalus* was practicing a crash dive, the main induction valves failed to close and water poured into the engine rooms. The submarine sank to the ocean floor more that 200 feet below the surface. The two engine rooms were closed off as well as the after torpedo room, entombing 26 men. The remaining 33 were eventually rescued. *See* C. La Vo, BACK FROM THE DEEP 32-61 (1994). The *Squalus's* travails are covered in more detail in N. Barrows, BLOW ALL BALLAST! (1941). The man who actually closed the bulkhead door was reported as saying, when rescued, "I wish to make it clear that I acted according to the requirements of my duty in closing the bulkhead door. I have the utmost sorrow for my

pits to keep fires from spreading through a mine.[67] But again these cases are not analogous to the trolley situation. They are usually situations, like the climber situation, in which it is not the case that a decision is made to save some by sacrificing others who would otherwise have lived, but rather situations in which all will die if nothing is done. They are, moreover, also situations in which the person making the decision is a quasi-public authority, like the captain of a ship or the superintendent of a mine.

How this type of situation might be handled under German or French law is difficult to ascertain. Article 122-7 of the French *nouveau code pénal* provides that a person who, in the face of a danger to himself or another, performs an act necessary to safeguard the personal safety of himself or of another is not subject to criminal punishment unless there is a disproportion between the means employed and the gravity of the threatened danger.[68] The comments to the code indicate that the interest sacrificed must be of inferior value to the interest that is saved.[69] The only discussion in these comments that is at all germane to the possibility of having to sacrifice the safety of one individual to save another concerns the abortion of a fetus to safeguard the life or health of a pregnant woman. It would hardly seem plausible to interpret this provision to authorize one to kill an innocent person who poses no threat to oneself in order to save one's own life. To use this provision to justify the killing of one innocent in order to save the lives of a greater number of other innocent persons would require a finding that the lives of five innocent people are of greater value than the life of one innocent person. This presumably is what Foot and Thomson believe, at least in the trolley situation but not in the tyrant or organ transplant situations. I am skeptical as to whether the French *nouveau code pénal* would be so construed. Article 34 of the German Criminal Code declares that someone who commits an act to avoid an

---

shipmates who died, but I would not hesitate to do the same thing if similar circumstances required . . . ." *Id.* at 172.

[67] P. Rakes, *Casualties on the Homefront: Scotts Run Mining Disasters During World War II*, 53 W. VA. HIST. REV. 95, 111 (1994) describes an instance in which, after the failure of a two-day attempt to extinguish a fire in a mine, the mine officials abandoned the search for a missing miner and sealed off the affected area.

[68] C. PEN. art. 122-7 (author's translation).

[69] *See* C. PEN. art. 122-7 (95th ed. *petits codes*, Dalloz).

imminent and otherwise unavoidable danger to himself or another does not act unlawfully if, taking into account all the conflicting interests, the interest protected significantly outweighs the interest which he harms. [70] This general statement merely begs the question at the core of our discussion. Does the interest in saving five innocent lives outweigh the interest in preserving an innocent person from the deliberate taking of his life?[71]

An examination of the law of national legal systems does not, however, exhaust the legal sources that might bear on the difficult questions with which a universal audience, to which an appeal is made to permit the killing of one innocent person to save the greater number of innocent lives, would have to wrestle. There is, for example, an international convention, to which the United States and the United Kingdom and at least one hundred other countries including France and Germany are parties, that absolutely prohibits the use of torture and specifically states that "[n]o exceptional circumstances whatsoever, whether a state of war or a threat of war, internal political instability or any other public emergency, may be invoked as a justification of torture."[72] The convention, in addition, obliges signatory states to insure that "all acts of torture" and all attempts to commit torture shall be made criminal offenses. This convention dates from 1984 but no one pretends that the convention made new law. It only repeats in greater detail the prescriptions of Article 7 of the 1966 International Covenant on Civil and Political Rights, to which the United Kingdom, France, Germany, and most countries in the world are parties and to which the United States is a signatory.[73]

---

[70] STGB art. 34, translated in THE PENAL CODE OF THE FEDERAL REPUBLIC OF GERMANY 59 (J. Darby transl. 1987), hereinafter cited as STGB.

[71] George Fletcher maintains that German law would not permit the taking of innocent life to save the lives of a greater number of innocents. *See* G. Fletcher, RETHINKING CRIMINAL LAW §§ 10.2-10.2.2, at 774-88 (1978).

[72] Convention Against Torture and Other Cruel, Inhuman or Degrading Treatment or Punishment, U.N. GAOR, 39th Sess., Supp. No. 51, art. 2(2), at 197, U.N. Doc. A/RES/39/46 (1984), hereinafter cited as Torture Convention.

[73] International Covenant on Civil and Political Rights, Dec. 19, 1966, art. 7, 6 I.L.M. 368, 370, hereinafter cited as ICCPR.

The relevance of these provisions to our present inquiries can be clearly illustrated by considering the following case, which unfortunately is much less hypothetical than the trolley cases constructed by Foot and Thomson. A terrorist has been apprehended after he has placed a bomb that, if it detonates, will kill a large number of innocent people. Can we torture this terrorist to obtain the location of the bomb?[74] Let us assume that the terrorist has indeed even admitted planting the bomb and that he is taunting his captors. The international conventions to which we have just referred answer categorically, no. A universal audience that accepted the arguments of Foot and Thomson, and perhaps also those of the drafters of the Model Penal Code, *and* accepted the validity of the international conventions against torture would have to conclude that Bloggs can kill an innocent man to save the lives of five innocent men but a self-confessed terrorist cannot be threatened with death or physically tortured to save the lives of a large

[74] The Israeli security service has apparently sought to use torture in these circumstances and indeed has, in the past, been accused of actually using some forms of what many would consider torture. *See* B. Gellman, *Israeli First: Word 'Torture' Is Spoken: Attorney General Condemns Shaking of Arab Prisoners in Interrogation*, WASH. POST, Oct. 21, 1995, at A17. Soon after this report, the question was considered by the Israeli Supreme Court. Accepting for the moment a civil-rights lawyer's allegation that what the security services were engaged in was torture, that court was reported as having refused to uphold an injunction that had been issued by a lower court. *See id.* One of the judges described as "immoral" the position that a person could not be tortured when the lives of a thousand people could thereby be saved. *See* S. Schmemann, *Israel Allows Use of Physical Force in Arab's Interrogation*, N.Y. TIMES, Nov. 16, 1996, § 1, at 8. More recently, however, a nine-member panel of the Israeli Supreme Court held that the routine use of physically coercive measures such as violent shaking, forcing prisoners to crouch like frogs, and shaping them in contorted positions were illegal and must immediately be stopped. The court left open what would be the case in an emergency situation when the suspect would know of a "ticking bomb." *See* D. Sontag, *Israeli Court Bans Most Use of Force in Interrogations*, N.Y. Times Sept. 7, 1999, at A1. Article 4(1) of the Torture Convention, on the other hand as already indicated, specifically provides that the parties shall make acts of torture and all attempts to commit torture criminal offenses. It has been suggested that torture of the terrorist might be justifiable, in some instances, on the ground of self-defense. *See* E. Benveniste, *The Role of National Courts in Preventing Torture of Suspected Terrorists*, 8 EUR. J. INT'L L. 596 (1997). *See also* A. Enker, *Duress, Self-Defence and Necessity in Israeli Law*, 30 ISRAELI L. REV. 188 (1996). The most compelling case would be one in which the terrorist and his interrogator are confined in a small place and both will be killed if the bomb is not discovered and disarmed.

number of innocent people whom the terrorist has admitted he has put in danger of certain and imminent death. That would take quite a bit of mental gymnastics.

The relevance of international human rights law is not confined to the torture convention. Article 6 of the 1966 Covenant on Civil and Political Rights declares that "[e]very human being has the inherent right to life . . . [which] shall be protected by law," and it further provides that "[n]o one shall be arbitrarily deprived of his life."[75] The Covenant then provides for certain limitations on the imposition of the death penalty in those states that have not already abolished it. Finally the Covenant even expressly declares that no public emergency that threatens the life of the nation can justify a derogation from Article 6. It is hard to maintain that these provisions leave open the possibility that the killing of an innocent person to save a larger number of innocent lives may be legally authorized. Certainly the parties to the 1950 European Convention for the Protection of Human Rights and Fundamental Freedoms could not have thought so. Article 2 of that Convention declares that "[e]veryone's right to life shall be protected by law. No one shall be deprived of his life intentionally save in the execution of a sentence of a court following his conviction of a crime for which the penalty is provided by law."[76] The only exception are deprivations of life resulting "from the use of force which is no more than is absolutely necessary" in defense of a person threatened with unlawful violence, or to effect a lawful arrest or to prevent the escape of a person lawfully detained or in the course of actions lawfully taken to quell a riot or insurrection. The existence of war or other public emergency is expressly declared to permit "[n]o derogation" from this right to life "except in cases resulting from lawful acts of war."[77] In the face of all these provisions of international human-rights law, it would be hard to maintain, particularly in a nation that is a member of the European Community, that generally-worded national provisions on the lesser-evil defense in fact authorize the killing of innocent persons in order to save the lives of a greater number of innocent persons.

---

[75] ICCPR., art. 6(1), 6 I.L.M. at 370.
[76] European Convention for Protection of Human Rights and Fundamental Freedoms, Nov. 4, 1950, 5 EUROP. T. S. 3, hereinafter cited as European Convention.
[77] Id., art. 15(2), at 14.

And yet the fact remains that most philosophers who have considered the issue agree with the position of Foot and Thomson and conclude that Bloggs should throw the switch or, at least, that it is morally permissible for him to do so.[78] Furthermore, the drafters of the *Model Penal Code* strongly suggest that Bloggs should be legally justified in doing so. Why is there such a big discrepancy between what seems to be the law and what, all these people assert, is the morally correct solution and should be the legally correct solution? One possibility is that neither Foot and Thomson nor the drafters of the *Model Penal Code* have ever rigorously examined how the positions they espouse could fit in with other aspects of the legal system.

Suppose in the trolley situation, where it is urged that Bloggs should throw the switch and shunt the trolley on to a spur where it will certainly kill one helpless person rather than permitting it to continue on its way where it will certainly kill five helpless people, we add just one fact. Although helpless to avoid the trolley, should Bloggs throw the switch, the lone workman has a free hand and a revolver. Can he shoot Bloggs, if Bloggs attempts to throw the switch? I have never seen any authority in English or American law suggesting that he could not. Even the *Model Penal Code* accepts that one is so privileged if one *reasonably believes* that it is necessary to do so in order to protect oneself or another from death or serious bodily injury.[79] It is true that the *Model Penal Code* adds to the standard rubric that the privilege to defend onself or another only arises when one is threatened with unlawful force, but that does not help Bloggs. First, even under the *Model Penal Code*, it is not evident that Bloggs is not acting unlawfully. As noted above, the *Model Penal Code* expressly declares that one who can successfully invoke the lesser-evil defense is, nevertheless, liable in tort for the harm that he causes.[80] Second, under the *Model Penal Code*, all the workman needs to establish is that he *reasonably believes* that he was threatened with unlawful force. Moreover, it is clear that the *Model Penal Code*, in its self-defense provisions, was only concerned to make it clear that someone who was himself an aggressor

---

[78] *See* note 41, *supra.*

[79] OFFICIAL MODEL CODE §§ 3.04(2)(b), 3.05. *See also* RESTATEMENT (SECOND) OF TORTS §§ 65, 76 (1965).

[80] *See id.* at § 3.01(2), discussed at p. 97, *supra.*

could not claim self-defense if he injured a person trying to defend himself from the aggression. Indeed, under Anglo-American law an innocent person is entitled to defend himself even when threatened by force that is in no way culpable. Take a person, A, whose life is jeopardized by an imminent collision with a person, B, who, through no fault of his own, has lost his footing and is about to crash into A and knock him in front of a speeding locomotive. May A use all reasonable means to avoid being killed even if that means endangering B's life? Of course he may.

German law seems to raise the same considerations that we have discussed in connection with the *Model Penal Code*. Article 32 of the German Penal Code recognizes the right of self-defense and it defines self-defense as "that defense which is required in order to prevent a present unlawful attack upon oneself or another."[81] It is hard to believe that, under German law, the lone man who will be killed if Bloggs throws the switch is under an obligation under German law to allow himself to be killed even if he has the means of defending himself. The same may be said of French law. Article 122-5 of the *nouveau code pénal* declares that no criminal responsibility accrues to a person who, faced with an unjustifiable threat to himself or to another, performs an act dictated by the necessity of legitimately defending himself or another, unless there is a disproportion between the means used in the defense and the seriousness of the threat.[82]

If Bloggs were justified in throwing the switch, even if he would thereby kill an innocent man who is otherwise not threatened with injury, in order to save five other innocent people who are threatened with certain death, then it would seem to follow that Bloggs could shoot the man on the spur who is trying to prevent Bloggs from throwing the switch. But that seems rather odd. Either one must conclude that the lone man is under a legal and moral obligation *not* to try to defend himself or to fall back on the supposed distinction between justification and excuse. Bloggs would be justified in shunting the trolley on to the spur where it will kill the innocent man and, because he is so justified, Bloggs would also be justified in shooting that man in order to disable him from preventing Bloggs from throwing the switch. If the lone man shot Bloggs on the other hand, his

---

[81] STGB. art. 32 (J. Darby transl.).
[82] C. PENAL art. 122-5 (author's translation).

conduct would only be excused. This possibility is suggested by provisions of the German Penal Code. Article 34 provides that one who acts "to avert an imminent or otherwise unavoidable danger . . . *does not act unlawfully* if, taking into consideration all the conflicting interests, . . . the interest protected by him significantly outweighs the interest which he harms,"[83] and Article 35, which carries the heading "Necessity or excuse," declares that someone who "commits an unlawful act in order to avert an imminent and otherwise unavoidable danger to his own life . . . *acts without guilt.*"[84] Like many English-speaking authors, I find the justification/excuse distinction a difficult one outside of the situation in which excuse is used to describe cases where the acceptance of the excuse merely lessens the gravity of the offense charged rather than absolving the accused of criminal responsibility altogether. This is not the place to discuss this somewhat esoteric issue.[85] For present purposes, it suffices to note that none of the legal authorities that we have examined even remotely supports the possibility that the lone man (or his wife or any third party who saw him imperiled by Bloggs' action) would not be justified in trying to stop Bloggs by all necessary means. Indeed, by protecting his own life the lone man would be merely taking at face value the European Convention's declaration that no one shall be intentionally deprived of his life except in the execution of a lawful sentence or in the course of defense against unlawful force or resisting arrest or lawful actions to quell a riot or insurrection.[86]

The position that Bloggs would be justified in shunting the trolley that is espoused by Foot and Thomson, and seemingly by the *Model Penal Code,* and that is accepted by most of the other philosophers who have considered the question, can be explained in one of two ways. I have suggested that one explanation is the failure of its proponents to consider

---

[83] STGB art. 34 (J. Darby transl.) (emphasis added).

[84] *Id.* at art. 35 (emphasis added).

[85] *Compare* G. Fletcher, *The Right and the Reasonable,* 98 HARV. L. REV. 949, 971-76 (1985), with K. Greenawalt, *The Perplexing Borders Between Justification and Excuse,* 84 COLUM. L. REV. 1897, 1918-27 (1984). This subject is discussed at greater length in G. Christie, *supra* note 7, at 1034-35.

[86] *See* European Convention §§ 2(1), 2(2), and 15(2) discussed in notes 76 and 77, *supra,* and accompanying text.

the implications of the position that they are supporting. If they had, they might have been less confident in the validity of the positions they have espoused. The other possibility is that they are committed to the view that the public good is a collective good and that the individual is ultimately a means to the achievement of that collective good. Under this view, if we do not want to condone the torturing of an innocent because a tyrant has threatened to torture five innocents if we do not comply with his request, it must be because there is a collective good in not encouraging tyrants. The surgeon/transplant case is more difficult to rationalize in this way, but perhaps one could argue that, while saving five at the expense of one enhances the collective good, the mental anguish that we would all suffer if we were fearful that we might be snatched up as raw material for a set of transplants would result in a net diminution of the collective good that is not offset by the assurance that we might be beneficiaries of that arrangement. The argument for distinguishing the tyrant and surgeon cases from the Bloggs case would have to be that the choice of victim in those circumstances is determined by arbitrary human decisions whereas in the trolley situation the choice of victim is dictated by the circumstances. Although he has not wronged anyone nor done anything that in the least threatens the interests of others, the lone man just happens, regrettably for him, to be in a position where killing him will save five other people. A universal audience for whom the public good is a collective good might accept that argument. The universal audience to which current legal regimes are addressing themselves does not. For it, at least in the circumstances that we have been discussing, the primacy of the good of the individual sought to be sacrificed forbids making him a means to the achievement of the ends of others.[87]

---

[87] *Cf.* I. Kant, FOUNDATIONS OF THE METAPHYSICS OF MORALS 54 (L. Beck transl. 1959) (1785):

> The practical imperative, therefore, is the following: Act so that you treat humanity, whether in your own person or in that of another, as an end and never as a means only.

As is well-known, in a later work, Kant discussed the classic case of two drowning men struggling for possession of a plank and concluded that, even if legal sanctions are pointless in that situation, "there still cannot be any necessity that will make what is unjust legal." I. Kant THE METAPHYSICAL ELEMENTS OF JUSTICE 42 (J. Ladd transl. 1965) (1797).

CHAPTER 8

THE CONFLICT BETWEEN THE GENERAL AND THE PARTICULAR—SOME LEGAL BACKGROUND

A. *Some Historical Background and Examples*

A recurrent conflict, in both theoretical discussions of the law and in its practical application, is that between the intellectual urge to greater generality and the cautionary counsel of experience to focus as much as possible on the particular. The ideal or universal audiences to which legal argument is directed are constantly torn by these conflicting impulses. In the history of common-law adjudication, one of the principal areas in which this conflict has been played out is the field of tort law or what in other systems of law is generally called either the law of delict or the law of non-contractual obligations. After the law of torts developed as a separate field of law in the second half of the nineteenth century, scholars began to argue about whether the law of torts was just a convenient amalgam, for purposes of study and classification, of a large set of discreet types of actions which would continue to develop in their separate ways, or whether it now reflected the application of some broad general principles that were implicit in the structure of the older law and which would henceforth guide its future development.[1] That what is now the modern law of torts was historically a set of different forms of action each with its own peculiarities and restrictions, was indisputable. The question was whether it had evolved into something else.

The controversy was not merely a theoretical one. On the contrary, it had important practical implications. As the material and, more importantly, the social structure of society changed, the legal system was confronted with the problem of how it would deal with the new types of claims for legal redress that were produced by these changes. More specifically, the question was raised as to what should be the structure of the arguments made to the courts of law when new sorts of problems found their way into the courts. Would an ideal or universal audience to whom legal arguments are ultimately addressed want the argument to focus on

---

[1] For a good discussion and evaluation of the respective positions, *see* G. Williams, *The Foundation of Tortious Liability*, 1939 CAMB. L. J. 111.

whether the legal redress sought for new social problems fell within the scope of general principles that underlay the existing legal system, or would it prefer the argument to proceed by demonstrating in what ways the legal situation before the court resembled specific previous situations that had been adjudicated by the courts? For the advocate seeking to extend tort remedies to cover truly novel situations, it would seem easier to convince an audience committed to the general theory of tort law to make the desired extension than it would be to convince an audience that had a more particularized and historically based understanding of the scope of tort law.

Take what is now known as the concept of privacy. In 1890 Samuel Warren and Louis Brandeis argued that the law should recognize a broad right of privacy, and that such recognition was only a logical extension of existing tort remedies.[2] Warren and Brandeis noted a case[3] in which Queen Victoria's husband, Prince Albert, who had employed a printer to make copies for private distribution of etchings and drawings done by himself and the Queen, had secured an injunction preventing a person who had received unauthorized copies of these works from publishing a description of them. In another English case,[4] a woman who had employed a photographer to take her portrait secured an injunction prohibiting the photographer from selling copies of her photograph to a maker of Christmas cards. In a third case,[5] the son of the original Lord Clarendon was able to enjoin a person, to whom his father had given an original manuscript of his famous history, from reproducing and selling the work. In these cases recovery was granted either on a theory of implied contract or of a breach of trust or of a common-law copyright. It was Warren and Brandeis' argument that, despite the narrow reasons based upon property rights given by the courts that had decided them, these cases implicitly demonstrated that the law recognized a broader right, a right of privacy or, as it was also called by them, a right to be left alone.

Not surprisingly, it was not many years after the publication of Warren and Brandeis' article before a case raising the issues they discussed reached

---

[2] S. Warren and L. Brandeis, *The Right to Privacy,* 4 HARV. L. REV. 193 (1890).

[3] Prince Albert v. Strange, 41 Eng. Rep. 1171 (Ch. 1849).

[4] Pollard v. Photographic Co., 40 Ch. Div. 345 (1888).

[5] Duke of Queensbury v. Shebbeare, 28 Eng. Rep. 924 (Ch. 1758).

the courts. That case was *Roberson v. Rochester Folding Box Co.*,[6] which was decided by the New York Court of Appeals in 1902. The plaintiff was a woman whose photographic portrait, she alleged, was used on a circular advertising flour, 25,000 copies of which were distributed to all sorts of public places including saloons.   How the defendants obtained her photograph is not clear from the reported decision. Her complaint was upheld against demurrer by the trial court, a decision that was affirmed by the Appellate Division, New York's intermediate appellate court.   The defendants appealed the case to New York's highest appellate court, the New York Court of Appeals, which, in a 4-3 decision, reversed.   The majority examined the cases cited in the Warren and Brandeis article and found that they all involved the violation of some sort of property right. Since the plaintiff alleged violation of no such right, but merely a "so-called 'right of privacy,'" the majority concluded that she had not stated a cause of action against the defendants. The dissenters, in an opinion written by Gray, J., argued that whether the plaintiff could obtain judicial relief did not require the existence of "some precisely analogous case," so long as the plaintiff could show that the defendants had performed a "wrongful" act for which the plaintiff should be provided a remedy. Quoting from the Warren and Brandeis article, Gray, J., declared that "[t]he right to life has come to mean the right to enjoy life, the right to be left alone . . . and the term 'property' has grown to comprise every form of possession, intangible as well as tangible."[7] Gray, J., noted that the writer of a letter has a literary property that allows him to enjoin its unauthorized publication.   The plaintiff, in his view, had "the same property in the right to be protected against the use of her face for defendant[s'] commercial purposes."[8]

One of the reasons given by Parker, C. J., who wrote for the majority, for denying the plaintiff a remedy was that he could not see how courts could establish the limits of a so-called right of privacy.   He could understand that a "legislative body could very well interfere and arbitrarily provide that no one should be permitted for his own selfish purposes to use the picture or the name of another for advertising purposes without his

---

[6] 171 N.Y. 538, 64 N.E. 442 (1902).
[7] *Id.* at 563, 64 N.E. at 450.
[8] *Id.* at 564, 64 N.E. at 450.

consent."[9] But, he continued, "[t]he courts . . ., being without authority to legislate, are required to decide cases upon principle" and so are embarrassed by precedents created by "an extreme, and therefore unjustifiable, application of an old principle." Indeed, undoubtedly prompted by, Parker, C. J.'s suggestion, the New York legislature, in 1903, in fact adopted a statute that made it a misdemeanor, and also provided civil remedies against the offender, for any person to use "the name, portrait or picture" of another "for advertising or for the purposes of trade without written consent."[10] From that time onward recognition of a right to privacy has become almost universally recognized in the United States, usually by judicial decision and usually in a form that is much more encompassing than the protection against commercial appropriation afforded by the New York statute.

Thus far, the so-called right of privacy has not been recognized in the United Kingdom.[11] The difficulties encountered in the United States in establishing the boundaries of any such right of privacy may explain why. From its origins, in the aftermath of the *Roberson* case, it evolved into almost a claimed universal right that was used as one of the reasons for striking down state statutes that restricted the sale of contraceptives, even to married couples,[12] and laws restricting a woman's ability to secure an abortion during the period before the fetus became viable.[13] Reference to "private rights" was even made by one state court in striking down a statutory provision making it mandatory for motorcyclists to wear a helmet.[14] No other court followed this lead, nor have the courts been generally prepared to recognize any rights of privacy claimed by persons

---

[9] *Id.* at 545, 64 N.E. at 443.

[10] N.Y. CIV. RIGHTS LAW §§ 50, 51, as amended (McKinney 1992).

[11] *See* W. Pratt, PRIVACY IN BRITAIN (1979). On whether the recent statutory incorporation of the European Convention on Human Rights into domestic law (Human Rights Act, 1998, c. 42) will affect this situation, *see* B. Markesinis, *Privacy, Freedom of Expression, and the Horizontal Effect of the Human Rights Bill: Lessons from Germany,* 115 LAW. Q. REV. 47 (1999).

[12] Griswold v. Connecticut, 381 U.S. 479 (1965).

[13] Roe v. Wade, 410 U.S. 113 (1973).

[14] People v. Fries, 42 Ill.2d 446, 250 N.E.2d 149 (1969).

being prosecuted for smoking marijuana.[15] When pushed to these limits, the so-called right of privacy became a shibboleth with only symbolic and no predicative value in legal argumentation.

Even in the core area of tort law, some of the same difficulties have arisen as the courts struggled to establish the dimensions of the new tort of "invasion of privacy." Moving beyond the cases involving commercial appropriation of a person's name or likeness, the cases recognizing a right of privacy came to be classified under three additional subheadings.[16] The first, false-light invasion of privacy, need not detain us. It merely provides a remedy for false statements of fact about a person that are not defamatory but nevertheless embarrassing. As such, it usually carries with it the defenses and limitations applicable to actions for defamation. The other two categories are intrusions into the plaintiff's private space and the publication of truthful but embarrassing information about the plaintiff. From the beginning, certain difficulties were experienced in applying the notion of privacy to give redress in such situations. Indeed, even in cases of commercial appropriation, the courts, from the beginning, were obliged to recognize that the publication of a person's name or likeness in newspapers or magazines sold to make a profit did not constitute a commercial appropriation if the published material were newsworthy. The publication in a newspaper of a couple kissing in a public market on a fine spring day has, for example, been held to meet this newsworthiness test.[17]

Moreover, the courts have accepted not only that someone walking on the public streets could not object to being photographed but also that a person could not object to being followed when he appeared in public so long as his physical safety was not thereby threatened.[18] Any other

---

[15] *See, e.g.*, People v. Aguiar, 257 Cal. App.2d 597, 65 Cal. Rptr. 171, *cert. denied*, 393 U.S. 970 (1968); State v. Kantner, 53 Haw. 327, 493 P.2d 306 (1972); Commonwealth v. Leis, 355 Mass. 189, 243 N.E.2d 898 (1969). In Ravin v. State, 537 P.2d 494 (AK 1975), although the court was not prepared to hold that the possession and smoking of marijuana was a fundamental constitutional right under the Alaska constitution, the possession of small amounts of marijuana, and the smoking of it, in one's home was within the constitutionally protected rights of privacy under the Alaska constitution.

[16] The standard four-part division of the tort law of privacy is attributable to the late Dean William L. Prosser. *See* W. Prosser, *Privacy*, 48 CAL. L. REV. 383, 389 (1960).

[17] *See* Gill v. Hearst Pub. Co., 40 Cal.2d 224, 253 P.2d 441 (1953).

[18] *See* Galella v. Onassis, 487 F.2d 986 (2d Cir. 1973).

conclusion would seriously compromise the freedom of others. Intrusion into the private space of another thus came to be confined to physical invasions of a person's home or office in situations that resembled trespassory invasions but were not technically trespasses. A classic case is that of a landlord who installs a hidden microphone in the bedroom of an apartment *before* he leases it to a married couple[19] or someone who taps the telephone lines leading into the plaintiff's home or office.[20] The latter conduct is now also criminally proscribed.[21]

The most difficult area has been the publication of embarrassing true, but little known, facts about a person. In 1931, an intermediate appellate court construed a provision in the constitution of the state of California, which declared that "[a]ll men . . . have certain inalienable rights among which are . . . pursuing and obtaining safety and happiness," to give an individual the right to prevent the publication of embarrassing private facts about himself. The case was *Melvin v. Reid*[22] and it involved the use of a woman's real name in a motion picture about a sensational murder trial in which the plaintiff, then a prostitute, had been acquitted of murder. The plaintiff alleged that she had abandoned "her life of shame" some seven years before the defendants made their motion picture and that she had married and, under her married name, taken a respectable place within society. While the court recognized that the defendants had a right to make the motion picture about a past notorious trial, it held that the defendants should not have used the plaintiff's real name in the motion picture.

Often cited as a correct statement of the law, it is hard to find many reported cases in which *Melvin v. Reid* has actually been applied. It was at one time tempting to dismiss the case as one involving a motion picture, a category of communication that was at the time perceived as largely entertainment and thus not entitled to the protections afforded to print media.[23] The Supreme Court of the United States put that notion to rest in

---

[19] *See* Hamburger v. Eastman, 106 N.H. 107, 206 A.2d 239 (1964).

[20] *See* Fowler v. Southern Bell Tel. & Tel. Co., 343 F.2d 150 (5th Cir. 1965).

[21] *See* 18 U.S.C. §§ 2510-20 (1994), first enacted in 1968.

[22] 112 Cal. App. 285, 297 P. 91 (1931).

[23] *See* Blumenthal v. Picture Classics, 235 App. Div. 570, 257 N.Y.S. 800 (1932), *aff'd on procedural grounds*, 261 N.Y. 504, 185 N.E. 713.

1952.[24] If *Melvin v. Reid* was still good law, it must, therefore, also apply
to the print media. And, indeed, in 1971, the Supreme Court of California,
in *Briscoe v. Reader's Digest Ass'n*,[25] held that *Melvin v. Reid* was in fact
applicable to a magazine article that identified a man by name in an article
about hijacking published some eleven years after he had been convicted in
Kentucky. In holding that the man had stated a cause of action, the court
held that, in order to receive constitutional protection, even truthful
publications must be newsworthy and not reveal facts so offensive as to
shock the community's notions of decency. The case was remanded for
trial on the merits, whereupon it was removed to a federal court which
granted summary judgment to the defendants on the ground, *inter alia*, that
the "publication disclosed no private facts about the plaintiff."[26]

Subsequent to the *Briscoe* case, the Supreme Court of the United
States, in two cases, struck down state statutes making it a crime to reveal
the names of the victims of sex crimes. In the first case, the reporter had
learned the name of the victim from an examination of the indictments
made available for inspection in the courtroom.[27] In the second, the reporter
copied the name of the victim from a police report posted in the police
department pressroom in which there was also a sign stating that the names
of rape victims were not matters of public records.[28] In these cases, the
United States Supreme Court has come close to declaring that the
publication of truthful information can never be proscribed as long as the
publisher has come by the information in question lawfully and has not
violated any duty of confidentiality in publishing the information. The
Duke of York had, so to speak, marched up the hill and down again. The
intellectual desire for generality captured in the notion of a so-called right
of privacy had come upon the obstacle presented by the other goals and
purposes of the legal system. What started out in *Melvin v. Reid* as a
celebration of the individual's right to keep the details of his private life
from public scrutiny had ended up in a series of cases suggesting that the
individual was largely at the mercy of the curiosity of his fellows. If redress

---

[24] *See* Joseph Burstyn, Inc. v. Wilson, 344 U.S. 495 (1952).
[25] 4 Cal.3d 529, 93 Cal. Rptr. 866 (1971).
[26] 1972 WL 7259 (C.D. Cal. 1972).
[27] Cox Broadcasting Corp. v. Cohn, 420 U.S. 469 (1975).
[28] The Florida Star v. B. J. F., 491 U.S. 524 (1989).

was to be had, it would only be in certain narrowly defined circumstances. What began as the recognition of a broad right of recovery had ended up as reaffirmation of the notion that the law consists of sets of particulars.

The longing for some general theory that would unify the law of torts has, however, proved hard to resist. Despite the inevitable disappointments, the urge to construct a universal theoretical foundation of the law of torts constantly manifests itself in the course of judicial decisionmaking. As this book amply illustrates, there seems to be something in the nature of our concept of the ideal audience that craves generality. In 1946, some forty years after it had turned its back on the effort to establish a broad right of privacy in *Roberson*, the New York Court of Appeals was presented with the following case.[29] The defendants, a large tobacco company and its advertising agency, produced a weekly national radio program that claimed to present the nine or ten currently most popular songs. The plaintiff was a musical publishing company. It claimed that, although some of its songs were in fact among the top nine or ten songs at various periods, its songs were either not listed at all among the top nine or ten songs or listed in a lower order of popularity than was justified under the selection criteria purportedly used by the defendants. All this resulted, it was claimed, in lower sales of the plaintiff's sheet music. Although the plaintiff's claim was a novel one, the trial court thought that it had stated a valid cause of action. The Appellate Division reversed and ordered the case dismissed. The New York Court of Appeals in turn reversed the Appellate Division's order and remanded the case for trial. Quoting some language from a late nineteenth century English case, as well as from a 1904 decision of the United States Supreme Court, written by Oliver Wendell Holmes, Jr., the New York Court of Appeals declared that the "'intentional infliction of temporal damage . . . is a cause of action, which . . . requires a justification if the defendant is to escape.'"[30] There is the strong suggestion in the court's opinion that it believed that the ideal or universal audience consisting of all right-thinking human beings would subscribe to that proposition. The court then went on to hold that the plaintiff had alleged "such a prima facie tort."

---

[29] Advance Music Corp. v. American Tobacco Co., 296 N.Y. 79, 70 N.E.2d 401 (1946).

[30] *Id.* at 83-84, 70 N.E.2d at 403.

The case does not on its face seem to involve any questions of major importance but the emergence of the so-called "*prima facie* tort" proved to be a significant potential threat to civil liberty. Most of the things we do have a potentially adverse effect on others and we are often very much aware of that possible effect at the time we act. Although very rarely invoked, and probably now largely moribund, the doctrine was used as the basis upon which a group of electric power companies prevented the circulation of a letter from the American Institute of Certified Public Accountants to its members from April 15, 1959 until July 7, 1959.[31] The letter related to how, in the opinion of the Institute, the deferred potential tax liability generated by the use of accelerated depreciation should be treated in constructing a company's balance sheet. The plaintiffs' argument was that circulation of the letter, before seeking comments from the entire accounting community, while the United States Securities and Exchange Commission was considering the adoption of mandatory accounting rules on the subject, would intentionally inflict temporal damage upon them because the method proposed by the defendant accounting institute would increase the liabilities side of their balance sheets. This in turn would make it more difficult for them to borrow from institutional investors the vast amounts of money regularly required by electric-power-generating companies to increase their capacity. None of the federal courts that considered the case on its merits thought that the plaintiffs had stated a good cause of action but, because the case was governed by New York law and arguably came within the definition of a *prima facie* tort, both the federal district court and the United States Court of Appeals for the Second Circuit kept in place the temporary injunction obtained by the plaintiffs at the commencement of the law suit until the plaintiffs had exhausted their avenues of appeal. Justice Brennan[32] finally ended the farce by refusing to stay the mandate of the Second Circuit while the plaintiffs' petition for certiorari awaited disposition by the United States Supreme Court.

---

[31] The case in question is Appalachian Power Co. v. American Institute of Certified Public Accountants, 177 F.Supp. 345 (S.D.N.Y. 1959) *aff'd per curiam*, 286 F.2d 844 (2d Cir.), *cert. denied*, 361 U.S. 887.
[32] 80 S.Ct. 16 (1959).

B. *The Scope of the Modern Tort of Negligence*

The most recent manifestation of the felt demands of an ideal audience for universality has arisen as much in Great Britain as it has in the United States. It also affects more central aspects of tort law and thus would have more serious practical consequences were it fully to succeed. I am referring to disputes as to the nature and scope of the modern tort of negligence, one of the central, if not *the* central, category of contemporary Anglo-American tort law. The core concept of negligence law is that one must act in relation to his fellow human beings as would a reasonable person. And, if he fails to act in the manner that a reasonable person in his circumstances would have acted, he must compensate those who have been injured as a result of his unreasonable conduct. One of the principal features of the law of negligence is the notion of foreseeability, that is what could one reasonably foresee as the consequences of his behavior. It is a notion that is used to determine both the persons towards whom one has a duty of care, that is a duty of reasonable behavior, and the extent of liability to those whom one has injured as a result of not exercising due care, that is of not behaving as would have a reasonable person in his situation.

Although the notion of foreseeability has long played a major role in the development of tort law, and the law of negligence in particular, it has assumed even greater importance in recent years as a result of a number of developments. One of these is the gradual extension of liability for negligent conduct to areas which were previously thought only to allow for liability premised on intentional or at most reckless conduct. For example, in the nineteenth century, barring special circumstances, to bring a tort action for misrepresentation one had to show fraud, that is to say an intention to mislead or a reckless indifference to whether one misled others.[33] In the course of the twentieth century, the courts, first in the United States and then in England, came increasingly to recognize the possibility of bringing an action for misrepresentation based merely on negligence. The question then arose as to who were the persons to whom one would be liable for any negligent misrepresentations he might make.

---

[33] *See* Derry v. Peek, 14 App. Cas. 337 (1889).

Ronald Dworkin, whose work we shall examine in greater detail in the next chapter and a great proponent of the need to bottom the law on general principles, has declared that, if a legal system "appeals to the principle that people have a right to compensation from those who injure them carelessly, as its reason why manufacturers are liable for defective automobiles, it must give full effect to that principle in deciding whether accountants are liable for their mistakes as well."[34] And some American courts have, in fact, extended the liability for negligent misrepresentation to all those who might foreseeably be injured should one negligently supply false information.[35]

The English courts, and the majority of the American courts as well, have, however, not been prepared to go so far. For liability to accrue under English law, it is not enough that injury to the plaintiff is foreseeable if false information is negligently supplied. The defendant must have assumed some special responsibility towards the plaintiff. In an important recent case, the House of Lords held that shareholders who bought additional shares on the strength of a negligently prepared auditor's report could not bring an action against the auditors.[36] In an even more recent case, a majority of the House of Lords held that a surveyor who negligently altered his report to allow a ship to sail with only temporary repairs, instead of the permanent repairs he had initially recommended, had not assumed any responsibility to act with reasonable care to the owners of the ship's cargo, which was lost when the temporary repairs failed and the ship sunk.[37] A few months earlier, however, a divided House of Lords had held that a solicitor who had negligently delayed preparing a new will had assumed a duty to act with reasonable care to the prospective beneficiaries whose hopes were frustrated when the testator died before the new will was prepared and executed.[38] This case is difficult to reconcile with the ship-surveyor case except on the policy ground that, if the disappointed beneficiaries cannot bring an action, there is no possible redress, while the cargo owners can and undoubtedly had insured themselves against the loss

---

[34] R. Dworkin, LAW'S EMPIRE 165 (1986).
[35] *See, e.g.,* Rosenblum v. Adler, 93 N.J. 324, 461 A.2d 138 (1983).
[36] Caparo Industries PLC v. Dickman, [1990] 2 A.C. 605.
[37] Marc Rich & Co. v. Bishop Rock Marine Co., [1996] 1 A.C. 211 (1995).
[38] White v. Jones, [1995] 2 A.C. 207.

of their goods. The cases can certainly not be reconciled on the basis of the degree of foreseeability of injury.

In the United States, most states follow the *Restatement (Second) of Torts* and restrict the liability of the defendant to the person or the limited class of persons for whose benefit and guidance the defendant intends to supply the information "or knows that the recipient [of the information] intends to supply it."[39] The defendant must furthermore intend that the information should influence the transaction in question or know that it will do so. This is a long way short, *pace* Dworkin, of liability to all those who might reasonably be foreseen to rely on the information.

Why would the ideal audience to whom legal arguments are ultimately addressed be prepared to accept these conceptually messy resolutions of legal controversies? We will explore some of the possible reasons in the next chapter when we consider the urge for general principles from a more theoretical perspective. To further set the stage and to illustrate the importance of the question, some further legal examples in Anglo-American law of the conflict between the continuing aspiration for generality and the constant claim made by the exigencies of practical life for a more particularized, a more cramped if you will, resolution of legal controversies will be helpful.

The area of negligent misrepresentation is not the only area of modern tort law in which English and many American courts have been attracted by the idea of finding some general principle that would apply to all cases of negligence only to feel obliged, in time, to fall back on a more compartmentalized view of the law. Two additional related examples immediately present themselves. The first involves the question of when damages may be recovered for the negligent infliction of emotional distress. The second revisits the questions raised in our discussion of negligent misrepresentation. Why should there not be a general right to recover pure economic damages in a negligence case not merely in a case of negligent misrepresentation but in any case of negligently caused economic loss? In the cases that we shall examine in the course of that discussion, we shall find the fullest judicial discussion of the issue we have been discussing,

---

[39] RESTATEMENT (SECOND) OF TORTS § 552 (1977). *See, e.g,.* Bily v. Arthur Young & Co., 3 Cal. 4th 370, 11 Cal. Rptr. 2d 51 (1992).

namely whether there are certain universal general principles upon which Anglo-American tort law is ultimately based.

Initially the law did not permit recovery for the negligent infliction of emotional distress in the absence of some sort of direct or indirect physical contact with the person of the plaintiff.[40] This position was gradually abandoned, first in England and then in the United States, to allow recovery to people within the zone of danger, that is, those who could plausibly maintain that they were close enough to the physical source of the danger that threatened them although, happily for them, they had escaped being hit by the source of danger. Certainly such distress was a clearly foreseeable consequence of the defendant's negligence. But surely it is also reasonably foreseeable by the defendant that, if he injures someone, those who witness or in some way observe the injuries inflicted by the defendant's negligent conduct may very well suffer serious mental trauma even if they themselves have not been physically threatened with injury. New York and a number of other American jurisdictions have recognized this possibility but on policy grounds have refused to extend liability beyond the class of people who are themselves physically threatened by the defendant's conduct.[41] What is possibly a majority of American jurisdictions, however, have been prepared to extend liability beyond these limits, and this is the position of English law.[42] *Dillon* v. *Legg*,[43] a 1968 California case that started this trend in American law, specifically relied on the concept of reasonable foreseeability.

This triumph of principle had hardly taken place before some serious questions started to be presented. What is it to witness a distressing event? What if one witnesses the event live on television?[44] What if one comes upon the aftermath of a distressing event,[45] or sees the victim of a

---

[40] *See, e.g.*, Mitchell v. Rochester Ry., 151 N.Y. 107, 45 N.E. 354 (1896); Victorian Ry. Comm'rs v. Coultas, 13 App. Cas. 222 (1888) (P.C.).

[41] *See* Bovsun v. Sanperi, 61 N.Y.2d 219, 473 N.Y.S.2d 357 (1984). *See also* Consolidated Rail Corp. v. Gottshall, 512 U.S. 532 (1994), which adopted the same doctrine with regard to tort actions governed by political law.

[42] Dating at least since Hambrook v. Stokes Bros., [1925] 1 K.B. 141 (C.A.).

[43] 68 Cal.2d 728, 69 Cal. Rptr. 72 (1968).

[44] *See* Alcock v. Chief Constable of the So. Yorks. Police, [1992] 1 A.C. 310 (1991).

[45] *See* Dziokonski v. Babineau, 375 Mass. 555, 380 N.E.2d 1295 (1978).

horrendous event in the hospital?[46] And what is a distressing event, the witnessing of which entitles one to recover damages for any emotional distress he might have suffered as a consequence?

The American cases have largely limited recovery to people who have witnessed the actual injury to a family member or who have witnessed a situation in which serious injury to a family member seemed reasonably likely. After flirting with a more extensive liability, the Supreme Court of California, the court that relied on the principle of reasonable foreseeability to start the American trend to expand liability beyond the class of those who themselves were threatened with physical injury, has decided that, to recover, the family member must be present at the time of the accident.[47] Coming upon the aftermath is not enough. Moreover that same court, as almost all other American jurisdictions, has refused recovery to cohabiting adults.[48] A marriage or blood relationship is almost always necessary with some possibility of recovery by step-parents and step-children. It is ironic that a trend that began because a distinction based upon whether a person was himself threatened with physical injury was thought to be arbitrary should now rely on distinctions that some may feel are equally arbitrary.

Something similar seems to have transpired in Great Britain. The law there seems to be that, although a bystander—now called a secondary victim—may recover for witnessing injury to another, he must not only be close to the incident in time and place and in some sense have directly perceived it, but he must also have a close tie of love and affection with the person killed, injured, or imperilled.[49] The relationship of being a brother to the primary victim is not itself enough since "the quality of brotherly love is well known to differ widely."[50] For a bystander, who does not meet these criteria, recovery is only possible if, as in America, the bystander is himself

---

[46] *See* McLoughlin v. O'Brian, [1983] A.C. 410 (1982).

[47] Thing v. La Chusa, 48 Cal.3d 644, 257 Cal. Rptr. 865 (1989).

[48] Elden v. Sheldon, 46 Cal.3d 267, 250 Cal. Rptr. 254 (1988).

[49] White v. Chief Constable of the So. Wilts. Police, [1999] 1 All E.R. 1 (1998) (H.L.); Page v. Smith, [1996] 1 A.C. 155 (1995).

[50] Alcock v. Chief constable of the So. Yorks. Police, [1992] A.C. 310, 406 (1991), (per Lord Ackner).

a primary victim, that is, someone actually threatened with physical injury as a result of the defendant's negligence.

In all these jurisdictions, it is obvious that the fear of too great a potential monetary liability has overcome the desire to establish, once and for all, the principle of reasonable foreseeability as *the* principle for determining when compensation may be obtained for injuries caused by negligence. Is this a solution that could or should be accepted by an ideal audience? The discussion in the next chapter may help us respond to that question. In the meantime one more modern legal illustration of the tension that we have been exploring requires at least some brief description because of its very great practical importance and because the principle cases presenting this tension carry forward the debate begun in the negligent misrepresentation and negligent-infliction-of-emotional-distress cases that we have already examined.

During the same period in which the courts were wrestling with the question of the limits of liability for the negligent infliction of emotional distress, many courts were also struggling with the question of whether the principle of reasonable foreseeability also governed recovery for what is often called pure economic loss. If a person is physically injured, among the injuries he may have suffered is loss of income because of inability to work. This is obviously an economic injury and the law will provide him with compensation for this loss, but, since this economic loss is the result of physical injury to his person, it is not considered "pure economic" injury. Traditionally, except for certain intentional business torts such as misrepresentation and unfair competition, the law had not allowed for the recovery of pure economic loss.

We have seen, however, that over the course of the twentieth century the common law has come to allow, to a limited extent, recovery for pure economic loss in cases of negligent misrepresentation. In the latter half of the twentieth century, as the principle of reasonable foreseeability was taking hold as *the* principle governing liability of negligently caused injury, some courts began to question the general exclusion of pure economic loss from the category of recoverable injury. If pure economic loss could be recovered for negligent misrepresentation, why should there not be recovery of pure economic loss in other situations? Certainly, in many cases, such losses were clearly foreseeable consequences of the defendant's negligence.

For example, if one negligently destroys the electric cables leading to a construction site, one could obviously foresee damage to the owner of the power cables that have been destroyed and would therefore have to compensate the owner of the cables for that loss. One could also easily foresee that, owing to the loss of electric power, the construction will not be completed on time and this will often lead to serious loss to the contractor and/or the owner of the building under construction. Nevertheless, this loss, which is pure economic loss, traditionally had not been recoverable no matter how foreseeable it was. Even a person whose property, say an office building, had been physically damaged, so as to entitle him to compensation for that loss, would not receive any compensation for the loss of rent that he might suffer while his building was being repaired, or was being rebuilt if it had been totally destroyed. Admittedly, in the case of the total destruction of the building, the fair market value of the building before its destruction may, because of its location or other factors, reflect more than the cost of its physical reconstruction, but, to the extent that this premium did not include the entire loss that the owner of the building would suffer from the loss of the building, he went uncompensated. A prudent building owner would have purchased business interruption insurance.

In the 1970's, by which time the possibility of recovery for negligent misrepresentation and negligent infliction of emotional distress had already been recognized, although the extent of that liability was still being debated, the situation began to change. Undoubtedly prompted by the seemingly imminent triumph of the reasonable foreseeability test that was captured in the writings of Ronald Dworkin—recall Dworkin's assertion, quoted above, that liability for negligent misrepresentation should be governed by the same principles as govern the negligent manufacture of an automobile—the traditional distinction between pure economic loss and loss occasioned by physical injury began to be questioned in England. A key case was *Anns* v. *Merton London Borough Council*,[51] decided by the House of Lords in 1977. The plaintiffs were the lessees of a group of flats that had been completed in 1962 and that, as it was subsequently discovered, had been constructed with inadequate foundations. The basis for the claim against

---

[51] [1978] A.C. 728 (1977).

the Council was that the Council's inspectors had negligently inspected and approved the foundations even though they had not conformed to the Council's building code. The House of Lords affirmed the Court of Appeal's conclusion that the plaintiffs could bring an action against the Council for the cost of repairing the foundations. The principal speech was delivered by Lord Wilberforce. Although he said that an action would "only arise when the state of the building is such that there is present or imminent danger to the health or safety of persons occupying it,"[52] Lord Wilberforce made a number of statements in his speech that, for a number of years thereafter, were to have a profound effect on the law of torts. Among the most important was his declaration that "the position has now been reached that in order to establish that a duty of care arises in a particular situation, it is not necessary to bring the facts of that situation within those of previous situations in which a duty of care has been held to exist."[53]

It is uncanny that, in 1977, the House of Lords was engaged in the same inquiry as to whether there was some general theory underlying tort law that had so divided the New York Court of Appeals in 1902 when it decided the *Roberson* case, which we discussed earlier in this chapter. Instead of trying to find a close fit between the instant situation and some previous case, Lord Wilberforce thought that one had to ask two questions. First, was there "a sufficient relationship of proximity or neighbourhood such that ... [it was] in the reasonable contemplation of the [defendant that] carelessness on his part [would] be likely to cause damage [to the plaintiff]—in which case a *prima facie* duty of care arises?"[54] Second, if that were the case, one would then consider "whether there are any considerations which ought to negative, or to reduce or limit the scope of the duty or the class of person to whom it is owed or the damages to which a breach of it may give rise."[55] Negligent misrepresentation was among the examples that he gave of situations in which such limitations might be appropriate.

---

[52] *Id.* at 760.
[53] *Id.* at 751.
[54] *Id.* at 751-52.
[55] *Id.* at 752.

Although the scope of *Anns* could be somewhat confined because it could be said to involve physical damage to property, Lord Wilberforce's speech obviously raised the question whether the traditional distinction between pure economic loss and other sorts of loss was about to be discarded by a "more principled" mode of analysis. And, indeed, in a series of cases ending in 1982, the House of Lords came very close to adopting that position in *Junior Books Ltd.* v. *Veitchi, Co. Ltd.*,[56] a case in which the owner of a building was allowed to recover, *inter alia*, the loss of profits it had incurred because construction work had not been completed in time as a result of the defendant subcontractor's negligent installation of a defective floor in a factory. The action lay in tort because there was no contractual privity between the parties. Except for a lone dissenter, all of their lordships agreed with Lord Roskill who, to the argument that allowing recovery in such cases would "open the floodgates," replied that although "policy considerations have from time to time been allowed to play their part in the tort of negligence since it first developed . . . yet today I think its scope is best determined by considerations of principle rather than of policy."[57]

This apparent triumph of the principle of foreseeability in the economic loss cases had been foreshadowed a few months previously by some of the language used in *McLoughlin v. O'Brian*.[58] In *McLoughlin*, the House of Lords allowed recovery of damages for emotional distress by a mother who had not physically witnessed the serious injury to her children and husband in an automobile accident. She first saw them a few hours later in a dazed and battered condition in the hospital, where she was also informed that one of the children had been killed. The most interesting speeches were those of Lord Scarman and Lord Bridge of Harwich. The latter concluded that, with regard to the question of the limits of liability for the infliction of nervous shock, there were "no policy considerations sufficient to justify limiting the liability of negligent tortfeasors by reference to some narrower criterion than that of reasonable foreseeability."[59] He expressed regret that

---

[56] [1983] 1 A.C. 520 (1982) (Sc.).
[57] *Id.* at 539.
[58] [1983] 1 A.C. 410 (1982).
[59] *Id.* at 443.

Lord Edmund-Davies criticized his conclusion. Not only did Lord Edmund-Davies criticize Lord Bridge of Harwich's conclusion, he also rather pointedly disagreed with the conclusion of Lord Scarman, who in a brief speech expressing his agreement with Lord Bridge of Harwich asked, "Why then should not the courts draw the line, as the Court of Appeal [which denied recovery on policy grounds] manfully tried to do in this case?"[60] To which question Lord Scarman declared, "[s]imply, because the policy issue as to where to draw the line is not justiciable. The problem is one of social, economic, and financial policy. The considerations relevant to a decision are not such as to be capable of handling within the limits of the forensic process." This of course, like Lord Roskill's declaration in *Junior Books*, was again pure Dworkin, whose work, as already noted, we shall discuss in greater detail in the next chapter when we move from these legal examples to a more theoretical discussion. To Lord Scarman's argument, Lord Edmund-Davies replied that his proposition was "as novel as it is startling."[61] He found it novel because it had never been mentioned in argument and "startling because in my respectful judgment it runs counter to well-established and wholly acceptable law."

These cases represented the highwater mark of the ascendency of principle over what was viewed as the pragmatism of policy. We have already seen that English law has restricted, although not by any means done away with, the ability of bystanders to bring actions for emotional distress. In the realm of recovery for pure economic loss, however, the House of Lords did a complete *volte-face*, which soon led it to declare that *Anns* had been wrongly decided and that all the cases decided on the basis of *Anns* should be overruled.[62]

A similar, but less dramatic, process took place in the United States. Starting in the mid 1960's a few state courts held that recovery would lie for pure economic loss in products liability cases[63] and several federal courts of appeal intimated that this principle mandated a similar renunciation of

---

[60] *Id.* at 431.

[61] *Id.* at 427.

[62] Murphy v. Brentwood District Council, [1991] 1 A.C. 398 (1990).

[63] *See, e.g.,* Santor v. A. & M. Karagheusian, Inc., 44 N.J. 52, 207 A.2d 305 (1965); Oksenholt v. Lederle Labs., 294 Or. 213, 656 P.2d 293 (1982); City of La Crosse v. Schubert, Schroeder & Assocs., 72 Wis.2d 38, 240 N.W.2d 124 (1976).

the traditional distinctions in admiralty cases as well.[64] But again a reaction set in. For example, in a case decided in 1965, the New Jersey Supreme Court held that a retail purchaser of what was described as "Grade #1" carpet was able to recover the cost of replacing that carpet from the manufacturer who was several steps removed in the distribution scheme from the retail purchaser, and of whose name the retail purchaser was unaware at the time he bought the carpet.[65] Twenty years later the New Jersey Supreme Court refused to apply that doctrine in an action involving what it called "commercial" parties, hardly a distinction based upon principle.[66] An additional year later, in 1986, the Supreme Court of the United States, *in East River S.S. Corp v. Transamerica Delaval, Inc.,*[67] held that damages for pure economic loss could not be recovered in a product liability action brought in admiralty, regardless of whether the action was brought under a strict liability theory or a negligence theory, a position that now has been taken with regard to all products liability actions by the *Restatement (Third) of Torts.*[68]

For the moment the position that has prevailed in both Great Britain and the United States is that parties who wish to protect themselves against pure economic losses can provide for their recovery either by contract or by the purchase of business interruption insurance. In the *East River S.S.* case, for example, the unsuccessful plaintiffs had entered into long-term bare boat charters of tankers that proved to have defective turbines. They were unable to recover either for the cost of repairing the engines or their loss of profits during the period in which the ships were out of service while being repaired.

What lesson applicable to the study of legal argument is to be learned from this brief review of contemporary legal developments? We have seen that at least two major common-law nations have rejected the notion that all cases of negligence should be governed by the same principles of liability whether they involve emotional distress, the liability of accountants, or the

---

[64] *See, e.g.,* Union Oil Corp. v. Oppen, 501 F.2d 558 (9th Cir. 1974); In re Kinsman Transit Co., 388 F.2d 821 (2d Cir. 1968).

[65] Santor v. A. & M. Karagheusian, *supra* note 63.

[66] Spring Motors Distub. v. Ford Motor Co., 98 N.J. 555, 489 A.2d 660 (1985).

[67] 476 U.S. 858 (1986).

[68] RESTATEMENT (THIRD) OF TORTS (PRODUCTS LIABILITY) § 21 (1998).

more general question of pure economic loss. Would an ideal or universal audience condemn these legal systems for doing so? Would it perhaps grudgingly accept this result as a practically necessary one but pine for the day when such concessions to pragmatic considerations would be unnecessary? Or could one conceive of an ideal or universal audience applauding this more particularized approach to discreet practical situations? These are questions that we shall consider in the next chapter.

CHAPTER 9

THE CONFLICT BETWEEN THE GENERAL AND THE PARTICULAR—THEORETICAL PERSPECTIVES

One could give endless additional illustrations of the practical force of the perennial desire for some general principle around which to organize as much as possible of the legal universe and the subsequent retreat to a more particularized view of the law in the face of the stubborn reality of complex social conditions. From the perspective from which this book is written, the presentation of additional examples would be pointless. There are, however, some more basic observations that can be made about this recurrent phenomenon and especially about the context in which some particular manifestation of this phenomenon appears. The phenomenon has generally manifested itself in judicial decisions and scholarly work aimed at a relatively small professional legal audience. The controversy over whether there is a general right to privacy that we discussed above fits that model. The same may be said about the American cases concerning recovery for pure economic loss to which we have also referred. But, in England, the discussion of whether pure economic loss was recoverable in tort was undoubtedly influenced, as we have already indicated, by the work of Ronald Dworkin. This made a significant difference. While Dworkin himself is of course a lawyer, his work is directed at a much wider audience than the narrow professional audience of practicing lawyers and the law school professors who teach concrete legal subjects like torts or contracts. Under his prompting, questions such as whether pure economic loss should be recoverable in tort mutated from being relatively narrow legal issues into inquiries as to the nature of legal reasoning itself and even as to the nature of moral reasoning. That is, the resolution of these legal issues has raised the question of what the ideal form of legal argument addressed to an idealized universal audience would look like.

A. The Case for General Principles Put Forth by Dworkin

Ronald Dworkin first attracted attention by his attack on the legal positivism of H. L. A. Hart.[1] Hart conceived of law as a rule-driven

---

[1] *See* R. Dworkin, *The Model of Rules*, 35 U. CHI. L. REV. 14 (1967) *reprinted in* R. Dworkin, TAKING RIGHTS SERIOUSLY 14 (1977) (hereinafter cited as TAKING RIGHTS

enterprise but he accepted that, at its margins—its penumbras so to speak—law was uncertain. For Hart the task of the judge, when he dealt with cases that fell within the penumbras of the law, was to resolve the uncertainty as best he could, given the legal sources available to him. In the performance of this task, according to Hart, the exercise of some degree of judicial discretion was inevitable. In his criticism of Hart, Dworkin started with a view of the legal system of a mature society as consisting not only of rules but also of principles.[2] Like Hart, Dworkin accepted that there were occasions when the existing rules of law did not cover a case or when the existing rules of law were in conflict. But he differed with Hart's conclusion that, in such circumstances, a judge was obliged to exercise his discretion. Rather, in such situations, in which the conventional sources of law (namely the statutes and previously decided cases) did not provide clear answers, judges could, should, and did resort to the "principles" embedded, so to speak, in the legal system to ascertain the correct decision of the case.

Dworkin purported to give two examples of actual legal decisionmaking that illustrated his thesis. One involved the question of whether someone who had murdered a testator could nevertheless inherit the testator's estate under the will;[3] the other involved the question of whether contractual disclaimers of liability for physical injuries suffered by consumers as a result of a defectively manufactured consumer product barred a person who was physically injured by the product from bringing an action for damages against the manufacturer and retail seller of the product.[4] Whether a close legal analysis of these cases would support

SERIOUSLY) attacking H. Hart, THE CONCEPT OF LAW (1961).

[2] There is of course a superficial resemblance between this view of a legal system and Roscoe Pound's well known and more complex division of the legal universe as an amalgam of *rules* which, like Hart and Dworkin, he viewed as the practical core of a legal system, *principles, conceptions* (or categories of legal thought), *doctrines* (or schemes of fitting together the components of legal thought), and *standards* (the limits of permissible human conduct, such as the reasonably prudent man standard of tort law). *See* R. Pound, *Hierarchy of Sources and Forms in Different Systems of Law,* 7 TUL. L. REV. 475, 482-86 (1933).

[3] *See* TAKING RIGHTS SERIOUSLY at 29. The case he was commenting on is Riggs v. Palmer, 115 N.Y. 506, 22 N.E. 188 (1889).

[4] *See* TAKING RIGHTS SERIOUSLY at 23-24. The case he was commenting on is Henningsen v. Bloomfield Motors, Inc., 32 N.J. 358, 161 A.2d 69 (1960).

Dworkin's assertion that they illustrated his thesis is another matter.[5] But since, in the vast legal literature to which Dworkin's thesis has given rise, it has been assumed that his thesis has a factual basis, it is not worth pursuing that issue here. It is also, for the same reasons, not worth pursuing here the question of whether principles are anything more than broadly worded rules[6] or even whether a rubric such as "no one should profit from his own wrongdoing" should be classified as a principle rather than as a statement of social policy.[7] Nevertheless, taking Dworkin at face value, it was his insistence that judges were always meaningfully constrained by principle that led Dworkin to reject any suggestion that, in difficult cases, judges were obliged to resort to policy. Policy was not law. As we saw in the previous chapter, this was precisely the tack taken by Lord Scarman in *McLoughlin v. O'Brian*, where he asserted that reasonable foreseeability must be the test of tort liability because "the policy issue as to where to draw the line is not justiciable."[8] Dworkin could not have put the point better himself.

This book, of course, is not about legal doctrine. Particular series of cases have only been used to illustrate certain general features of legal argument. We are not merely interested in how Dworkin's thought has undoubtedly influenced contemporary judicial decisionmaking but in the broader question of what drives people to believe that arguments addressed to an ideal or universal audience must be general in scope and possess a certain form. Since Dworkin has had a lot to say about these questions and has had a major influence on contemporary jurisprudential thought, it will

---

[5] In G. Christie, *The Model of Principles*, 1968 DUKE L. J. 649, I submitted that they do not.

[6] This point has been well made in K. Greenawalt, *Policy, Rights and Judicial Decisions*, 11 GAL. REV. 991 (1977); K. Greenawalt, *Discretion and Judicial Decision*, 75 COLUM. L. REV. 359 (1975).

[7] One might note, in this regard, that in discussing, McLoughlin v. O'Brian, [1983] A.C. 410 (1982), Dworkin asserted that the proposition: "People have a moral right to compensation for reasonably foreseeable injury but not in circumstances when recognizing such a right would impose massive and destructive financial burdens on people who have been careless out of proportion to their moral fault," is a statement of principle. R. Dworkin, LAW'S EMPIRE 241 (1986), hereinafter cited as LAW'S EMPIRE. How this proposition differs from what most people would call "policy" escapes me.

[8] [1983] 1 A.C. at 431.

be necessary to continue our discussion of the evolution of Dworkin's thought and how it bears on the ultimate questions examined in this book.

From the beginning, Dworkin recognized that a number of principles could point in competing directions and might even directly conflict.[9] A means for weighting principles was thus obviously required if his theories were to have any practical application. Neither Dworkin nor anyone else, however, has yet produced that weighted list of principles. Recognizing his inability to produce such a list, Dworkin thus began to take a slightly different tack as his thought evolved. He asserted that, in difficult cases (the so-called hard cases), it was the task of the judge "to find a coherent set of principles" that would justify his decision. These guiding principles were to be selected "in the way that fairness requires" in light of the "institutional history" of a society's legal structure.[10] Pursuing this suggestion further, Dworkin next claimed that in nearly all cases, at least in advanced and complex societies with long legal traditions such as the United States or Great Britain, one set of principles, and the decision they justified, would provide a better fit with that society's basic legal structure than would a competing set of principles pointing to a different or even contrary decision.[11] Dworkin did not, however, support this assertion; he assumed that it was obviously true. He also came to assume that there was some notion of "normative consistency" that could be relied on to support his position.[12] Furthermore, when one of those rare cases arose in which no one set of principles was accepted as dispositive by most of the participants in the legal enterprise, Dworkin thought that recourse should be had to what he called "moral facts."[13] These moral facts in some way proceed from political theory and ultimately produce moral rights. In hard cases, when conventional legal theory cannot produce the right answer, the right answer might therefore still be found by asking what moral rights are at stake.

---

[9] *See* TAKING RIGHTS SERIOUSLY at 22-31, 35-36.

[10] R. Dworkin, *Hard Cases*, 88 HARV. L. REV. 1057, 1098-99 (1972) *reprinted in* TAKING RIGHTS SERIOUSLY, at 81, 120-21.

[11] *See* R. Dworkin, *No Right Answer?*, 53 N. Y. U. L. REV. 1, 30 (1978), *reprinted in* R. Dworkin, A MATTER OF PRINCIPLE 119, 143 (1985), hereinafter cited as A MATTER OF PRINCIPLE.

[12] A MATTER OF PRINCIPLE at 142.

[13] *Id.* at 138.

Dworkin claimed that it would be an "extremely rare" case, if any such case "exist[s] at all," for which there would be "no right answer."[14]

In trying to meet the objections of his critics, Dworkin thus came to assume that there are almost always "right answers" to the moral questions confronting a society. Otherwise, under Dworkin's theory, there could not almost always be right answers to legal questions. Seeking to support this thesis, Dworkin broadened the scope of his intellectual interests. He became interested in interpretation and the similarity he detected between the task of the literary critic trying to come up with the *best* interpretation of a literary text and the task of the judge trying to come up with the *best* decision in the light of his society's legal traditions—traditions informed ultimately by the basic morality underpinning that society. In the course of expanding his intellectual focus, Dworkin openly came to acknowledge that legal decisions are a species of political decision, not merely because they necessarily involve the application of power by state organs, but also because they are and must be motivated by basic political theory.[15] While some might think that law and politics are diametrically opposed, Dworkin seemed driven to equate them. For him, politics is ultimately premised on morality, and, as we have seen, it is only through resort to morality that the legal system attains the closure that permits us to claim that there are indeed right answers to (almost) all legal questions. Finally, in his major work, *Law's Empire*,[16] Dworkin set out to present a coherent restatement of the epistemological basis of his position as it had evolved over the course of his academic career.

Dworkin's principal argument in *Law's Empire* is that, if we wish to understand law, we must adopt the interpretive attitude. That is, we must accept that law must have a point, and we must construe individual legal provisions in the light of what we conceive that point to be. For Dworkin's argument, however, it is essential that the interpretive attitude we adopt *not*

---

[14] *Id.* at 144.

[15] *See* R. Dworkin, *Law as Interpretation*, 60 TEX. L. REV. 527 (1982), *reprinted in* A MATTER OF PRINCIPLE at 146.

[16] LAW'S EMPIRE, cited note 7, *supra*. I have reviewed this book at some length in G. Christie, *Dworkin's Empire*, 1987 DUKE L. J. 157, and much of the present discussion is taken, in greatly compressed form, from that work, which may be consulted by those who are seeking a more extended discussion of Dworkin's work.

be a form of "conversational interpretation" that "assigns meaning in the light of the motives and purposes and concerns it supposes the speaker to have, and reports its conclusions about his 'intention' in saying what he did."[17] Rather the interpretation of a social practice like courtesy or law is like "artistic interpretation." They are, in short, types of "creative interpretation."

Because Dworkin lays so much importance on the similarity between the creative interpretation of social practices and artistic interpretation, he was obliged to defend his assertion that artistic interpretation is not "inevitably a matter of discovering some author's intention[,] . . . a factual process independent of the interpreter's own values."[18] Dworkin embraced the suggestion that "[a]n insight belongs to an artist's intention . . . . when it fits and illuminates his artistic purposes in a way he would recognized and endorse even though he has not already done so."[19] This technique, of course, can be applied to authors that have long been dead. Most importantly, Dworkin contended that this approach "brings the interpreter's sense of artistic value into his reconstruction of the artist's intention in at least an evidential way, for the interpreter's judgment of what an author would have accepted will be guided by his sense of what the author should have accepted, that is, his sense of which reading would make the work better and which would make it worse."[20] Applying this approach to the interpretation of social practices such as law, Dworkin rejected "the thesis that creative interpretation aims to discover some actual historical intention" but nevertheless he maintained that "the concept of intention . . . provides

---

[17] LAW'S EMPIRE at 50.

[18] *Id.* at 55.

[19] *Id.* at 57.

[20] *Ibid.* I do not claim to be a trained literary critic, and am therefore somewhat reluctant to say much about the validity of Dworkin's methods when applied to literary criticism. To demonstrate my naïveté, if, in interpreting a text, the critic endeavors to make it the best literary work he can, why should he not also make the text the best text that he can? What if there are some (small) gaps in the text because portions of the manuscript have been destroyed? To change perspectives, what about someone faced with the task of restoring an old painting. What is his function? To make the painting the best he thinks it can be? Or is it to restore it, as nearly as possible, to the painting Valasquez or Michelangelo or some unknown artist painted? *See Profiles,* THE NEW YORKER, Mar. 16, 1987, at 44.

the *formal* structure for all interpretive claims."[21]   Interpretation, he submitted,

is by nature the report of a purpose; it proposes a way of seeing what is interpreted—a social practice or tradition as much as a text or painting—as if this were the product of a decision to pursue one set of themes or visions or purposes, one "point," rather than another.[22]

This is true even when what is being interpreted is a social practice, that is, "even when there is no historical author whose historical mind can be plumbed."[23]

The notion that Dworkin wished to carry forward from his discussion of methodology is that, in interpreting a social practice like courtesy or law, one is not engaged in reporting what the participants in the practice mean but in determining "what *it* means."

Dworkin's ultimate purpose, in *Law's Empire,* accordingly, was to propose a model of law that he calls "law as integrity."[24] Law as integrity accepts law and legal rights wholeheartedly and presumes that the constraints of the law benefit society "not just by providing predictability or procedural fairness, or in some other instrumental way, but by securing a kind of equality among citizens that makes their community more genuine and improves its moral justification for exercising the political power it does."[25] Law as integrity is a more general conception of law. As such, it "must also have external connections to other parts or departments of political morality and, through these, to more general ideological and even metaphysical convictions."[26] According to what Dworkin terms "law as integrity," propositions of law are true if they figure in or follow from principles of justice, fairness, and procedural due process that provide the best constructive interpretation of the community's legal practice. That is,

---

[21] *Id.* at 58.

[22] *Id.* at 58-59.

[23] *Id.* at 59.

[24] *Id.* at 94.

[25] *Id.* at 95.

[26] *Id.* at 101. Unlike conventionalism, a theory he rejects, Dworkin is not concerned only with what people *believe* is good and bad.

a judge seeking to decide a particular case must decide whether "legal practice is seen in a better light if we assume the community has accepted" one principle rather than another.[27]

Having set forth this theoretical framework, Dworkin, in *Law's Empire*, proceeded along grounds he had made familiar in much of his writings. He analogized the development of the law to the writing of a chain novel in which each succeeding author is obliged to search for the interpretation of the text supplied to him that best fits that text, which interpretation he will then use to write his section of the chain novel. In the law one is of course interested in coming up with "the best story from . . . the standpoint of political morality, not aesthetics"[28] as would be the case of someone participating in the writing of a chain novel. But, just as in the writing of a chain novel one must proceed as if it were the work of a single author, so in the unfolding of law as integrity in the context of a particular legal community "[t]he adjudicative principle of integrity instructs judges to identify legal rights and duties, so far as possible, on the assumption that they were all created by a single author—the community personified— expressing a coherent conception of justice and fairness,"[29] a requirement that many people would dismiss as an impossibility.

In applying his view that law is a political activity—albeit a political activity with morally correct solutions—Dworkin argued that the Supreme Court of the United States should have upheld an affirmative action scheme that it struck down and that that Court might also have been justified in refusing to accept clear and unambiguous expressions of legislative intent in a controversial endangered species case.[30] In this process of

---

[27] *Id.* at 172-73.

[28] *Id.* at 239. To illustrate how the process he described works in practice, Dworkin resorted to his alter ego, Hercules, a super judge, with whom readers of Dworkin's previous work were well familiar, and he strives to show how a lesser judge, whom he called Hermes, would be driven to adopt the interpretive approach of Hercules.

[29] *Id.* at 225.

[30] Dworkin's reason for rejecting a legislator's express statement about an issue, is that given "her more general opinions" the statement of the legislator in question "about the snail darter is . . . a mistake." *Id.* at 333. Dworkin was commenting on TVA v. Hill, 437 U.S. 153 (1978), in which the Court enjoined the completion of a virtually complete federal dam and power project. Congress subsequently overruled that decision. Dworkin

reformulating and extending his basic thesis, Dworkin has been forced to compromise one of the principal claims that catapulted him to the forefront of contemporary jurisprudence, namely that legal cases, if properly analyzed, have only one demonstrably right answer. Throughout *Law's Empire* Dworkin readily conceded that judges operating in good faith, even when using Dworkin's methods, will often arrive at different solutions to legal questions.[31] They will undoubtedly each strive to achieve what for them is the right answer, but that of course is a different matter. Nevertheless, Dworkin attempted to maintain some consistency with his earlier assertions by insisting that it is still meaningful to talk of right answers even when it is contestable what those right answers are, and even if we shall often never be able to agree on what the right answer is. The important point is that legal decisions, although ultimately political decisions, are also ultimately moral decisions and, as moral decisions, have certain features. Legal decisions are capable of being correct or incorrect, because moral questions, in a given social milieu, are capable of right answers, *and* they are reached by a process in which they come to express a coherent conception of justice and fairness and portray the social and political institutions in the society in which they are made in the best possible light.

Applying Dworkin's analysis to our examination of the way notions of an ideal audience figure in legal argument, we reach the following conclusions: An argument in a court of law that would win the assent of an ideal or universal audience must be based on a legal principle or a set of legal principles that is itself ultimately based upon generally accepted moral principles. Furthermore, the legal principle or set of principles so based must present the institutional and social history of a particular society in the best possible light. It is no wonder that, when Dworkin applies his philosophical approach to concrete legal questions, he is attracted to the

---

presumably would have been appalled by the Court's literal interpretation of the Federal Tort Claims Act in the *Smith* case, which was discussed at length in Chapter 5 in the course of our examination of differing approaches to statutory interpretation. *See* Chapter 5, *supra*, at pp. 53-55.

[31] Dworkin repeated this concession a few years later in a book denoted the "moral reading of the American Constitution." *See* R. Dworkin, FREEDOM'S LAW 83 (1996).

possibility that liability for negligence, whether of accountants or of automobile manufacturers, should be governed by the same standard, namely the standard of "reasonable foreseeability." But when, as we have seen, an attempt is made to apply some general organizing concept to tort law, whether it be the notion of a general right of privacy, or the principle that the intentional infliction of temporal damage is prima facie actionable, or the concept of reasonable foreseeability as determining the scope of liability in all negligence actions, the courts are eventually forced to resort to distinctions that are no less "unprincipled" than the distinctions that the courts had previously abandoned because they were "unprincipled."

Is this just another illustration of a point that is at least as old as Aristotle?[32] Namely, that our language is not rich enough to encompass, in a succinct verbal formula, all the possible situations that arise in practice, even if our minds were facile enough to foresee all the possible situations that might reasonably be expected to arise, which of course they are not. For Aristotle, the application of law called for the exercise of φρόνησις, or practical wisdom, by which we can overcome the deficiencies of the general nature of written legal prescriptions and arrive at the equitable (τό ἐπιεικές) or more suitable or appropriate solution. Arriving at the appropriate solution, is, of course, what Dworkin was trying to do, but Dworkin's point seems to be that we make up for the deficiencies of generally-worded legal prescriptions by resort to a different class of generally-worded prescriptions.

B. Additional Factors Prompting the Search for General Principles

Our inquiry is concerned with the nature of the reasons that a judge will give when he is called upon to decide a case in which the existing legal sources either give little direction or dictate a solution that the judge seems to consider clearly inappropriate. Must these reasons be general in nature, even if they are not what Dworkin would accept as principles, or can they be something more particular? Furthermore, if there is a preference for general reasons, does it necessarily follow that, in theory at least, legal and moral disputes can almost always actually be resolved by resorting to some

[32] *See e.g.* Aristotle, NICOMACHEAN ETHICS, Bk. v, c.10.

overarching general moral or legal reasons, even though, as was shown in previous chapters, we are not able, or at least thus far have been unable, to state what those general reasons might be.

Let us discuss the demands for generality first. That some amount of generality in language and in thought is inevitable is indisputable. If each experience were unique in the sense that it could only be described in language appropriate for that situation and no other, social life would be impossible. Some notion of sameness, as well as of difference, is essential. From an epistemic point of view, the problem is how broad our terms of reference must be to permit us to function properly in the world, and the answer to that inquiry will surely depend on the circumstances, although for reasons of facilitating theoretical discussion or perhaps even by temperament we may prefer as general a set of terms to organize our experience as is possible. Many of these same imperatives operate in the normative universes of law and morality. Some of these are practical concerns. Law, as St. Thomas has said, is a rule and a measure of human acts[33] as, of course, also is morality. Law tells us what is to be done and enables us to judge the legality of what has been done. It thus enables us to predict the reactions of others to what we do. This requires that the law should exhibit some degree of generality.

In performing all these functions, moreover, law is also supposed to be objective, and it is normally felt that generality is a prerequisite of objectivity in legal (and moral) reasoning. At the same time, as we have already seen, we may in our quest for general reasons reach the point at which these general reasons lose their utility because they lead to conclusions that we are not prepared to accept. We then start to qualify these general reasons to such an extent that we seem in danger of abandoning the possibility of any coherent general organizing principles and descending into a world of particulars, the very world from which we sought to escape. It is a mistake, however, to believe that the type of generality that has proved so difficult to achieve in practice is a necessary component of objectivity. In an interesting and important paper, Amartya Sen reminds us that we can meaningfully talk of "positional objectivity," namely an objectivity that is relative to specificity of location and any other

---

[33] St. Thomas Aquinas, SUMMA THEOLOGIAE, Part One of the Second Part, Q. 90, Art. 1.

condition that might influence our observations.[34] In the limiting case, we might be prepared to accept that our reactions might be wrong from the perspective of others and even, if we had had the luxury of other perspectives, that we too would accept that they are wrong, but our observations can nevertheless be said to be objective if we are prepared to assert that any other person who was similarly situated would have reached the same conclusions that we did. That is, if he were similarly situated, he would accept the same view of the world that we have and, if required to act, would act in the same way that we have felt obliged to act. For a ground of decision to have any validity in legal or moral reasoning, it would seem to require at least this minimal amount of generalizability.

The law recognizes positional objectivity when, as we have seen, it allows a person to use force, even sometimes deadly force, to defend himself or a third party when he reasonably believes it is necessary to do so to achieve that purpose.[35] That person may be wrong—say he was not in fact being threatened—but if his mistake was a reasonable one for a person in his circumstances he is not subject to either criminal or civil sanctions. This is only one particular instance of the fact that arguments presupposing the validity of positional objectivity are routinely addressed to an ideal or universal audience. We noted earlier in this book how the Supreme Court of the United States, faced with the prospect of having to invalidate seldomly enforced anti-miscegenation laws at the time it was trying to implement its school-desegregation decisions, relied on a questionable procedural expedient to avoid having to rule on the merits of the case.[36] Alexander Bickel, it will be recalled, asserted that we would be prepared to accept the legitimacy of the Supreme Court's use of a questionable procedural expedient to avoid ruling on a socially divisive issue whereas we would not be prepared to accept the legitimacy of a decision on the merits that we believed was both legally and morally wrong, however much it

---

[34] *See* A. Sen, *Positional Objectivity*, 22 PHIL. & PUB. AFF. 126 (1993).
[35] *See* RESTATEMENT (SECOND) OF TORTS §§ 65, 76 (1965); MODEL PENAL CODE §§ 3.04, 3.05 (Official Draft and Revised Comments 1985). These provisions were discussed in Chapter 7, *supra*, at p. 106.
[36] *See* the discussion in Chapter 4, *supra*, at p. 46.

preserved social peace.[37] We also hypothesized a case in which a judge whose wife and children had been threatened with death, were he to rule in a particular way in a pending case in circumstances where the state was powerless to protect him and his family, might appeal to the universal audience to, if not accept, at least understand and empathize with the decision which he felt obliged to make.[38]

In both political and legal argument, the impetus for seeking general reasons is governed, however, not only by the belief that general reasons are more likely to be objective than particular reasons but also by the belief that decisions based upon general reasons are more likely to be correct. Underlying this quest for generality is the belief, well-expressed by Dworkin, that difficult legal and moral questions are capable of solution and that the reason that they are capable of solution is that certain general principles exist which, if they were properly understood, would be capable of leading us to the correct solution.

In our earlier discussions of the arguments given, for and against, on the issue of affirmative action,[39] we saw that the dispute often boiled down to a conflict between two contrasting visions of the good. Under one vision the common good was ultimately a communal value. It was not merely the aggregation of the good of discreet individuals but something that was different from and even independent of the good of the particular individuals who might be members of the particular social or political group in question. Since the pursuit of the common good, as so defined, would often entail the sacrifice of what many individuals would consider their own individual good, it became incumbent upon those advocating particular policies to give reasons that those affected by those policies might be prepared to accept, so that the policies might at least be grudgingly accepted as legitimate, or possibly even correct. If therefore the difficult questions of public policy could be said to have correct solutions, and better still, if the correct solutions could be arrived at by the application of general principles or reasons, the task of legitimating political decisions that

---

[37] *See ibid.*, n.7.
[38] *See* Chapter 4, *supra*, at p. 45.
[39] *See* Chapter 6, *supra*, at pp. 70-75.

adversely affected the interests of discreet individuals would be immensely eased.

This of course is the driving force behind Dworkin's work and of his insistence that there are correct answers even to difficult legal questions, the so-called hard cases. As we have already noted for such a decisionmaking process to work, one would need to know the legal principles that are applicable in any given case and how to weight them. Indeed, in his early work, Dworkin even intimated that his life's work might be devoted to providing us with a method of weighting principles when they pointed in conflicting directions in some particular case.[40] No one of course has come up with a scale against which the force of competing principles can be compared. Nor is the inability to produce such a scale compensated for by the suggestion that the decision of difficult legal questions is at bottom a political question that ultimately must be decided on the basis of a society's basic morality. It just changes the inquiry into the quest for the morally correct decision and presupposes that there are correct answers to most, if not all, moral questions, answers based likewise on some generally applicable moral principle. To make any such scheme of moral reasoning produce these sorts of correct answers, there must again be some principle that, in cases of conflict, will ultimately prevail over all other principles. That principle might be some variation of the greatest good of the greatest number of utilitarianism, or of the primacy of equality and particularly, in political matters, of the equality of the fair value of people's abilities to enjoy political liberty, as maintained by John Rawls,[41] or of the right to equal respect and concern as maintained by Dworkin.[42]

---

[40] *See The Model of Rules, reprinted in* TAKING RIGHTS SERIOUSLY 14, 44-45.

[41] *See* the discussion in Chapter 3, *supra,* at pp. 28-29.

[42] *See* R. Dworkin, *The Original Position,* 40 U. CHI. L. REV. 500, 531 (1973), *reprinted in* TAKING RIGHTS SERIOUSLY at 150, 180-83. This was a review essay of John Rawls, *A Theory of Justice,* and Dworkin maintained, quite plausibly, that Rawls' theory was ultimately premised on the primacy of the principle of equality of equal respect and concern. Dworkin has relied on this principle to distinguish between discrimination based on race that is premised upon prejudice or contempt for the discriminated race—which is and should be prohibited—and discrimination based on race that is not so premised and which may be permitted in affirmative action schemes for good social reason. *See* R. Dworkin, A MATTER OF PRINCIPLE 293-315 (1985); TAKING RIGHTS SERIOUSLY at 223-39

C. Counter-Arguments

Historically, the question of whether there are objective general principles that can correctly resolve moral conflicts has arisen most frequently in the context of the long philosophical tradition of the natural law. Most if not all natural lawyers have followed Aquinas in accepting that the natural law consists of primary or first principles and also of secondary principles that are derivative of the primary or first principles. They are also generally agreed that there are multiple primary or first principles and not just one such principle, except perhaps in the vacuous sense of "do good and avoid evil" which then reopens the same question by shifting the inquiry from whether there are multiple ultimate moral principles to whether there is one pre-eminent good or whether there are multiple pre-eminent goods. Accepting that there are multiple primary or first principles of moral conduct or that there are multiple ultimate or basic goods, what is to be done when the different primary or first principles of moral conduct or the different ultimate or basic goods dictate that specific moral questions should be decided in different ways?

To simplify the discussion, I shall concentrate on the question of the good. One could of course focus on the first principles of moral conduct, that is of action—the eventual conclusions would be the same—but the merit of any so-called first principle of action must ultimately depend on the conclusion that the end sought to be achieved by the principle of action in question is a good. Despite his insistence on the "priority of the right over the good," Rawls must surely believe that a society in which, say, the value of each person's ability to enjoy political liberty is of equal worth is a good society, and Dworkin must surely likewise believe that a society in which people enjoy equal respect and concern is a good society. Few people would of course be prepared to dispute these conclusions. The only point of contention would be whether these are such preeminent goods that, when there is a conflict between the goods that may be achieved by social action, all other goods must be sacrificed to these hierarchically superior goods.

("the right to treatment as an equal is fundamental, and the right to equal treatment, derivative." *Id.* at 227). These are all essays that first appeared in the *New York Review of Books*.

In his important book, *Natural Law and Natural Rights*, John Finnis lists seven basic goods. They are "life," "knowledge," "play," "aesthetic experience," "sociability or friendship," "reasonableness" (shades of St. Thomas), and "religion."[43] These are goods for each individual human being. We would undoubtedly agree with him that the decision to limit the list of basic goods to seven is somewhat arbitrary, although Finnis maintains that most, if not all, of the things we consider good can be derived from his seven. We might also not all agree with him that "religion" is one of these basic goods but, if we replaced that term with "freedom of belief and conscience," we would probably come close to achieving that agreement. Finnis, of course, is concerned as much with the choices that people must make as individual human beings as he is with the choices that those in public authority must make. We, on the other hand, are concerned with choice in the domain of law, that is with choices that have to be made in a social context. But that does not change the nature of our problem. Unless we are prepared to take the position that the creation or preservation of a society in a particular form trumps all other goods, we are forced to choose between goods that we accept as basic.

Whether these basic goods are considered from an individual or a social perspective does not matter. For most people the notion of the good is probably considered from a melange of both perspectives, although with a preference for one or the other perspectives. The point is that whatever we accept as a basic good is just that. It is a basic good and it cannot be considered subordinate to some other higher basic good. That of course makes the decision of the so-called hard case doubly difficult. We may be obliged to decide but we have no formula to decide. Whatever we do, something we consider a fundamental good will be sacrificed. Approaching difficult legal and moral questions from this perspective might understandably lead one to try as far as possible to avoid making a choice between two goods which he accepts as basic. He might prefer a solution that would decide a case on a relatively narrow ground, a ground that permits reaching a socially acceptable result, without requiring a definitive choice between the goods that he has recognized as being basic. He also might, in some circumstances, wish to deny himself the power to decide.

---

[43] J. Finnis, NATURAL LAW AND NATURAL RIGHTS 81-95 (1980).

The person, for example, who refuses to accept the argument that it is better to sacrifice the life of one innocent than to allow a greater number of innocents to die is not thereby committed to the view that the life of one innocent person is more important than the lives of a greater number of innocent persons. He might be prepared to concede that that would be absurd. His argument is rather that it is not for him to decide who should live and who should die. That is, it is not for him to choose among the goods at stake. Chance or whatever has created the situation and the cards must be played as they lie. He is not God with the authority to reshuffle the deck.

Of course, sometimes people do feel obliged to play God. But generally those decisions are, as we noted earlier in Chapter 7, reserved for those exercising political authority and, most importantly, generally reserved for instances in which the very existence of society is at stake. Moreover, as we have also previously noted, it is generally accepted that the decision by the public authorities as to whom to sacrifice should be made on the basis of neutral criteria. The problem presented by hiring preferences is not the goal sought to be achieved—such as diversity in the workplace or in educational institutions—but that the means chosen requires the sacrifice of something accepted as a basic political good in most Western societies, namely that people should not be subject to differential treatment on the basis of either their sex, race, or religion, that is that each person, in the words of the United States Constitution, should enjoy "the equal protection of the laws."[44] The problem is particularly acute because there are few proponents of preferences who are prepared to assert that diversity is itself a *basic* good on a par with those mentioned by Finnis, and fewer still who are prepared to assert that diversity is a more basic good than the principle of equality before the law. The most that most proponents would argue is that violating the principle of equal treatment under the law now will lead to a better society in which the principle of equal treatment under the law will be more nearly attained in the sense that the legal equality thereby attained will be more meaningful to all the members of the society in question.[45]

---

[44] U.S. Const., Amend. 14.
[45] *See* Chapter 6, n. 32, *supra*, at p. 74.

Let us assume that the ideal audience to whom legal arguments are addressed accepts that there are multiple goods and, more importantly, that, in case of a conflict between basic goods, there is no generally accepted weighting principle that allows one to give priority to one basic good over another. Does this mean that there is therefore no acceptable procedure for deciding a really difficult case even if, in the circumstances of that case, avoiding decision is not a practical option? That would certainly seem to follow *if* all legal cases had to be decided on the basis of general principle and *if* two or more basic principles each encapsulating a basic good were equally applicable to the case but unfortunately pointed in conflicting directions.

In common-law systems there are some built-in mechanisms for handling these sorts of situations. It has, for example, been characteristic of the common law to eschew attempts at achieving global consistency and settling for what, following Joseph Raz's approach, we might wish to call "local consistency."[46] In the previous chapter, we presented a number of instances in which the courts in England and America actually abandoned efforts to achieve global consistency in favor of more limited grounds of decision that they believed were more compatible with the demands of justice and fairness, demands that are always made by ideal audiences. It is not a feature of legal reasoning that appeals to Ronald Dworkin as the best possible method but, from his point of view, at least one good thing could be said of it. It still relies on principles. The principles are just less general and are confined to discreet areas of the law. They are also not so clearly related to the fundamental moral principles of the society whose law is under examination.

It is, moreover, possible to describe a method of common-law adjudication in which there are even fewer resorts to widely-shared normative general principles, other than a commitment to consistency in adjudication and a recognition of the primacy of legislation. I have discussed the operation of such a system of legal decisionmaking—which indeed resembles how the common-law system of adjudication actually

---

[46] *See* J. Raz, *The Relevance of Coherence*, 72 B. U. L. REV. 273 (1992), discussed in Chapter 5, *supra*, at p. 55.

works more accurately than Dworkin's model—at length elsewhere.[47] I shall here merely present a brief outline of how such a system works and then explain why such a method of legal decisionmaking might appeal to an ideal audience. Unlike Dworkin's model, such a system of judicial decision making is interested not so much in reaching *the* correct answer to a legal question but rather, in the words of Chief Justice John Marshall in "convincing [the parties] . . . that the case has been fully and fairly considered, that due attention has been given to the arguments of counsel, and that the best judgment of the Court has been exercised on the case."[48]

Under the approach to legal reasoning now to be described, so-called rules or principles are merely rubrics that serve as the headings for classifying and grouping together the cases that constitute the body of the law in a case-law system. In such a system even statutes are no more than the set of cases, if any, that have construed the statute together with the set of what might be called the paradigm cases that are, at any point of time, believed to express the meaning of the statute. All that is necessary under this view is that there be general agreement that certain marks on paper are cases and statutes and that certain bodies, i.e. courts, are recognized as having the authority to decide disputes that are brought before them. It is an empirical fact that there is such agreement and such recognition. In argument to a court, the parties will cite the statutes and cases that they claim control the instant case.

Under the model, the court is free to decide the instant case in a manner different from that of the decided cases and from the paradigm cases under the statutes claimed to be relevant only if it can point to a significant difference between the instant case and each of the decided cases and the paradigm cases.[49] What is a significant difference is whatever the participants in the legal process are prepared to accept as a significant difference. What the previously decided cases have decided is or is not significant will be important—as for example previous cases holding that

---

[47] *See* G. Christie, *Objectivity in the Law*, 78 Yale L. J. 1311 (1969).

[48] Mitchell v. United States, 34 U.S. (9 Pet.) 711, 735 (1835).

[49] One would have to consider also all hypothetical cases proposed by the parties that are not considered significantly different from the decided cases and the accepted paradigm cases.

the color of a plaintiff's hair or of his skin are not significant—as will also be the state of scientific knowledge. Such knowledge might, for example, justify the conclusion that there is no difference, from the causal perspective, between a case of intentional homicide in which the victim dies immediately from an intentionally inflicted gun shot wound and one in which the victim of an intentional shooting lingers for a few hours and then succumbs despite the best efforts of competent physicians. Similarly, in a suit to enjoin the operation of an airport as a nuisance, the total yearly traffic of the airport will be of more practical importance in distinguishing among the cases than the assertion that "the public interest requires airports," and the decibel level of sound created by the planes will be more important than the maxims *"sic utere tuo"* or *"cujus est solum, ejus est usque ad coelum."* Even the most fervent member of the critical legal studies movement who believes that a judicial decision to impose or not impose responsibility on airports is purely a political decision will concede that the level of noise is a relevant consideration.

Under traditional models of legal reasoning, two cases are considered similar if they illustrate the same general rule and significantly different if they illustrate conflicting or inconsistent rules. Because there are often any number of rules—many conflicting and inconsistent—for which two cases can stand, this is not a particularly helpful test unless there is some way of choosing, in terms sufficiently concrete to be useful, the "true" or "correct" rule for which a case or group of cases stands, and experience indicates that there is no such method. It is this obvious feature of the traditional model of legal reasoning that is used by the members of the so-called critical legal studies movement to support their claim that legal decisions are just political decisions clothed in a misleading robe of apparent objectivity. Under the alternative model, on the other hand, the significant differences between cases that will justify differences in result will lie in the factual circumstances of the cases rather than in the rules or principles which they supposedly illustrate. As a logical matter this criterion is easier to meet. It is logically more stringent to insist that, before any two instances can be classed as similar, one must construct a general rule or definition such that all other instances which one might wish to characterize as similar will fall within it, than it is to provide that any two cases will be considered similar if, according to whatever criterion of similarity is imposed, they are within a certain degree of proximity. In other words, the contention is that it is easier to decide whether a group of cases are significantly different from one another according to any given factual criterion than to decide the "proper" rule or rules under which all the cases should be grouped. The validity of this point is in some ways acknowledged by John Rawls when he accepts that people who have very different basic sets of beliefs can nevertheless agree on specific solutions to specific political problems.[50]

The advantage of this common-law method of adjudication is that it avoids, as much as it is humanly possible to do so, the necessity of deciding among basic conceptions of the good (and the principles that embody those conceptions). It does so by finding some other less contentious way of deciding a case. Seeking to avoid, if possible, the need to choose among basic conceptions of the good is not merely a plausible and historically supportable approach to legal reasoning. It is also, as the reference we have just made to John Rawls illustrates, a method for deciding contentious issues of public policy in the larger arena of public life. It certainly is an approach that might appeal to Aristotle's statesman who is trying to bring practical wisdom to the resolution of contentious political issues. If, for example, the debate between proponents and opponents of a woman's right to an abortion turns on the truth or falsity of the proposition that the foetus is a person with a right to life or of the proposition that a woman's right to autonomy trumps whatever rights the foetus may have, the issue will never be resolved peacefully at the present time. On the other hand, it may be possible to secure agreement on two more modest propositions. The first is that any policy requiring for its success the imprisonment of several million women and their doctors will be no more successful than the so-called war on drugs. The second is that, insofar as is possible, people should be left to make their own decisions so that, all other things being equal, there is a presumption against state coercion in a free and democratic society. In permitting abortion under such circumstances, society is neither

---

[50] *See* J. Rawls, POLITICAL LIBERALISM, 10-11, 15, 35-43, 134-35, and passim (1993), in which Rawls accepts that in democracies a "diversity of reasonable comprehensive religions, philosophies and moral doctrine . . . is a permanent feature of public culture," *id.* at 36, but that does not preclude political agreement on specific measures. *See also* J. Rawls, *The Idea of Public Reason Revisited,* 64 U. CHI L. REV 765, 769-71 (1997).

endorsing it as a moral right nor grudgingly condoning it as a necessary evil. Society is rather trying, as much as possible, to avoid ruling on the moral merits of abortion, just as laws regulating the drinking age neither endorse nor condemn the drinking of alcoholic beverages. For those for whom the prohibition of abortion is an ultimate basic good that is even more important than the basic good of preserving social peace and individual freedom, this arrangement will prove inadequate. For others, the real possibility that some people may actually insist on the primacy of some single ultimate principle is evidence that an ideal or universal audience should view the good as multifaceted and reject all greater good theories.

Obviously, sometimes basic choices cannot be avoided even by an audience that prefers a particularized approach to legal and moral questions. The most that such an audience can hope for is that the choice between competing basic goods should be made only in the most pressing of situations and on the most neutral criteria possible, such as, wherever possible, focusing on what most people are prepared to accept as significant factual differences among the situations under discussion. As already emphasized, it is not necessary that they should all agree on the reasons why those factual differences are significant. Moreover, the decision encapsulating the choice between the basic goods should be restricted to the narrowest possible scope. Anything else would be disrespectful of the basic good that we have been regretfully forced to sacrifice due to the exigencies of actual life. We are like a mother forced to choose between two of her children when, if she does nothing, both will die. She might decide to choose by lot or, if there is a significant age difference between the two, she might choose to save the younger or, if she lived in a country with a high mortality rate from disease, choose to save the healthier one.

* * *

I have tried in this and the previous chapter to explain why it is that the recurrent drive to found legal and moral argument on general principles is almost always followed, in the practical world, by a retreat to a more particularized form of argumentation. It is not because the general principles that are often set forth by the courts are ones that most people disagree with. If that were so, the problem would be that we have not come up with the correct general principle. The problem rather lies elsewhere. It is perhaps evident that I personally am inclined to a more narrow, a more particularized form of legal and moral reasoning. It is not, however, my purpose in this book to convince others of the correctness of this view. My purpose instead has been to set forth the historical and theoretical reasons why the ideal audience which we construct as the auditor of legal and even moral argumentation might vacillate between the two views and why, at any one time, it might choose one rather than the other.

CHAPTER 10

AMBIVALENT ATTITUDES WITH REGARD TO DISCRETION

A. Introduction

The universal audiences to which the participants in the legal process address their arguments will have different conceptions of the amount of freedom that a decisionmaker, such as a judge or other public official, should have. In our previous discussion, we contrasted a universal or ideal audience that considered the public good to consist of a composite of individual goods with a similar audience for which the public good was more than the summation of individual goods. It is probably the case that an audience that considered the public good as something more than the summation of individual goods would, as a practical matter, prefer a more open-ended decisionmaking process, at least at some point in the decisionmaking process.[1] Indeed, one of the criticisms directed towards Dworkin's work was that his so-called model of principles was an attempt to cloak the broad-ranging judicial legislation that marked the United States Supreme Court during the Chief Justiceship of Earl Warren with an aura of respectability by arguing that, because a superhuman judge, such as Dworkin's Hercules, could show that the Warren Court's decisions flowed from some of the more basic principles of the American legal system, those decisions were not as free-ranging as they appeared.[2]

The tension between the competing preferences for a more open-ended and a less open-ended style of legal reasoning is intertwined, often inseparably, with another type of tension within and among legal systems. This other tension concerns the decisional leeway that various legal systems are prepared to grant to decisionmakers at different levels of the judicial process. A particular legal system might prefer an open-ended style of decisionmaking at the highest levels of the judicial hierarchy but, at the same time, insist on a more narrow focus for subordinate decisionmakers. Conversely, it is possible, although less likely, that a particular legal system would insist on a circumscribed type of decisionmaking at the highest level but tolerate a more unconstrained type of decisionmaking at lower levels in

---

[1] *Cf.* the discussion of Professor Damaška's work in Chapter 6, *supra* at 63-68.
[2] *See, e.g.*, S. Letwin, Book Review THE AM. SPECTATOR, Jan. 1986, at 33-40 (reviewing R. Dworkin, A MATTER OF PRINCIPLE (1985)).

the judicial hierarchy. This chapter will be concerned with first examining the contexts in which the tension between these two styles manifests itself in the day-to-day operation of a sophisticated legal system. It will then explore some of the historical reasons why, even within a particular legal system, an ideal audience might prefer one or the other styles of legal decisionmaking at different periods of time. Finally, in the next chapter, we shall address the question whether certain types of legal systems, and the ideal audiences presupposed by those legal systems, might have an inherent bias towards particular ways of resolving these tensions.

At least among English speakers, much of the discussion between those who favor a more constrained and those who favor a more open-ended style of legal decisionmaking is subsumed under the rubric of "discretion." A brief exegesis of how that term is used in legal discourse will therefore be a useful prolegomenon to our endeavor. When one examines the operation of a mature legal system, such as, for example, that of the United States, what becomes immediately apparent is that, despite the constant use of the term "discretion" in legal discourse, those who use it do not agree on its meaning. It is universally accepted that discretion has something to do with choice but, beyond this, the consensus breaks down. And, if there is little agreement about the meaning of discretion, there is even more controversy, as we have already noted, about its desirability.

The problem of evaluating the desirability of discretion is complicated by the fact that, while almost everyone will accept with Aristotle that the exercise of some degree of discretion is unavoidable in any legal system, the actual participants in the legal process, as well as the observers of that process, take a schizophrenic view of the value contributed by the discretionary element to the legal decisionmaking process. Sometimes, in some contexts, they praise the discretionary element and sometimes, in other contexts, these same people will execrate it. In the course of our discussion, we will examine the conflicting attitudes various audiences have towards discretion and why these attitudes will probably always remain ambivalent. Nor, of course, is the question exclusively a legal one. Although this book is mainly concerned with legal decisionmaking, the notion of discretion operates in a much broader context because the exercise of discretion relates to the way that people interact with each other in a political context. Discretion inevitably involves power relationships and thus ultimately and inevitably relates to the ways that people work out these relationships in an ongoing political system.

B. An Analytical Framework

At least in the United States, two of the most important and useful discussions of discretion are those of Maurice Rosenberg[3] and Ronald Dworkin.[4] In the judicial context, Rosenberg distinguishes between primary discretion and secondary discretion. Primary discretion arises when a decisionmaker has "a wide range of choice as to what he decides, free from the constraints which characteristically attach whenever legal rules enter the decision process."[5] Used in this sense, discretion can mean simply that a person has the authority to decide. Courts, judges, and legal scholars often use the term discretion in this sense of referring simply to authority to decide, that is the ability to make an unconstrained choice. For example, in his dissent in *Heckler v. Day*,[6] Justice Marshall declared: "Although Congress has delegated to the Secretary 'full power and authority to make rules and regulations and to establish procedures,' 42 U.S.C. § 405(a), that discretion is limited by the requirement that procedures be consistent with the Social Security Act. . . ."[7] Presumably, if the discretion had not been limited it would have been equivalent to the unconstrained authority to decide. Legal scholarship provides another example of this usage of the term discretion in Peter Westen's statement: "'[D]iscretion' means . . . an area within which the discretion-holder has authority to adopt, or not to adopt, whatever rule he deems fit."[8] When used in this sense, discretion is quintessentially associated with variability of result. Rosenberg contrasts this "primary" form of discretion with "the secondary form, [which] has to

---

[3] M. Rosenberg, *Judicial Discretion of the Trial Court, Viewed from Above*, 22 SYRACUSE L. REV. 635 (1971).

[4] R. Dworkin, *The Model of Rules*, 35 U. CHI L. REV. 14 (1967), reprinted in R. Dworkin, TAKING RIGHTS SERIOUSLY 14 (1977) (hereinafter cited as TAKING RIGHTS SERIOUSLY).

[5] M. Rosenberg, *supra* note 3, at 637.

[6] 467 U.S. 104, 120 (1984) (Marshall J., dissenting).

[7] *Id.* at 124.

[8] P. Westen, *The Meaning of Equality in Law, Science, Math and Morals: A Reply*, 81 MICH L. REV. 604, 642 (1983).

do with hierarchical relations among judges."[9] The secondary form of discretion

enters the picture when the system tries to prescribe the degree of finality and authority a lower court's decision enjoys in the higher courts. Specifically, it comes into full play when the rules of review accord the lower court's decision an unusual amount of insulation from appellate revision. In this sense, discretion is a review-restraining concept. It gives the trial judge a right to be wrong without incurring reversal.[10]

To summarize Rosenberg's argument in capsule form, in the limiting case, the choice made by a person exercising *primary* discretion is by definition the correct choice. The correctness of the choice cannot be attacked because there are no external legal criteria on which to base such an attack. When, on the other hand, *secondary* discretion is involved, one can attack the correctness of a choice, although the authority of the person to make that choice may be beyond attack. Secondary discretion thus involves the authority to make the wrong decision. To illustrate secondary discretion, Rosenberg describes two famous incidents from American college football.[11] In the 1940 Cornell-Dartmouth game, a confused official allowed Cornell a fifth down in which they scored to win the game. In the 1961 Syracuse-Notre Dame game, a Syracuse player fouled a Notre Dame player *after* Notre Dame had unsuccessfully attempted a field goal as time ran out in the fourth quarter. Once the player had kicked the ball, however, Notre Dame no longer had possession. Accordingly, under the rules governing American football, the penalty against the Syracuse team could not rightfully extend the game. Nevertheless, the officials gave Notre Dame another chance. This time the field-goal kick was successful, and Notre Dame won 17-15. In both cases, everyone agreed that the officials were clearly wrong; but, in both instances, no redress for those errors was possible.

Rosenberg of course only uses the football examples to dramatize his point. He is concerned with the effect of secondary discretion on appellate courts' treatment of certain contested rulings of trial courts, particularly procedural rulings such as denials of motions for new trials. Naturally, in

---

[9] M. Rosenberg, *supra* note 3, at 637.

[10] *Ibid..*

[11] *Id.* at 639-40.

any hierarchically-organized bureaucratic structure, there are limits to the amount of perverseness that superiors are prepared to tolerate in their subordinates. In practice, therefore, Rosenberg's secondary discretion—the authority to make wrong decisions—usually boils down to the authority to make decisions to which reviewing authorities will in varying degrees accord a presumption of correctness. The reviewing authority will intervene only if the initial decisionmaker *abused* his discretion.

A cynic might contend, however, that Rosenberg's notion of secondary discretion merges with what he calls primary discretion when an inferior is given the authority to make wrong choices that cannot be overturned. There is no practical difference between the authority to make whatever decision one chooses and the authority to make decisions that will be enforced even if they are considered to have been wrong. And, indeed, primary and secondary discretion do sometimes seem to merge at the edges, but one clear distinction exists—different types of criticism can be leveled at decisions made under different types of discretion. Any decision, whether decided in the exercise of primary or secondary discretion, can be criticized by an audience, whether it is an ideal audience or not, for such failings as being dumb, stupid, immoral, impractical, or counterproductive. But, under the analysis outlined here, only decisions made through the exercise of secondary discretion can additionally be criticized as wrong. Obviously, in a legal context, this distinction assumes that one can determine the legally correct solution. Keeping this point in mind, let us approach the notion of discretion from Dworkin's point of view.

Dworkin initially asserts flatly that "[t]he concept of discretion is at home in only one sort of context: when someone is in general charged with making decisions subject to standards set by a particular authority."[12] He then proceeds to identify two "weak" senses of discretion. In the first, "we use 'discretion' in a weak sense, simply to say that for some reason the standards an official must apply cannot be applied mechanically but demand the use of judgment."[13] As we have observed in prior chapters, it is well known that Dworkin claimed that what principally characterizes the role of a judge is authority to exercise discretion in something like this weakened sense. In the second usage identified by Dworkin, "we use the term in a

---

[12] TAKING RIGHTS SERIOUSLY, at 32.
[13] *Ibid.*

different weak sense, to say only that some official has final authority to make a decision and cannot be reviewed and reversed by any other official. . . . Thus we might say that in baseball certain decisions, like the decision whether the ball reached second base first before the runner, are left to the discretion of the second base umpire, if we mean that on this issue the head umpire has no power to substitute his own judgment if he disagrees."[14] This second weak sense of the term "discretion" looks very much like what Rosenberg called secondary discretion.

Dworkin distinguishes these two "weak " senses of discretion from a "stronger" sense: "We use 'discretion' sometimes not merely to say that an official must use judgment in applying the standards set him by authority, or that no one will review that exercise of judgment, but to say that on some issue he is simply not bound by standards set by the authority in question."[15] To illustrate his point, Dworkin gives the example of a sergeant ordered to take five men on patrol. If the captain had amplified his order to enjoin the sergeant to take his five most experienced men on patrol, the sergeant would only have discretion in the weak sense, whereas if the sergeant were simply told to take five men on patrol, he would have discretion in the strong sense. Although this "discretion in a stronger sense" looks very much like what Rosenberg characterizes as primary discretion, it does not seem to fit within Dworkin's broader analytical scheme. A discrepancy exists between Dworkin's basic position that "[t]he concept of discretion is at home in only one sort of context: when someone is . . . charged with making decisions *subject to standards* set by a particular authority"[16] and his statement that when a decisionmaker has discretion in the strong sense he is "*not controlled by a standard* furnished by the particular authority" in question.[17] Dworkin of course is not saying that either of these hypothetical decisionmakers is beyond criticism. He recognizes that (almost) all decisions can be criticized. Depending on the context, we might, as already noted, attack a particular decision as being dumb, irrational, unfair, malicious, or careless, but such criticisms are different from the criticism that those decisions failed to conform to a set of standards. The criticisms

---

[14] *Id.* at 32-33.
[15] *Id.* at 33.
[16] *Id.* at 32 (emphasis added).
[17] *Id.* at 34 (emphasis added).

only become the same if by a "set of standards" one means broad notions of rationality and fairness to which all people—and, by extension, all decisions—are subject. In that sense, all decisions are discretionary. But surely the notion of standards governing decisions would lose much of its utility if one defined "standards" so broadly.

Even if the criteria for such criticisms were much more concrete than vague notions of rationality and fairness, it might not be desirable to call all decisions discretionary. Consider, for example, the choice of a wife made by a man who attended a small, socially elite college, graduated first in his class at a major law school, and has associated with rich and fashionable people all his life. For years, this man confided to all his friends that the woman he married must be beautiful, intelligent, and, most importantly, rich. Suddenly, however, he decides to marry a plain, not exceptionally intelligent woman of humble background, whose entire employment history consists of jobs in fast-food restaurants, and who is neither pregnant nor thought to be pregnant at the time of the marriage. Observers could criticize this man's choice of a wife on the basis of various criteria. With such different backgrounds it is hard to imagine that the couple could have enough in common upon which to base a happy marriage. In addition, the choice of a wife who possessed none of the characteristics ostensibly sought is totally irrational in the absence of any evidence that the man has changed his value system. Still, we cannot say that this person abused his discretion, because he is not *accountable* to us. Although we may also want to say that he has made the "wrong" decision, it was not a wrong to us. Admittedly, one of the subsidiary dictionary meanings of "discretion" is prudence or sound judgment, and all human choice, especially the choice of a marriage partner, engages the exercise of prudence. But criticizing a person for acting imprudently or indiscreetly, or for failing to show or exercise discretion, is not the same thing as criticizing him for abusing his discretion, or for making a decision that was beyond his discretion, or for claiming to have any discretion in the first place.

Only where there is accountability can we meaningfully speak of discretion in choice. Contrary to Dworkin's contention, *accountability*, not the existence of standards, is the chief identifying feature of contexts in which discretion is "at home." In other words, the notion of discretion arises when some people are attempting to exercise power in a political context and other people are prepared, at least on occasion, to challenge these attempts. Discretionary choices are sometimes, but not always, made in contexts in which there are fairly specific criteria or standards that we can use to judge the soundness of the choice; recall Dworkin's "strong sense" of discretion—the type of discretion Rosenberg calls "primary"—that by definition exists when there are no such standards. This absence of standards does not immunize a decision or the person who made it from criticism, including, most importantly, the criticism that the discretion has been exercised improperly because it has been abused. To distill the essence of this discussion of various types of discretion, we may say that discretion is "at home" in contexts in which people who are accountable in some way to others can expect to be subjected to criticism for the choices they make.

Judges, by definition, make choices for which they are accountable. So, of course, do other public officials, including legislators. According to the analysis thus far presented, it makes sense to say that all these officials exercise discretion. Nevertheless, the situation of the legislator seems different from that of the judge. First of all, one might say, accepting the thesis of Edmund Burke,[18] that, although a legislator is accountable to his constituents, his only obligation is to vote his conscience as to how best to promote the public good. This sort of accountability is too attenuated, it might be urged, to justify calling the legislator's role a discretionary one. It is an empirical fact, however, that most legislators and most of their constituents believe that legislators have a higher degree of accountability to their constituents than this often-repeated theory of legislative responsibility maintains is appropriate. Nevertheless, although the legislator may be accountable to the persons who elected him for the choices he makes, his range of choice on any given issue is so great that it seems odd to describe legislative choices as discretionary. A legislator, moreover, is expected to make choices on a larger number of issues than is a judge. And of course there is the practical problem, that we shall discuss in the next section, of how to supervise legislators, judges, and other decisionmakers.

Identifying the theoretical difference between legislative choice and judicial choice is, however, a difficult matter, and one that has received

---

[18]   E. Burke, *Speech to the Electors of Bristol* (Nov. 3, 1774), WORKS, Vol. II, at 94-98 (1869).

much critical attention. I suggest that the distinction does not necessarily lie in the range of choice that is available to the decisionmaker in making some particular decision. There are many legislative decisions that seem obvious and foreordained, just as there are many judicial decisions that are impossible to predict and that will be difficult to make. The difference between legislative and judicial choice lies, rather, in the potential sources of assistance that are available to the decisionmaker for the making of his choices. No official has a totally unconstrained range of criteria of choice. The range of criteria to which different public officials may properly resort is dictated partly by the role played by each official and partly by societal expectations. One can argue that judicial choices, no matter how difficult, and even if, as is sometimes the case, there are no standards against which their validity or correctness can be assessed, must nevertheless be made on the basis of a circumscribed set of considerations and in a certain stylized sort of way, whereas legislative choice is not so constrained. It might, for example, be unobjectionable for a legislator to take his fourteen-year-old daughter's advice about how to vote on an issue, but intolerable for a judge to decide a difficult case on the same basis.

Countless factors that are vague and indeterminate and that we cannot completely capture in a formalized system circumscribe a decisionmaker's possible choices. Indeed, there is no necessary connection between the formalization of decisional constraints and the achievement of decisional restraint. That is, the effectiveness of decisional restraints is not a logical matter. The procedures decisionmakers must employ and the form of the justifications they must give can limit their choices as effectively as the considerations they are either directed or forbidden to take into account. In sum, to repeat, the presence or absence of criteria for choosing is not the crucial determinant of what makes a choice a discretionary one. If people are accountable for their choices, they have discretion. If they are not accountable for their choices, then talk of discretion is out of place. Furthermore, whether people are or are not accountable to others for the choices they make is as much determined by empirical considerations such as public expectations and the social role played by a decisionmaker as it is by formal legal criteria. As we have repeatedly emphasized, political and legal decisions are made with an audience in mind and the expectations of these audiences are ignored by decisionmakers at their peril.

C. The Irresistible Urge to Narrow the Scope of Discretion

Despite the inevitable omnipresence of discretion in any form of social organization, the existence of discretion in *other* people often creates a sense of unease. We feel uncomfortable with the idea that we will be bound by some other person's best judgment about what is appropriate, and we seek ways to constrain that person's exercise of his authority. Sometimes, of course, the people to whom a decisionmaker is accountable, who collectively can be considered to count as one of his audiences, are unable to exercise very much ongoing supervision of the decisionmaker's performance. A legislator, to use an example from the previous section of this chapter, is accountable to his constituents. But these constituents form an amorphous group, able to exercise their right to discipline their legislative representatives only at discrete intervals that may be separated by substantial periods of time. Under these conditions, the constituents can neither specify all-inclusive, all-encompassing sets of criteria for the legislator to consider in making choices nor enforce conformity to these criteria on a day-to-day basis. They must inevitably be prepared to accept relatively untrammeled decisionmaking from their legislative representatives, and this acceptance will be projected onto the ideal audiences that are presupposed as the addressees of political and legal argument.

This is not to say that constituents are powerless. A well-organized group of constituents may be able to make it perfectly clear what the legislator must do regarding a particular issue under pain of risking defeat should he seek reelection. In these matters the legislator's "discretion" is quite constrained. Nevertheless, as a practical matter legislators will generally have comparative freedom of decision over a wide area. The vast range of questions over which legislative choices must be made, coupled with the constituents' inability to exercise close supervision, may thus account for the feeling that legislative choices perhaps should not be described as instances of discretion at all.

Admittedly, final appellate courts are not subject to the close supervision of superior authorities either, and, as we have already intimated many people would say that such courts have the ability to make choices that are almost as wide-ranging as those of a legislature. Even here, however, there are some special constraints that apply to judicial choices that do not apply to legislative choices. A legislature may, for example, "overrule" judicial decisions and this feature can, on occasion, inhibit a judge. Moreover, judges, as members of an elite profession, are subject to the expectations of their co-professionals. These expectations, as already pointed out in Chapter 2, influence judges' perception of their role in a way that affects their decisionmaking. Likewise, as was pointed out in Chapter 4, the stylized ways in which judges are required to justify their decisions also impose some limitations on the decisions they make, as do the restrictions on the sources they may consult that were noted earlier in this chapter when we discussed the persons whom judges may consult in the course of their deliberations. Finally, insofar as the procedural requirements for instituting litigation circumscribe the ability of people to obtain judicial redress, the opportunities for courts to exercise wide-ranging and unconstrained discretion will be limited. Nevertheless, it must be conceded that lack of effective close supervision of judges or of other decisionmakers will inevitably lead to the exercise of, and an audience's toleration of, a wider range of choice by people like judges, particularly judges on final appellate courts, who are ostensibly accountable to that audience.

The converse of this axiom is, however, equally true. The more capable we are of closely supervising people ostensibly accountable to us, the more likely we are to try to exercise that supervision by curtailing the range of choices available to those people. And of course the desire to exercise some supervision of these choices will be reflected in the expectations of the ideal audiences that we inevitably construct. We may try to exercise that supervision by specifying the criteria that the decisionmaker must take into account in making choices, or, less ambitiously, we may specify criteria that a decisionmaker is prohibited from considering but otherwise leave the choice of criteria to the decisionmaker.[19] We can also facilitate the supervision of decisionmakers by requiring the prompt reporting of decisions so as to give a higher authority the opportunity to reverse the decision of a subordinate decisionmaker. In the typical case, of course, a combination of methods will be used.

---

[19] *See, e.g.* J. Raz, PRACTICAL REASON AND NORMS 35-48 (1975). Raz discusses what he calls "exclusionary reasons," i.e. reasons for not taking certain otherwise applicable considerations into account.

In discussing appellate courts' control over exercises of discretion by trial courts, Rosenberg notes that the "ultimate type of [an] unreviewable trial court order is the judge's declaration of a mistrial in a jury case."[20] As Rosenberg succinctly puts it, "[s]ince no appellate court can put Humpty Dumpty together again once the jury has been discharged and has disbanded, the trial court's decision is immune to appellate reversal for any ground or on any basis." This was the point of Rosenberg's football examples. That is, although trial courts may be accountable to appellate courts, appellate courts are unable to do anything about some of the choices trial courts make.

But where accountability is joined with effective power in the superior body, the situation is markedly different. Rosenberg notes a number of instances in which appellate courts accepted trial courts' so-called discretionary decisions while intimating that they did not agree with them, but he also notes other instances in which appellate courts intervened on the ground that the trial court had "abused" its discretion, even in the absence of express criteria supposedly governing the purported exercise of discretion. One has the impression that something rather quixotic is happening. Many of the cases are hard to explain. All one can say is that appellate courts will sometimes use the power they have over trial courts to second-guess them. When they will, and when they will not, very often seems rather subjective. We can nevertheless safely conclude that accountability to a superior authority conjoined with power in the superior authority to intervene often leads to reviewability, even when the decisions being subjected to review are said to have been "discretionary" in the widest sense of that term. This inclination seems to be a natural and universal human characteristic. The urge to restrict the scope of discretion can, moreover, also lead to review in cases where the superior authority simply has power, and no accountability has previously been thought to exist. Consider, for example, the use of peremptory challenges in the United States to strike prospective jurors from the venire. Traditionally, counsel had not been accountable for their exercise of peremptory challenges. As one court remarked, "[w]hen peremptory challenges are subjected to judicial scrutiny, they will no longer be peremptory."[21] Since 1965,

[20] M. Rosenberg, *supra* note 3, at 650.
[21] Neil v. State, 433 So.2d 51, 52 (Fla. App. 1983), *rev'd,* 457 So.2d 481 (Fla. 1984).

however, courts in the United States have increasingly used their power to control the exercise of peremptory challenges, thus eroding an area of decisionmaking formerly within the exclusive province of counsel.

It would not be profitable in a book such as this one to review in detail this significant development in the law of the United States.[22] It is enough to note that the supreme courts of several states and, finally, the Supreme Court of the United States, in *Batson v. Kentucky,*[23] held that peremptory challenges may not be used to strike jurors solely on the basis of race. While the first cases involved peremptory challenges by the prosecution the same strictures have been applied to the use of peremptory challenges by defendants.[24] The prohibition against the use of peremptory challenges to strike jurors because of counsel's belief in the existence of "group bias" has, not surprisingly, led to attacks on peremptory challenges based upon "sex, race, color, creed or national origin."[25] Indeed, in one case it was seriously argued that convicted felons—who in most states are barred from jury duty—constituted a "discrete group" whose blanket exclusions from jury duty was unconstitutional.[26]

Three reasons have been given for this development. They are worth briefly describing because they figure in the expectations that at the present time are ascribed to the ideal audiences to whom legal and political arguments are typically addressed. The first is the assumption that a fair jury is one that includes people of countervailing shared group biases. If this is true, it would seem to follow that the more varied and disparate the group biases of jurors, the better. But, of course, seating a group of wildly assorted jurors with no shared perspectives may result in a total impasse. As one perceptive criticism of these developments has noted, one basic function of a jury is to agree, especially when unanimous verdicts are required.[27] It would be foolish to make extraordinary efforts to impanel

---

[22] For a more detailed examination of the development, see G. Christie, *An Essay on Discretion*, 1986 DUKE L. J. 747, 757-64.

[23] 476 U.S. 79 (1986).

[24] Georgia v. McCollum, 505 U.S. 42 (1992).

[25] *See, e.g.*, Commonwealth v. Soares, 377 Mass. 461, 387 N.E.2d 499, *cert. denied* 444 U.S. 881 (1979).

[26] *See* Rubio v. Superior Court, 24 Cal.3d 93, 154 Cal. Rptr. 734 (1979).

[27] *See* S. Salzburg & M. Powers, *Peremptory Challenges and Clash Between Impartiality and Group Representation*, 41 MO. L. REV. 337, 354-55 (1982).

juries whose internal dynamics would make hung juries more likely, particularly when there is no reason to believe that the clash of diverse social perspectives necessarily enhances the ability of juries to arrive at correct decisions. Aristotle perceptively suggested that collective judgments may be better than individual judgments, not because opposing biases will hopefully cancel each other out but, rather, because the contribution of each individual's best qualities *may* permit a collective judgment to be superior even to the judgment of the most gifted of individuals.[28]

A second reason given for allowing courts to restrict the scope of peremptory challenges is to reduce reliance on stereotypes. But the judicially imposed solution does not eliminate the resort to stereotypes. Indeed, given the limited time and resources available for examining members of the venire, the parties must resort to stereotypes. Cases like *Batson* merely attempt to restrict resort to one stereotype—race—and some few other stereotypes. But there is no logical reason to focus only on those few stereotypes. It is not at all clear that race, sex, or national origin are more important than classifications based on educational level, economic class, or physical disability. Moreover, the cases do not, as a practical matter, preclude counsel's ability to rely even on those group associations recognized as suspect. Unlike counsel's attempts to challenge a juror for cause, the courts only require counsel seeking to use a peremptory challenge to strike a member of a suspect group to articulate a "reasonable" or a "bona fide" reason for challenging that juror. The objections must only seem plausible; they need not necessarily be well-founded.

A third reason given for courts seeking to control the exercise of peremptory challenges is to enhance the public's perception that the criminal process is a fair one. Whether the fairness of the process will be enhanced in the eyes of the participants in the legal process is another matter. Take a black male accused of raping a black female who would have wanted to use his peremptory challenges to remove black females from the jury. Would the process seem fair from his perspective?

The problems presented by the use and abuse of peremptory challenges is particularly acute in states allowing large numbers of peremptory

---

[28] *See, e.g.*, Aristotle, METAPHYSICS, Bk α, c.1 993a 30-993 b3; POLITICS, Bk. 3, c.11 1281a43 -1281b10.

challenges.[29] Given the complexity of the problem there is some logical force behind the contention that peremptory challenges should be completely abolished, but it would require the jettisoning of almost 800 years of history in which the practice of peremptory challenge has always been considered to be one of the guarantors of a fair trial.[30] It is an issue on which I do not wish to express an opinion in this book. I merely use the peremptory-challenge controversy as an illustration of the observation that, if a decisionmaker has the power to control a subordinate powerholder, he will almost inevitably be inclined to find a way to exercise that power. This universal human inclination furthermore will find expression in legal argumentation. The ideal or universal audience will expect that arguments challenging the choices made by subordinate powerholders will be made to superior powerholders and that those superior holders will not automatically refuse to consider those arguments.

D. Structural and Ideological Factors Behind the Urge to Broaden the Scope of Discretion

In the course of our discussion it has, not surprisingly, become clear that the amount of discretion that will be claimed by a particular decisionmaker, and that will be tolerated by a society when it is exercised, will be decisively influenced by the perspective from which the question of discretion is viewed. If viewed from the perspective of a person about to exercise discretion, it will seem natural to him to claim a relatively broad range of discretion, free from the second-guessing of others, and, in his arguments, he will assume that an ideal or universal audience would approve of his exercising such a discretion. If viewed, however, from the perspective of a person who has the power to control the exercise of discretion by a subordinate official, there will be a natural inclination to

---

[29] For example, in California, each side has twenty-six peremptory challenges in a capital case. CAL. PENAL CODE. § 1070 (a) (West 1985).

[30] "The right of challenge comes from the common law with trial by jury itself, and has always been held essential to the fairness of trial by jury. As was said by Blackstone, ... in criminal cases, or at least in capital ones, there is . . . allowed to the prisoner an arbitrary and capricious species of challenge to a certain number of jurors, without showing any cause at all, which is called a [peremptory challenge]'." Lewis v. United States, 146 U.S. 370, 376 (1892).

believe that the power to control creates an obligation to control. For surely the ideal audience to whom a superior official addresses his arguments could not expect him to leave undisturbed incorrect decisions that he has the power to overturn and correct.

These contradictory tendencies are always in operation and people in an organized social milieu will be inclined one way or another depending upon the perspective they have of a decisional situation at any particular time. On a more modest scale, it is somewhat like yesterday's radical who is today's government minister and whose view of the legitimacy of the exercise of political power to preserve the economic and social status quo has undergone a complete change. The difference in the more complex legal situations that we have explored is that the same individual can, at any given period of time, function in both capacities, namely as someone who decides at first instance and as someone who has the power to control the decisions that are initially made by other people. This is different from the situation in which a change in a person's political position leads to a more or less permanent change of perspective.

Our attitudes towards the proper scope of discretion, however, are sometimes strongly influenced by factors that go well beyond structural features, such as the shifting perspectives experienced by different people depending on the role they play in the social and political functioning of the society in which they live. Sometimes certain intellectual movements take hold that favor one or another of the differing views about the appropriate scope of discretion, regardless of the perspective from which a particular exercise of discretion is viewed. One such movement took place in the legal universe in northern Europe and the United States in the latter part of the nineteenth and the early twentieth centuries. During an era of explosive economic growth and rapid social change, the law administered in the courts came to seem overly formal and often far removed from the realities of contemporary life. The notions of people like von Savigny[31] and

---

[31] None of von Savigny's many works seem to have been translated into English. His most influential work on the matters discussed in the text is *Von Beruf unserer Zeit für Gesetzgebung und Rechtswissenschaft* (1814) (Of the Vocation of our Age for Legislation and Jurisprudence).

Puchta[32] in Europe and James C. Carter[33] in the United States—that the law administered by the courts was a self-contained body of doctrine that reflected and indeed was the product of the natural evolution of the society whose law it was—seemed less attractive.

At a time when everything seemed to be in a state of flux, the contention that large-scale purposeful legal change was bound to be an unwise intrusion into the natural processes of social evolution came increasingly to be regarded as unconvincing. The competing Austinian view, that law was merely the expression of the will of the political sovereign, seemed equally unsatisfying because it was incomplete. Law was more than the logical arrangement of the rules and doctrines promulgated by the supreme law maker. The dissatisfaction with these traditional models of the legal process was accentuated by the fact that, to many people, decisions that ostensibly purported to be derived from tradition and/or the logical application of legal concepts seemed clearly driven by unexpressed ideological considerations.[34]

Rudolf von Jhering's epic work *Der Zweck im Recht* (*Purpose in Law*) clearly reflected this changed intellectual climate. The English title of the first volume of that work, *Law as a Means to an End*, first published in 1877 put "Interest instead of Will at the basis of law."[35] Since interest suggests purpose, von Jhering therefore concluded that "there is no legal rule which does not owe its origin to a purpose, *i.e.*, to a practical motive."[36] The work of European scholars like von Jhering attracted the attention of the indefatigable Roscoe Pound who introduced this insistence upon the instrumental nature of law to the English-speaking world. There it found a welcome audience, particularly in the United States and for readily

---

[32] G. Puchta, OUTLINES OF JURISPRUDENCE AS THE SCIENCE OF RIGHT (W. Hastie transl. 1887) (reprinted 1982).

[33] J. Carter, LAW: ITS ORIGIN, GROWTH, AND FUNCTION (1907).

[34] One of the most famous and influential expressions of this point of view was that of Oliver Wendell Holmes, Jr. "Behind the logical form lies a judgement as to the relative worth and importance of competing legislative grounds, often an inarticulate and unconscious judgement, it is true, and yet the very root and nerve of the whole proceeding." O. Holmes, Jr., *The Path of the Law*, 10 HARV. L. REV. 457, 466, (1897).

[35] R. von Jhering, LAW AS A MEANS TO AN END, liii (transl. I. Husik 1924) (Author's Preface).

[36] *Id.* at liv.

understandable reasons.[37] At the turn of the century the American body politic was confronting the challenge of the United States' emergence as a great economic power with vast human and natural resources. Large railroads and industrial combines, such as Standard Oil, that were constituted on a scale never before seen anywhere in the world, were amassing an economic strength that, to many, seemed frightening.

Among one portion of the American elite, who came to be called the "Progressives," the situation called for government regulation. In the post-civil-war period, many of the individual states had tried their hand at regulation, particularly of railroad rates, but it had become clear by the latter part of the century that some federal regulation was necessary. Federal regulation of railroads began in 1887 with the passage of the Interstate Commerce Act and the establishment of the Interstate Commerce Commission.[38] The Sherman Antitrust Act was enacted in 1890;[39] and the Pure Food and Drugs Act followed in 1906,[40] from which beginnings the present Food and Drug Administration eventually evolved.[41] To many well-educated people, it seemed obvious that the economy could not be left to the clash of conflicting private interests subject to whatever piecemeal and fitful control could be exercised by the courts using traditional legal remedies. Moreover, the complexity of the modern economy could not be managed simply by legislation. Legislation was necessary but the economy needed day-to-day supervision and regulation by trained professionals.

It is was of course no coincidence that this was a period in which the social "sciences" were being established and were claiming that the social and economic structure of society could be studied with the same precision and objectivity as was claimed for the physical sciences. The notion that modern times needed a more interventionist state and that this intervention was best removed from the political arena and entrusted to trained professionals seemed, to these people, the only rational answer to the

---

[37] *See, e.g.*, R. Pound, *Mechanical Jurisprudence*, 8 COLUM L. REV. 605 (1908). Pound was so influential that much of what he wrote seems completely common-place because of its almost universal acceptance by subsequent writers. This has had the perverse effect of leading to his work being largely ignored by contemporary scholars.

[38] 24 Stat. 379 (1887).

[39] 26 Stat. 209 (1890), *as amended*, 15 U.S.C. § 1 *et seq.* (1994).

[40] 34 Stat. 768 (1906), *as amended*, 21, U.S.C. § 301 *et seq.* (1994).

[41] 102 Stat. 3120 (1988), *as amended*, 21 U.S.C. § 301 *et seq.* (1994).

challenge of modernity. This vision of the requirements of modern life was not confined to political scientists or to political radicals. One of the people to whom this vision seemed at the time the appropriate perspective from which to view modern social problems was the noted jurist, Learned Hand.[42] As a young lawyer, and in his early days as a judge, Hand was a committed supporter of this movement which, in the guise of the Progressive Party under Theodore Roosevelt, mounted a serious challenge for the presidency in 1912. By siphoning off a large portion of the Republican vote, Roosevelt's "Bull Moose" candidacy was undoubtedly responsible for the Democrat, Woodrow Wilson, defeating the Republican incumbent, William Howard Taft.

The prosperity of the 1920s temporarily checked the political expression of this approach to government. But in the universities, and especially in some of the elite law schools, particularly Columbia and later Yale, the ideas underlying the progressive movement took hold.[43] Moreover, it was not merely in the domain of public law that the scientific attitude could bear fruit. It was also claimed that, in the domain of private law, a properly trained lawyer, that is one with a thorough training in the social sciences and a thorough grasp of the needs and interests of the parties involved in legal transactions, could, even as an advocate but especially as a judge and occasionally as a legislator, make the law more responsive to the needs of society. It was this school of thought that formed the core of what came to be called "legal realism."

Implicit in the writing of "realists" like Herman Oliphant and Karl Llewellyn was the assumption that, if we knew more about how society works and more about the concrete problems of people engaged in the various types of legal disputes, the right answers to these disputes would somehow jump out at us.[44] They accepted Oliver Wendall Holmes Jr.'s

---

[42] See G. Gunter, LEARNED HAND: THE MAN AND THE JUDGE 190-270 (1994).

[43] See, e.g., L. Kalman, LEGAL REALISM AT YALE, 1927-60 (1986); W. Twining, KARL LLEWELLYN AND THE REALIST MOVEMENT (1973).

[44] See H. Oliphant, A Return to Stare Decisis, 14 AM. BAR ASS'N J. 71 (1928); K. Llewellyn, A Realistic Jurisprudence—The Next Step, 30 COLUM. L. REV. 431 (1930). Llewellyn captured some of the same sentiment in his later work when he extolled "Situation Sense," and what he called "The Law of the Singing Reason," namely "a rule which wears both a right situation-reason and a clear scope-criterion on its face." K. Llewellyn, THE COMMON LAW TRADITION DECIDING APPEALS, 60, 183 (1960). One can

assertion that a body of law was most rational when the judges were willing and able to articulate the policy judgments that underlay their judicial decisions.[45] Whether Holmes in fact ever accepted their additional belief that the articulation and weighing of the policy reasons and factual presuppositions underlying a particular problem would actually reveal the appropriate social response to a particular type of legal problem is another matter. Be that as it may, with this impetus the approach to legal reasoning, known variously as interest balancing or as factor analysis, had a profound effect on the teaching of law in the United States and it became the dominant trend in discussions of the appropriate method of legal decisionmaking.

Interest balancing appealed to a vision of an ideal audience that had lost faith in the traditional rule-and-precedent-bound theories of legal reasoning and preferred, instead, to leave the decision of legal issues to the sound discretion of legally trained social experts. The late William Prosser applied interest balancing in drafting the *Restatement (Second) of Torts*, and it figures even more prominently in the *Restatement (Second) of Conflicts*. We shall explore these developments shortly. Interest balancing was of course put forward to increase the rationality of judicial decisions by making them more sensible accommodations of the often conflicting imperatives of public policy. The result, however, was, as we shall see, to increase the area of judicial choice without necessarily leading to the "better" decisions that the realists hoped interest balancing would produce.

There are many reasons why, for all its continued attraction, interest balancing or, to use the more technical term, factor analysis, has not produced the satisfaction for which its proponents had hoped. At the outset, an adequate theory of interests must confront the problem of defining and identifying what is meant by an "interest." Writing during his heyday as a realist, Llewellyn argued that the "interests" bandied about in common speech were nothing more than aphorisms. Expressions like "security of transactions" were merely rubrics or what Llewellyn called "a red flag to

---

compare François Gény's assertion that legal interpretation "finds the necessary objective support only in the *nature of the subject matter of its inquiry*." F. Gény, MÉTHODE D' INTERPRÉTATION ET SOURCES EN DROIT PRIVÉ POSITIF (2d ed.), No. 157 (J. Mayda transl. 1963) (emphasis in original).

[45] O. Holmes, Jr., *supra* note 34, at 469.

challenge investigation in certain general directions."[46]   For Llewellyn, interests were "*groupings* of behavior claimed to be significant."[47]   When talking about interests, it was important to examine "the objective data, the *specific* data, *claimed* to represent an interest."[48]   When this is done "[w]hat is left, in the realm of *description*, are at the one end the facts, the groupings of conduct (and demonstrable expectations) which may be claimed to constitute an interest; and on the other the practices of courts in their effects upon the conduct and expectations of the laymen in question."[49]   Thus defined, interests are complex entities that are difficult to summarize in a few words and difficult to identify in individual cases.

Furthermore, even if a court could come up with relatively concise and yet meaningful statements of the interests involved in a particular case, one would next face the problem of deciding whether the interests identified were really comparable enough to permit balancing them against each other. Roscoe Pound long ago pointed out that one cannot directly weigh social or public interests against individual interests.[50]   That would be like comparing apples and oranges. To weigh individual interests against social interests, the individual interest in, say, security of the person, would have to be translated into the *social* interest in the security of the individual. Even assuming that all the necessary translations could be made so that all the interests being considered were in the same universe of discourse, the ultimate problem would remain: how should courts *weight* the interests? This is the same type of problem that Dworkin later confronted in his initial

---

[46]   *A Realistic Jurisprudence, supra* note 44, at 445.

[47]   *Ibid.*

[48]   *Id.* at 446.

[49]   *Id.* at 448. Llewellyn recognized that given his behavioral approach to law, there was something to be said for defining who officials were by examining the functions performed by the participants in the legal process rather than accepting doctrinal categorizations contained in statute books, *see id* at 457, but he did not bother to do so. He accepted instead the standard doctrinal definitions of who was a "layman" and who was an "official."

[50]   *See, e.g.*, R. Pound, *Individual Interest of Substance—Promised Advantages*, 59 HARV. L. REV. 1, 1-3 (1945). Among his earlier work on the same subject is, *Interests of Personality*, 28 HARV. L. REV. 343 (1915).

work on the primacy of principles and, as we have seen, even he was unable to solve it by telling us how to weight "principles."[51]

With this background in mind, let us turn to an example from the *Restatement* and the *Restatement (Second) of Torts* which illustrates both why the temptation to expand judicial discretion arises and why that effort so often fails to produce the more "rational" legal decisions that were promised. Section 520 of the *Restatement of Torts*, which appeared in 1938, subjected the operator of an "ultrahazardous activity" to strict liability if the activity miscarried, and it defined such an activity as one that (a) "necessarily involves a risk of serious harm" to others and (b) "is not a matter of common usage." The common-usage exception was intended to accommodate Lord Cairns' declaration in *Rylands v. Fletcher*[52] that the liability established in that case was limited to the "non-natural use" of land. One practical implication of the common-usage exception posed some difficulties. What about, for example, fumigation of commercial buildings? It certainly was a common activity; indeed, in many cities it was required by law. Nevertheless, the Supreme Court of California held that, although fumigation might be a common activity, only a very small number of professionals performed fumigation and thus it was not a matter of common usage.[53] Accordingly, the court could appropriately classify it as an ultrahazardous activity subject to strict liability. The court cited the commentary to section 520 as support for its conclusion.[54] The Oregon Supreme Court took a different approach, classifying cropdusting as an ultrahazardous activity[55] despite the fact that the court actually did consider it a matter of common usage. The court found the dangerousness of the activity alone sufficient to justify this classification.

When Volume III of the *Restatement (Second)* was published in 1977, several changes had been made in section 520. Instead of "ultrahazardous activity," the *Restatement (Second)* used the term "abnormally dangerous activity." More to the point, the *Restatement (Second)* replaced the two-pronged test of the *Restatement* with a factor analysis that included interest

---

[51] *See* the discussion in Chapter 9, *supra*, at 132.

[52] L.R. 3 E. & I. App. 330 (1868).

[53] Luthringer v. Moore, 31 Cal.2d 489, 500, 190 P.2d 1, 8 (1948).

[54] *Ibid.* The court cited Restatement of Torts § 520, comment b (1938).

[55] Loe v. Lenhardt, 227 Or. 242, 253-54, 362 P.2d 312, 318 (1961).

balancing. The full text of section 520 of the *Restatement (Second)* merits quotation:

In determining whether an activity is abnormally dangerous, the following factors are to be considered:

(a) existence of a high degree of risk of some harm to the person, land or chattels of others;

(b) likelihood that the harm that results from it will be great;

(c) inability to eliminate the risk by the exercise of reasonable care;

(d) extent to which the activity is not a matter of common usage;

(e) inappropriateness of the activity to the place where it is carried on; and

(f) extent to which its value to the community is outweighed by its dangerous attributes.[56]

This statement of the test leaves the overriding question: how is the required factor analysis or interest balancing to be done? That is, how should a court weight the six factors that are to guide the determination whether an activity is abnormally dangerous? The commentary declares that the determination is to be made by the court, and not by a jury, "upon consideration of all the factors listed in this Section, and weight given to each that it merits upon the facts in evidence."[57] This is hardly much of a weighting method. Moreover, the commentary, if taken literally, seems to suggest that each case is sui generis. Thus, in any case involving an activity not covered four-square by a precedent, one would have to litigate up to the highest court of the jurisdiction before knowing how the activity would be classified. The value of precedents covering other activities would be minimal. Whether or not one liked the old test, it was certainly easier to administer, since it asked only whether the activity involved "a risk of serious harm" to others that "[could not] be eliminated by the exercise of the utmost care," and whether the activity was "a matter of common usage," both of which questions are in theory questions of fact.

Some might contend that the *Restatement (Second)* merely made explicit the factors courts already considered. This contention misses the point, however. Of course, in any close case, a court is likely to consider

---

[56] RESTATEMENT (SECOND) OF TORTS § 520 (1977).

[57] *Id.* at comment l. As noted in the text, this decision is to be made by the judge. *Ibid.* Why this is a question for the judge, while questions such as whether a product is defective are jury questions, is never adequately explained.

individual equities like the comparative wealth of the parties and the social importance of the activity, and these factors will undoubtedly in some way influence the decision. It is unrealistic to expect a court always to ignore what some might term individual equities. But to recognize that a court will be *influenced* by individual equities in deciding some legal issue is not the same as saying that these individual features themselves *are* the legal issue.

An enormous range of legal decisions could all be plausibly justified under section 520 of the *Restatement (Second)*. For example, it was held in Maryland that operating a neighborhood gas station, whose leaking storage tanks fouled the well of an adjoining landowner, was an abnormally dangerous activity.[58] An Oregon court disagreed.[59] In a Florida court, a mine operator seriously urged, again on the basis of the new version of section 520, that a mine producing phosphatic wastes was not an abnormally dangerous activity because of the location of the mine and its social importance.[60] The court ruled against the mine operator because of the size of the activity and the possibility of enormous damage if the activity miscarried.

From the litigant's point of view, the expense and delay of the type of judicial decisionmaking envisioned by section 520 of the *Restatement (Second)* are staggering. Consider from the litigant's perspective *Doundoulakis v. Town of Hempstead*,[61] a case in which the New York Court of Appeals adopted section 520 of the *Restatement (Second)*. The case involved "a hydraulic landfilling project . . . on 146 acres of swamp meadowland abutting plaintiffs' houses." In remanding, because of lack of an evidentiary basis for applying the analysis of section 520, the court declared:

The pivotal issue is whether it was established that hydraulic dredging and landfilling, that is, the introduction by pressure of . . . massive quantities of sand and water is, under the circumstances, an abnormally dangerous activity giving rise to strict liability.[62]

. . . .

---

[58] Yommer v. McKenzie, 255 Md. 220, 222-27, 257 A.2d 138, 139-41 (1969).

[59] Hudson v. Peavey Oil Co., 279 Or. 3, 8, 566 P.2d 175, 178 (1977).

[60] Cities Service Co. v. State, 312 So.2d 799, 801-03 (Fla. App. 1975).

[61] 42 N.Y.2d 440, 398 N.Y.S.2d 401 (1977).

[62] *Id.* at 445, 398 N.Y.S.2d at 402.

There is little if any information, for example, of the degree to which hydraulic landfilling poses a risk of damage to neighboring properties. Nor is there data on the gravity of any such danger, or the extent to which the danger can be eliminated by reasonable care. Basic to the inquiry, but not to be found in the record, are the availability and relative cost, economic and otherwise, of alternative methods of landfilling. There are other Restatement factors, and perhaps still others, which the parties may develop as relevant about which there is little or nothing in the record.[63]

From the litigant's standpoint, a more easily applied standard that would allow him to ascertain his legal position more readily might be preferable. That was the attraction of the original version of section 520 of the *Restatement of Torts*, which focused merely upon the dangerousness of the activity and the degree to which it was not a "matter of common usage." As we have already noted, some courts were even prepared to eliminate the common usage justification.

Section 520 of the *Restatement (Second) of Torts* is not an isolated instance of the urge to inject factor analysis into judicial decisionmaking. For example, under the original *Restatement of Torts*, an intentional invasion of another's interest in the use and enjoyment of land was unreasonable (and hence a nuisance) "unless the utility of the actor's conduct outweigh[ed] the gravity of the harm."[64] The *Restatement (Second)* has now added an awkwardly-worded provision declaring that the invasion may also be unreasonable if "the harm caused by the conduct is serious and the financial burden of compensating for this and similar harm to others would not make the continuation of the conduct not feasible."[65] Admittedly, under the original *Restatement,* which tracked the traditional common law, courts were obliged to make the potentially open-ended decision about the utility of the defendant's conduct. Courts must still make that determination under the *Restatement (Second)*, but now, even if courts decide that the utility outweighs the harm, they must make the additional

---

[63] *Id.* at 448-49, 398 N.Y.S.2d at 404.

[64] RESTATEMENT OF TORTS § 826 (1939).

[65] RESTATEMENT (SECOND) OF TORTS § 826(b) (1977). To flesh out § 826, the RESTATEMENT (SECOND) OF TORTS has added a new section, § 829A which provides that "[a]n intentional invasion of another's interest in the use and enjoyment of land is unreasonable if the harm resulting from the invasion is severe and greater than the other should be required to bear without compensation."

problematic decision as to whether it is nevertheless "feasible" for the defendant to compensate the plaintiff.

The *Restatement (Second) of Conflicts* provides a more extreme example of how the use of factor analysis by courts leads to an enormous range of plausibly justifiable decisions. In section 6(2), seven factors are set out as being relevant to choice-of-law problems. Then additional, more topic-specific, factors are set out for applying the principles of section 6 to tort and contract disputes.[66] The regime set up by these provisions is clearly the provision of a methodology or approach rather than a statement of "law."[67]

Constitutional adjudication also provides illustrations of decisionmakers' attempts to broaden the scope of their discretion. Consider the question of how to determine whether some particular punishment in a noncapital case is cruel and unusual punishment under the Eighth Amendment. In *Solem v. Helm*,[68] the Supreme Court, in a 5-4 decision, held that imposition of life imprisonment upon a defendant who had been convicted previously of six similarly minor felonies was unconstitutional. The majority, writing through Justice Powell, declared that "a court's proportionality analysis under the Eighth Amendment should be guided by objective criteria, including (i) the gravity of the offense and the harshness of the penalty; (ii) the sentences imposed on other criminals in the same jurisdiction; and (iii) the sentences imposed for commission of the same crime in other jurisdictions."[69] The dissent, written by Chief Justice Burger, argued that "[w]hat the Court means is that a sentence is unconstitutional if it is more severe than five justices think appropriate."[70] Quoting from a previous case upholding a sentence of life imprisonment after conviction for a third nonviolent felony, the dissenters declared that "drawing lines

---

[66] RESTATEMENT (SECOND) OF CONFLICTS § 145(2) (1977) (torts; setting forth four additional factors); *id.* at § 188(2) (contracts; setting forth five additional factors).

[67] *See* W. Reese, *Choice of Law: Rules on Approach*, 57 CORNELL L. REV. 315 (1972). This approach has been criticized in F. Juenger, *Conflict of Laws: A Critique of Interest Analysis*, 32 AM. J. COMP. L. 1, 12-50 (1984); L. Brilmayer, *Interest Analysis and the Myth of Legislative Intent*, 78 MICH. L. REV. 392, 429-31 (1980); J. Ely, *Choice of Law and the State's Interest in Protecting Its Own*, 23 WM. & MARY L. REV. 173, 212-13 (1981).

[68] 463 U.S. 277 (1983).

[69] *Id.* at 292.

[70] *Id.* at 305.

between different sentences of imprisonment would thrust the Court inevitably 'into the basic line-drawing process that is pre-eminently the province of the legislature' and produce judgements that were no more than the visceral reactions of individual Justices."[71]

Needless to say, even if judges making these kinds of decisions are making the sorts of decisions that are thought to be within the province of legislators, the judges are accountable for their decisions, and their choices are constrained in some ways that legislative choices are not. And yet, while these and other institutional factors might lessen the uneasiness felt by some over what courts seem to be doing, they do not by any means eliminate it. It is not, however, the purpose of this book to debate at length the merits of factor analysis as a technique of judicial decisionmaking. The purpose of the present discussion is rather to demonstrate how different conceptions of the ideal form of legal reasoning will have important practical consequences. While no legal system exclusively favors one style of legal reasoning over another at any given period of its historical development, nevertheless at various times during that historical development, for reasons that I have indicated, a legal system will display a systemic preference for one style of legal decisionmaking over another. In the situations we have been discussing, there has been a preference for a more open-ended, a more discretionary, a more legislative style, if you will, of legal decisionmaking.

Before finishing with this discussion, one final point must be mentioned. There is certainly no necessary connection between the preference for a more discretionary or open-ended form of decisionmaking and a commitment to a particular viewpoint on the nature of the public or common good, that is on whether it is merely a composite of the goods of individual people or rather something over and above the composite of individual goods.[72] Nonetheless, as exemplified in the type of factor analysis espoused by the *Restatement (Second) of Torts* in the examples we have just examined, a tendency to define the public good as more than a

---

[71] *Id.* at 308.

[72] The type of factor analysis required by the Supreme Court of the United States in death penalty cases, for example, certainly emphasizes the need for focusing on the individual deserts of the particular defendant being sentenced rather than merely broad social needs like deterrence or retribution. *See* Gregg v. Georgia, 428 U.S. 153 (1976).

composite of individual goods often clearly comes through. As we saw, section 520 of the *Restatement (Second) of Torts* states that one of the factors that is to be considered in deciding whether the regime of strict liability should apply to an activity is the "extent to which its value to the community is outweighed by its dangerous attributes." To use another illustration, among the 11 factors to be considered in deciding which state has jurisdiction of a tort action and the 12 factors to be considered in deciding which state has jurisdiction of a contract action, the *Restatement (Second) of Conflicts* lists "the needs of the interstate and international systems."[73] This is certainly the expression of a clear preference for legal solutions in which the individual goods of the particular litigants before the court are subordinated to notions of a transcendent public or social good. Clothing a final court of appeals with the express authority to make these kinds of ultimate decisions might thus appeal to an ideal or universal audience committed to such a transcendent view of the public good, at least if it had confidence in the political and social judgment of the judges. If it did not, it might be prepared to settle for a more constrained role for judges of final appellate courts as a second-best solution.

---

[73]   RESTATEMENT (SECOND) OF CONFLICTS § 6(2)(a) (1977).

CHAPTER 11

TOLERATION OF DIVERSE AND EVEN INCONSISTENT OUTCOMES

In any complex political structure, the ideal or universal audience to which legal as well as political arguments are addressed must confront the question of the extent to which it is prepared to tolerate different and often even conflicting answers to similar problems. "Subsidiarity" has become almost a shibboleth in recent years. It seems to be almost universally accepted that, in a democratic political structure, decisions that affect human beings should be made at the lowest political level possible. But much of the euphoria for "subsidiarity" assumes that the decision made at the local level will be the same as that which would have been made at the higher and more centralized level. What if it is not? How would an ideal audience then react? This is a problem that is not confined to what we may call the political arena. The same problem arises in the law and how it is resolved has crucial significance for the nature and form of legal argumentation, that is on the style of legal argument and on what we perceive as the purpose of legal decisionmaking.

We have observed that any court with the power to control the actions of an inferior tribunal will inevitably be inclined to exercise that power even when it is conceded that the inferior tribunal was vested with a great deal of discretion. The notion of "abuse of discretion" is familiar enough in all legal systems. The tendency for superior courts to second guess inferior courts is, however, also materially influenced by the differing structural features of the various major legal systems. We have noted Damaška's contention that the more rigid hierarchical organization of civil-law systems is more antithetical to the dispersion of decisionmaking authority than would be the case in a common-law system.[1] Some of this greater tolerance shown by common-law systems for the exercise of discretion by subordinate tribunals is undoubtedly owing to the traditional common-law use of trial by jury, even in civil cases, and to the preference for presenting the case to the tribunal in the form of live testimony in a trial in which the

---

[1] *See* Chapter 6, *supra*, at pp. 63 ff.

parties, through their lawyers, and not the judges shoulder the main responsibility for how the evidence is presented as the trial proceeds.[2]

Although almost all common-law jurisdictions, other than the United States, have now largely abandoned the practice of using juries in civil cases,[3] some of the traditional deference to the determinations of juries has been transferred to the determinations of trial judges sitting without juries. Some of this was inevitable given the common-law method of trial in which, compared to civil-law systems, the trial judge is a relatively passive observer. As we have already noted, this common-law method of trial already manifests a willingness of officials with authority, namely trial judges, to defer to the decisions of counsel as to what witnesses to call, what should be the order in which the witnesses are called, and what should be the questions posed to the witnesses. When this feature of common-law adjudication is combined with a very strong preference for presenting the case through the medium of live testimony through witnesses subject to the cross examination of opposing counsel, the ability of higher courts, in a common-law system, to monitor and control the trial process is even weaker than the already weakened ability of the common-law trial judge to control the outcome of litigation.

For example, under the Judicature Acts of the 1870s, appeals from decisions of trial judges are supposed to be "rehearings," an approach markedly different from that prevailing at English common law when trial by jury is said to have been the only way in which a civil action could be tried.[4] Nonetheless, in the *Benmax* case,[5] the House of Lords declared that not all findings of fact made by trial judges are open to reexamination in appellate courts. Their lordships distinguished primary facts—what Lord Simonds called "the finding of a specific fact"—from inferences based on those facts.[6] With regard to factual questions turning on the credibility of

---

[2] Montesquieu thought that the use of jurors, as in England, made the people the holders of "the power of judging." *See* Montesquieu (Charles Louis de Secondat), THE SPIRIT OF THE LAWS, Part 2, Bk. 11, c.6, at 158 (transl. A. Cohler *et al.* 1989).

[3] Defamation cases are perhaps the only category of civil cases in which juries are still widely used in common-law countries other than the United States.

[4] *See* A. Goodhart, *Appeals of Questions of Fact*, 71 LAW Q. REV. 402, 407 (1955).

[5] Benmax v. Austin Motor Co., [1955] A.C. 370.

[6] *Id.* at 373.

witnesses, an appellate court should rarely, and then only in cases of clear error, substitute its conclusions for those of the trial court.

In the United States, of course, the use of juries in civil cases is still very common and in no danger of extinction. Nevertheless, a great number of civil cases are now tried to a judge without a jury. Focusing on only the federal courts—since this is not a legal treatise in which attention to legal detail is essential—these cases include not only cases that at one time might have been tried to a judge and jury,[7] but also cases in which, traditionally, juries were not used, such as cases arising under the federal courts' equity jurisdiction and cases arising under the exclusive federal admiralty jurisdiction. These latter categories of cases used to be tried under what purported to be a civil-law method of trial with greater emphasis, particularly in equity cases, on written evidence. In such cases, when appeals were taken, the appellate courts were not bound by trial court determinations of fact but could instead make their own factual determinations upon an independent examination of the record. Over the years, however, rather than common-law cases tried without a jury being assimilated to the equity and admiralty procedure, with a few exceptions, the opposite took place.[8] Under the Federal Rules of Civil Procedure that now apply to all civil litigation in the federal courts, a trial judge's findings of fact must be accepted by appellate courts unless those findings are "clearly erroneous."[9]

There are of course no such limitations placed on the authority of appellate judges in civil-law countries—at least at some level of the judicial process—to substitute their determinations of fact for those of the judge at first instance.[10] One would not be surprised, therefore, if this difference in

---

[7] Cases brought under the Federal Tort Claims Act, although identical with traditional common-law actions except for the fact that the United States, having waived its sovereign immunity, is the defendant, *cannot* be tried before a jury. *See* 28 U.S.C. § 2402 (1994). In traditional common-law litigation involving only private parties, juries may now be waived.

[8] The history of these developments is traced in G. Christie, *Judicial Review of Findings of Fact*, 87 NW. U. L. REV. 14, 16-17, at n.n.4-5 (1992).

[9] FED. R. CIV. P. 52(a).

[10] I recognize of course that, when cases reach the level of *cours de cassation*, review is limited to questions of law, but the statement in the text holds true of inferior civil-law

approach to the question of the deference due to the findings of fact of inferior courts might even have some effect on the temperament of appellate judges operating in these two different legal systems that would manifest itself in how they would generally approach the exercise of discretion by inferior judges on all sorts of issues.

George Fletcher, a respected contemporary student of comparative law, senses what he calls "a preference for pluralism in legal thought" "in the thinking of Anglo-American lawyers."[11] He notes that the "prominence of 'reasonableness'" as a crucial category of legal thought in common-law adjudication illustrates that "the common law does not insist upon the right answer at all times but only a reasonable or acceptable approach" to a problem. This is an approach that accepts that "there are many reasonable answers to any problem."

A recent case, *McLeod v. United Kingdom*,[12] decided by the European Court of Human Rights, a court which follows a civil-law method of decisionmaking, provides an interesting example of how a particular legal problem might be approached differently by civil-law judges than it would be by common-law judges. In *McLeod*, following the applicant's divorce from her husband, an English county court made an order for the division of personal property in the matrimonial home which, under the terms of the divorce, was to be transferred to the applicant upon her paying her ex-husband the value of his interest in their home. The applicant failed to deliver the personal property listed in the court's order to her ex-husband's solicitors within the allotted time. She was then again ordered to deliver the property to her ex-husband and this order was backed by a threat of penal sanction. She again failed to comply and an order committing her to prison was issued on September 28, 1989, but its operation was suspended for seven days to allow her to deliver the property in question on or before October 6, 1989. At the close of the hearing, the ex-husband suggested that he come by and pick up the property on October 3rd. She said that she

---

appellate tribunals.

[11] G. Fletcher, *Comparative Law as a Subversive Discipline*, 46 AM. J. COMP. L. 683, 699 (1998).

[12] 27 Eur. H. R. Rep. 493 (1999) (decided Sept. 23, 1998).

would have to consult with her solicitor before agreeing to this proposal because she would want him to be present at the time.

Believing that the applicant had agreed to his proposal, the ex-husband arrived on the premises on October 3rd with his brother and sister and a representative from his solicitors, together with two police constables whom his solicitors had asked to be present in case there were any trouble. The applicant was not at home but her elderly, infirm mother, who was present, opened the door and was informed by the constables of the court order. Whereupon she stepped aside and the ex-husband and his siblings started removing the property mentioned in the court's order. One of the constables checked the property being taken to make sure that only property mentioned in the list supplied by the ex-husband's solicitors was taken. As the ex-husband was about to drive away with the second and last load of personal property, the applicant returned home and demanded that the property which had been removed be returned to the house. One of the constables intervened and insisted that she permit the property to be removed although he let her inspect the contents of the van. The applicant then instituted criminal proceedings against her ex-husband and his brother and sister. These were dismissed. The applicant then, together with her mother, brought civil actions against her ex-husband and his brother and sister, against the ex-husband's solicitors, and against the London Metropolitan Police. The first two actions were tried in the county court and resulted in judgments in the favor of the applicant for trespass to her land and property because the judge found that there had been no agreement that the ex-husband could take the property on October 3rd.[13]

The third action, the one against the police, was tried in the High Court and ultimately turned on whether the police, in entering the applicant's premises, had entered in the exercise of the common-law privilege enjoyed by the police to enter private property over the objection of its owner to prevent a breach of the peace. The trial judge found that the police constables had reasonable grounds for believing that a breach of the peace might take place and that therefore their entry was privileged. Accordingly,

---

[13] The applicant and the estate of her mother— the mother who had been recovering from a stroke and who had high blood pressure at the time of the events in question having died while the action was pending—recovered £1,950 with interest and costs.

he dismissed the case. An appeal was taken to the Court of Appeal.[14] As we have already noted, since the judicature acts of the latter part of the nineteenth century, appeals from the decision of trial judges sitting without a jury are considered rehearings but, as we have also already noticed, considerable deference is nevertheless accorded to the factual findings of trial judges. In the Court of Appeals, the trial judge's findings of fact and his reasoning were set out by Lord Justice Neill in a judgment concurred in by the two other judges who heard the case and who did not issue separate judgments. He then concluded "I, for my part, can see no basis for upsetting his decision on these facts."[15] The Court of Appeal refused permission to appeal to the House of Lords and, when the applicant sought leave from the appeals committee of the House of Lords, that body in turn also refused her request for leave to appeal.[16]

Finding herself foreclosed from further relief in Great Britain, the applicant sought relief from the European Commission of Human Rights on the ground, *inter alia,* that the actions of the police constables were in violation of Article 8 of the European Convention for the Protection of Human Rights and Fundamental Freedoms which provides that "[e]veryone has a right to respect for his private . . . life [and] his home" and that "there shall be no interference by a public authority with the exercise of this right except such as is in accordance with the law and is necessary in a democratic society in the interests of national security, public safety or the economic well-being of the country, for the prevention of disorders or crime" as well as for other reasons not presently germane. By a vote of fourteen to two the Commission declared its opinion that there had been no violation of the applicant's rights under Article 8 of the Convention. The case was then referred by the Commission to the European Court of Human Rights which, in a seven to two decision, noted the findings of the European Commission and of the British courts and then made its own finding that, although British law could provide for entry into someone's property against that person's objections to prevent a breach of the peace, under the circumstances of the instant case the entry by the constables was not

---

[14] [1994] 4 All E.R. 553 (C.A.).

[15] *Id.* at 560.

[16] *Id.* at 561.

necessary. The applicant's rights under Article 8 of the Convention were therefore violated.[17]

The English judge, Sir John Freeland, joined by one of his colleagues, dissented in an opinion which gave much greater emphasis to the findings of the British trial judge and chided the majority for giving "insufficient weight" to certain findings of the trial judge such as that, although the applicant had not been present when the initial entry was made to remove the property, the constables could not know that she might not return while the property was being removed and therefore could conclude that they should remain in the driveway until the removal of the property had been completed.[18] The majority had concluded, in contrast, that upon being informed that the applicant was not at home, the constables should not have entered the home because there was "little or no risk of disorder."[19] According to the majority, the fact that an altercation occurred upon her return home was "immaterial in ascertaining whether the police officers were justified in entering the property initially."

I am not concerned with the question of whether the constables were or were not justified in what they did. I merely use the *McLeod* case to illustrate my point that common-law judges, even when they have the power to substitute their findings of fact for those of the trial court, might be much more reluctant to do so than are continental judges. That is they are prepared to tolerate the sort of variability of result, which of course was inevitable when trial by jury was the norm in civil cases, as is still largely the case in the United States, than are judges trained in the civil-law tradition. This was the situation in the *McLeod* case, in which the English Court of Appeal, as well as the European Court of Human Rights, was faced *not* with a challenge to any specific fact found by the trial judge but, rather, with an attack on the trial court's conclusions based upon a consideration of the largely uncontested specific facts of record.

---

[17] The European Court of Human Rights declared that the finding of a violation of her rights was sufficient satisfaction for any non-pecuniary damage the applicant might have suffered. She was granted a judgment for £15,000 for costs and expenses.

[18] 27 Eur. H. R. Rep. at 519. (para. 5 of the dissent).

[19] *Id.* at 515. (para. 57 of the judgment).

One is left with the impression that there are other stylistic differences between the forms and methods of legal argumentation employed in civil-law countries and those employed in common-law countries that can have a profound influence on the results reached by the courts in those jurisdictions. It seems, for example, to be characteristic of civil-law jurisdictions that, as cases wind their way up the hierarchy of appellate courts, they come to lose their character as a discreet dispute between the parties and become the vehicle for sweeping theoretical and ahistorical assertions about the "law" to a greater extent than is characteristic of cases winding their way up the appellate ladder in a common-law jurisdiction, where the minutiae of the actual facts of the case and the historical development of the law applicable to the case always continue to figure in the reasoning of the highest appellate courts. This feature of civil-law adjudication is obvious in judicial bodies, such as the French and Belgian *Cours de Cassation* and the German Federal Court of Justice, to which appeal is permitted only on questions of law, but it can also manifest itself in other ways as well. We noted in Chapter 3 the marked contrast between the willingness of the German Constitutional Court to find a basis in the German Constitution for the recognition of welfare rights and the unwillingness of the Supreme Court of the United States to find any such abstract rights in the American Constitution.[20] There are obviously textual differences between the German Constitution and the American Constitution but is it too much to suggest that stylistic differences between civil-law and common-law adjudication, such as the preference of the former for an impersonal and rather abstract didactic style of opinion-writing, also play their part? Such a preference may also help account for the greater reluctance of civil-law jurisdictions to tolerate the exercise of discretion by subordinate decisionmakers because they are less likely to accept, as Fletcher put it, that there are "many reasonable answers to a problem."[21]

---

[20] *See* Chapter 5, *supra*, at pp. 61-62.
[21] *See supra*, p. 184, at n.11.

A good example is perhaps the case of *A v. The United Kingdom*,[22] another case decided by the European Court of Human Rights, whose procedures and style of judicial decisionmaking are, as we have already seen, patterned after a civil-law and not a common-law model and which, unlike *cours de cassation*, is prepared to explore factual questions. In that case, a nine-year-old boy had been "hit with a stick by his stepfather" on probably more than one occasion and sufficiently severely to leave a number of bruises on the boy's body. The stepfather was charged with assault occasioning actual bodily harm and tried in an English court before a judge and jury, as one would expect in a common-law jurisdiction. The stepfather's defense was based on the admitted fact that the victim was a "difficult boy" and that the beating had been a necessary and reasonable exercise of parental discipline. The trial judge instructed the jury that the burden was on the prosecution to prove, beyond a reasonable doubt, that the force used was unreasonable. The jury thereupon, by a majority verdict, voted to acquit the defendant stepfather. Whereupon a proceeding on behalf of the boy against the United Kingdom was brought before the European Commission of Human Rights which, in turn, eventually referred the case to the European Court of Human Rights. In reliance on Article 3 of the European Convention for the Protection of Human Rights and Fundamental Freedoms which declares that "[n]o one shall be subjected to torture or to inhuman or degrading treatment or punishment," the European Court of Human Rights found that the stepfather's acquittal violated the convention by not providing adequate protection against the "treatment or punishment" that he had received. It noted that children were "entitled to state protection in the form of effective deterrence." The boy sought compensation for the grave physical abuse he had suffered and for the emotional distress of enduring "the trauma of criminal proceedings" which resulted in the acquittal of his stepfather. The court awarded the boy £10,000 as "compensation for non-pecuniary damages" and up to £20,000 in costs.

In the course of the proceedings, the United Kingdom promised to amend its domestic law, but the European Court of Human Rights'

---

[22] 27 Eur. H. R. Rep. 611 (1999) (decided Sept. 23, 1998) which, as can be seen, was decided on the same day as the *McLeod* case. Both cases were heard by nine-member panels and four judges sat on both cases.

judgment does not indicate in what way.   By outlawing all forms of parental corporal punishment as a species of "degrading treatment" under Article 3 of the European Convention?[23] By specifying in greater detail what constitutes unreasonable force? By placing the burden of persuasion on the issue of reasonable force on the defendant? By making the jury's determination no longer final?   In the United States that would be constitutionally impossible. The finality of a jury's acquittal in a criminal case is in no way affected by its lack of reasonable basis. The same is true if a jury is waived and the case is tried to a judge alone. At any rate, to a common-law lawyer, it does seem odd to use one short sentence of an international convention to assess damages against a state for a jury's acquittal of a defendant, however perverse that acquittal might seem to others. If the state itself was not in any way implicated in the inhuman treatment of the plaintiff, in a common-law jurisdiction the plaintiff's only remedy would be an action against the person who injured him. Leaving this last consideration aside, the European Court of Human Rights' decision clearly reflects more than a disagreement with the British jury's finding of reasonableness. Is it too far-fetched to suggest that the case also evidences, in a more profound way, a hint of the same predilection to assert hierarchical control over subordinate decisionmakers that we have already noted in our discussion of the *McLeod* case?

Of course, even within a particular legal system, some judges either by temperament or basic philosophical outlook might be inclined to a more abstract or less abstract style of legal argument. A good example is the House of Lord's first decision in the *Pinochet* extradition case.[24] By far the

---

[23] The United Kingdom has now abolished corporal punishment in all schools, private as well as state-run or state-supported. *See* School Standards and Framework Act 1998, 1998, c. 31, § 131 amending § 548 of the Education Act, 1996. In Costello-Roberts v. the United Kingdom, 19 Eur. H. R. Rep. 112 (1995) (Mar. 25, 1993), the European Court of Human Rights, in a sharply divided judgment, refused to hold, in the circumstances of that case, that the corporal punishment administered was severe enough or sufficiently long-lasting in its effects to constitute inhuman or degrading punishment. There has not, however, been any legislation or convention specifically banning corporal punishment by parents.

[24] Regina v. Bow Street Metropolitan Stipendiary Magistrate, *ex parte* Pinochet Ugarte, [1998] 3 W.L.R. 1456 (H.L.).

two longest speeches were those delivered by Lord Slynn and Lord Lloyd, both of whom concluded that General Pinochet enjoyed immunity from judicial process in Great Britain for the offenses with which he had been charged by the Spanish magistrates who were seeking his extradition. They examined the historical development of the act of state doctrine in the British and American courts and the precedents in both of these common-law jurisdictions on the ability of national courts to exercise jurisdiction over current and former heads of state. They also considered the British Sovereign Immunity Act of 1978, which, by reference to an earlier act of the British Parliament, incorporated the provisions of the Vienna Convention on Diplomatic Relations of 1961. Although the text of that treaty is unclear as to its applicability to *former* heads of state, all of their lordships accepted that it did so apply. As so construed, the convention provided for immunity of former heads of state for all actions performed in their capacity as heads of state. Since the criminal acts that General Pinochet was accused of performing were performed while he was head of state, Lord Slynn and Lord Lloyd concluded that he enjoyed immunity from criminal prosecution in the United Kingdom. Both Lord Slynn and Lord Lloyd believed, furthermore, that the 1978 act gave Pinochet the same immunity from criminal process in the United Kingdom as he would have enjoyed at common law. Their two speeches took up almost 36 pages in the Weekly Law Reports.

The speeches of the three law lords who formed the majority and who held that Pinochet was subject to the jurisdiction of the British Courts to determine whether extradition to Spain was warranted took up only a little more than 12 pages in the Weekly Law Reports.[25] The longest of these speeches was delivered by Lord Nicholls. Although he made some reference to common-law-act-of-state cases, he declared that the principal question was whether Pinochet was entitled to immunity under the 1978 act. Given that the acts charged against Pinochet included torture and the taking of hostages, he concluded that the immunity granted by that act to former

---

[25] Since he gave the first speech, Lord Slynn's speech does contain more procedural detail than do the other speeches, but this would only account for one to two pages of the discrepancy between the length of the speeches of the two dissenters and the length of the speeches of the three members of the majority.

heads of state for official acts did not cover torture or the taking of hostages. Since torture and the taking of hostages are outlawed by international conventions that had been incorporated by statute into the law of the United Kingdom, such acts could not be considered performed by former heads of state in their capacity as heads of state. Lord Steyn reached the same conclusion and devoted even less space to the common-law-act-of-state cases. Lord Hoffmann simply agreed with the speeches of Lord Nicholls and Lord Steyn.[26]

It is hard to find a recent British case with such a marked difference in style of decision between the majority and the minority than that displayed in this case. For the majority, this was a relatively straightforward application of a few clear principles of international law. For the minority, it was a difficult case requiring a careful analysis of a long historical process and, in their speeches, they exhibited a great diffidence about the ability of judges to decide what purported acts of a head of state were properly to be considered acts of a head of state and which were not.

As is well known, of course, when the *Pinochet* case was reheard by a panel of seven, and not the usual five law lords, their lordships, in a 6-1 decision, held that Pinochet could only be extradited for acts of torture committed after December 8, 1988.[27] This was the date on which the United Kingdom's ratification of the International Convention Against Torture became effective and torture committed outside the United Kingdom became a crime punishable under the law of the United Kingdom. Their lordships noted that Chile's ratification of the Convention had become effective on October 30, 1988 and that, thus, torture was also now

---

[26] Is it merely coincidence that Lord Hoffmann and Lord Steyn were born in South Africa and received their initial legal training and began their legal careers there? *See* their respective entries in WHO'S WHO 1999. South African law is derived from Roman- Dutch law, although it has of course been influenced by English law. *See* T. Reynolds and A. Flores, FOREIGN LAW, Vol. III, entry on South Africa.

[27] Regina v. Bow Street Metropolitan Stipendiary Magistrate, *ex parte* Pinochet Ugarte (No.3), [1999] 2 W.L.R. 827 (H.L.). The case was reheard because it turned out that Lord Hoffman was chairman of a British fund-raising affiliate of Amnesty International which had been granted leave to intervene in the appellate stages of the case and this association was not disclosed to Pinochet's counsel. Regina v. Bow Street Metropolitan Stipendiary Magistrate, *ex parte* Pinochet Ugarte (No.2), [1999] 2 W.L.R. 272 (H.L.).

accepted by Chile as being unlawful under international law and punishable in Chile. Accordingly, no immunity granted by English law to former heads of state was available to Pinochet as to these crimes. It is a much more limited and less sweeping judgment than the one issued by the majority that heard the case the first time it was argued in the House of Lords.

It is not the purpose of this book to pass judgment on the merits of one or the other styles of legal reasoning. It would of course be disingenuous of me to pretend that I do not have a preference for a less abstract and a more particularized style of legal decisionmaking. Nevertheless, the point I wish to make here is that the accepted style of legal reasoning has a profound effect on the substance of the decisions that courts will make. Style is not a matter of mere form. It sometimes has a decisive influence on the decision of cases. That is one more reason why the way the members of a particular legal community view the form, structure and methods of the ideal legal argument—the argument that would be approved by the ideal or universal audiences presupposed by those legal communities—is an important subject for careful study. That is what I have been trying to do in this book.

CHAPTER 12

CONCLUSION

In this book we have examined how our concept of the ideal or universal audience profoundly affects the style, form and substance of legal argumentation. That each person constructs a vision of an ideal audience is indisputable. It is also indisputable that for most people this ideal audience is, to use Perelman's term that has also been adopted by Habermas,[1] a universal audience. One of the themes of this book is that these visions of an ideal universal audience are widely shared. That is, it is not merely the case that we, as individuals, conceive the ideal audience as a universal audience, but that our individual visions of the ideal audience coincide with the visions of others. Some of these visions are shared among people belonging to a certain culture. Other visions are shared by people who, although belonging to different cultures, attribute certain universal characteristics to certain forms of human endeavor. Finally, we have seen that some visions of an ideal audience are coming to be accepted as truly universal and applicable to all types of human endeavor.

The international convention against torture is one of many instances of the growing body of international civil-rights law that clearly illustrates that there is indeed a common vision as to some features of the ideal audience, a vision that is truly universal in every sense of that term. Our vision of the qualities required in a judge and our expectations as to how a judge should go about performing his functions share some of this truly universal character, but these universal expectations only apply to people insofar as they are acting in a judicial capacity. We have explored the content of these visions of the ideal audience[2] and noted that some of these truly universal features have also, to some extent, informed our understanding of what sort of behavior is appropriate for those who play the role of counsel in legal proceedings. Indeed, some of these universal features are accepted as applying even to those who participate in legal proceedings only as parties. They are expected, at the very least, to behave with a certain degree of decorum and to exhibit a certain degree of candor in dealing with the tribunal and especially with their counsel.

---

[1] *See* Chapter 3, *supra*, at p. 27.
[2] *See* Chapter 4, *supra*.

A substantial portion of this book has, finally, been devoted to exploring those features of the ideal audience that figure in legal argumentation and are widely shared within particular cultures but are not shared by members of other legal cultures. Our discussion of the different techniques of statutory interpretation prevailing in common-law as opposed to civil-law countries illustrates this point,[3] as does our discussion in the last few chapters of the different positions taken by different types of legal systems as to the scope of the discretion that will be granted to subordinate judicial decisionmakers. We have seen in those chapters how our attitudes to all these questions are influenced not only by the different substantive preferences shared by members of particular legal communities but also by the differing expectations of these discrete legal communities concerning the style and form of legal argumentation and the allocation of roles among the various participants in the legal process.[4]

The recitation of similarities and differences among various legal systems does not, however, exhaust our subject. No aspect of human social life is static, although some aspects are more deeply ingrained and longer lasting than others. Even within particular legal systems the felt need to respond to acute social pressure will influence how a legal system will respond to the question of the appropriate level of discretion that should be allowed not only to subordinate decisionmakers but also to the highest judicial tribunals themselves. Moreover, every question that we have considered is, as we have noted, ultimately influenced by the vision that members of a given political society have of the nature of the public good and of the purpose of the state. Is the public good largely a composite of individual goods or is it a collective social good that transcends the interests of mere individuals? Is the state a protector and accommodator of the needs and desires of its citizens as they are or does it have the further purpose of actually changing and forming their desires? While Mao's China is an

---

[3] *See* Chapter 5, *supra.*

[4] Consider the willingness of the German Constitutional Court to recognize judicially enforced welfare rights in contrast to the refusal of the United States Supreme Court to do so. *See* Chapter 5, *supra*, at pp. 59-60. Unlike the United States and German constitutions, many modern constitutions expressly recognize welfare rights. *See, e.g.,* Articles 21 and 22 of the Greek Constitution of 1975. To what extent such rights are judicially enforceable against the state is another matter.

extreme situation, all states, to some extent, use legally authorized coercion to engage in some amount of social reeducation. No one, for example, who examines the change in public attitudes to racial and sexual equality in the United States over the last fifty years can have any doubt about that[5] nor of the fact that most Americans would agree that this has been a good thing.

This book has also exposed some problems that will become increasingly acute. In the last few chapters, for example, we discussed a number of differences between the visions of the ideal audience entertained by different legal cultures that are not merely matters of intellectual interest among scholars and of those whose legal practice forces them to bridge different legal cultures. These differences are rather matters that will have important practical consequences for the vast majority of the members of those respective legal cultures. This is the inevitable consequence of developments such as the growing international recognition of individual human rights and obligations and also, and more importantly, to the growing acceptance of the possibility of international tribunals to adjudicate those rights and obligations, such as the European Court of Human Rights and the proposals for a permanent international criminal court to deal with war crimes and other crimes against humanity. At the same time as these manifestations of the increasing globalization of the world legal order are unfolding, the notion of subsidiarity, of decision on the lowest political level possible, has achieved prominence as the guarantor of democratic legitimacy. How will the twin imperatives of globalization and subsidiarity be reconciled?

The different visions of the ideal audience to which legal argument is addressed are partly the effect of historical development. They also, however, often reflect a profoundly different vision of the purpose and function of the state. Moreover, as we have seen, even if there is a shared vision of the purpose and function of the state, there are some very deep disagreements over how closely national tribunals must be supervised in order to insure uniformity in the application of the law. We saw, in the last

---

[5] It would be almost impossible to overestimate the importance of Brown v. Board of Education, 347 U.S. 483 (1954) and the subsequent federal civil rights legislation in bringing about a fundamental change in the attitude of most Americans on racial questions.

chapter, that European Court of Human Rights, in the *McLeod* case, was prepared to exercise a degree of scrutiny over the findings of trial courts that was much greater than is customary in common-law countries, particularly in the United States with its heavy reliance on juries in civil cases.[6] When we turned to criminal proceedings, we saw that the parallel suggestions, in *A v. The United Kingdom*,[7] that a state might be liable to its own citizens, because an international court found a jury's verdict of acquittal perverse, would be totally unacceptable in the United States. If these portions of the legal universe are to be governed by international law and if adjudication by international tribunals is to be expanded, the questions presented by these potential conflicts must be addressed.

Finally, one last point needs mention in this regard. It concerns not the question of appellate control over subordinate tribunals nor even the role and function of the state or the international legal order. It concerns how the internationalization of law and the growth of international tribunals might be affected by and in turn affect the style of legal argumentation. We have noted the obvious differences between the discursive, particularistic style of common-law adjudication with the more impersonal, didactic style of civil-law adjudication with its greater reliance on abstract principles. I would submit that the form in which the exercise of judicial power is authorized in statutory instruments may be the source of perhaps greater problems. In the previous chapter we saw that the *McLeod* case was brought under Article 8 of the European Convention for the Protection of Human Rights and Fundamental Freedoms which, in the portions quoted by the European Court of Human Rights, provides:

(1) Everyone has the right to respect for his private and family life, his home and his correspondence.
(2) There shall be no interference by a public authority with the exercise of this right except such as is in accordance with the law and is necessary in a democratic society in the interests of national security, public safety or the economic well-being of the country, for the prevention of disorder or crime, for the protection of health or morals, or for the protection of the rights and freedoms of others.

---

[6] *See* Chapter 11, *supra*, at pp. 183-86.
[7] *Id.* at 188-89.

It is worth considering whether there is a universal consensus that the ideal audience, to whom legal argumentation is addressed in constitutional adjudication, would be prepared to give a court such a *carte blanche* to decide what the needs of a democratic society are. And yet, the form in which human rights are described in the constitutions of many nations has increasingly taken the form in which Article 8, and several other articles of the European Convention are worded, including Article 10 which provides a guarantee of freedom of expression. For example, the "Constitution of Canada," guarantees a number of "fundamental freedoms," such as freedom of expression and of peaceful assembly, but these guarantees are subject to "such reasonable limits prescribed by law as can be demonstrably justified in a free and democratic society."[8] Poland,[9] South Africa,[10] and Nigeria[11] are among other countries with similar guarantees subject to exceptions on similar grounds. This contrasts with the absolute terms in which many of the provisions of the American Bill of Rights are worded. For example, the First Amendment to the American Constitution declares that "Congress shall make no law respecting an establishment of religion, or prohibiting the free exercise thereof; or abridging the freedom of speech, or the press." The Sixth and Seventh Amendments to the American Constitution provide for the right to a jury trial in criminal and civil cases, respectively, in similarly absolute terms. American courts may sometimes feel obliged to read some limits to these rights,[12] but they must do so in the full awareness of the

---

[8] The principal enumeration of personal rights is contained in the Canadian Charter of Rights and Freedoms, Schedule B, Part I, § 2 of the Constitution Act, 1982, but the rights enumerated in that and other sections are subject to the general statement in § 1, that "[t]he Canadian Charter of Rights and Freedoms guarantees the rights and freedoms set out in it subject only to such reasonable limits prescribed by law as can be demonstrably justified in a free and democratic society."

[9] Constitution of the Republic of Poland, 1997, art. 31.

[10] Constitution of the Republic of South Africa, 1996, art. 36.

[11] Constitution of the Federal Republic of Nigeria, 1989, § 43.

[12] Although the reluctance of American courts to countenance any prior restraints of the press are well known, many Justices have refused to rule out the possibility that an injunction might be available in wartime to restrain publication of the date upon which a convoy would sail. *See e.g.*, New York Times Co. v. United States, 403 U.S. 713 (1971), at 725 (Brennan, J., concurring); *id.* at 742 (Marshall, J., concurring). This was the famous *Pentagon Papers* case.

tension between their decisions and the actual text of the American Constitution. Other American constitutional guarantees are expressed in qualified terms, such as the Fourth Amendment affirmation of '[t]he right of the people to be secure in their persons, houses, papers and effects, against unreasonable searches and seizures," but, it should be noted, the qualification in that amendment focuses on the unreasonableness of the search and not upon the ultimate social purposes sought to be achieved by the search.[13] The due process clauses are also open-ended but, it should be noted, these have been used to restrict the power of government and not, as do the exceptions in the European Convention, to permit government to limit the freedom of individuals.

The universal audiences to whom modern democratic societies address their arguments would certainly all agree that freedom of expression is a basic human right. They would not all agree, however, that permitting limitations of that right by means of such loosely-worded exceptions clauses is an adequate means of protecting those basic rights. It certainly runs contra to the more absolute wording of the United States Constitution, which presupposes an ideal audience that is reluctant to give government officials the authority to decide when some notion of the public good can override the basic freedoms of discrete individuals. Obviously the ideal audiences presupposed as the addressees of constitutional argument in the other nations to whose constitutions we have just referred are less suspicious of the ability of public officials to balance the demands of the public good against the basic freedoms of the individual. In the United States, the broad-ranging type of potential state curtailment of individual liberty authorized by the European Convention would be considered intolerable. Only if there were a background of several hundred cases fleshing out what infringements of individual liberties are permitted in the light of what is "necessary in a democratic society" could one even imagine that such a provision in a basic declaration of individual rights might

---

[13]   It should not be forgotten that the Fourth Amendment was adopted against a background of resistance to the British Government's use of searches, pursuant to general warrants, to suppress political dissent. *See e.g.,* Entick v. Carrington, 95 Eng. Rep. 807 (K.B. 1765), cited and relied upon in Boyd v. United States, 116 U.S. 616, 626 (1886). That is, it was adopted to prevent reasons of state from being used to justify searches and seizures.

possibly receive the assent of the ideal audience to whom constitutional arguments in the United States are addressed.

It certainly is not the purpose of this book to attempt to dictate how the increasing globalization of the world should be reflected in international legal instruments. I merely wish to point out that it is not merely a question of getting people to agree that incorporating certain substantive provisions into international law would be a good thing. The question of *how* these provisions would be incorporated into international law is equally important and possibly an even more daunting problem.

MODEL PENAL CODE AND COMMENTARIES (OFFICIAL DRAFT AND REVISED
    COMMENTS 1985).

RESTATEMENT OF TORTS (1934).

RESTATEMENT (SECOND) OF TORTS (1965).

RESTATEMENT (SECOND) OF CONFLICTS (1977).

Comment, *Justice Story, Slavery, and the Natural Law Foundations of
    American Constitutionalism*, 55 U. CHI. L. REV. 273 (1988).

Alexander, L., *Self-Defense, Justification and Excuse*, 22 PHIL. & PUB. AFF. 60
    (1993).

Alexy, A THEORY OF LEGAL ARGUMENTATION (R. and N. MacCormick transl.
    1989).

Aquinas, Saint Thomas, SUMMA THEOLOGIA.

Aristotle, METAPHYSICS.

Aristotle, NICOMACHEAN ETHICS.

Aristotle, THE POLITICS.

Aune, B., KNOWLEDGE, MIND, AND NATURE (1967).

Austin, J., LECTURES ON JURISPRUDENCE (R. Campbell ed. 1885).

Barrows, N., BLOW ALL BALLAST! (1941).

Benvenisti, E, *The Role of National Courts in Preventing Torture of suspected
    Terrorists*, 8 E.J.I.L. 596 (1997).

Bickel, A., THE LEAST DANGEROUS BRANCH (1962).

Bohlen, F., *Incomplete Privilege to Inflict Intentional Invasions of Interests of
    Property and Personality*, 39 HARV. L. REV. 307 (1926).

Brodie, F., AN INTIMATE HISTORY (1974).

Carter, J., LAW: ITS ORIGIN, GROWTH, AND FUNCTION (1907).

Christie, G., *The Defense of Necessity Considered from the Legal and Moral
    Points of View*, 48 DUKE L. J. 975 (1999)

Christie, G., *Dworkin's Empire*, 1987 DUKE L. J. 157 (1987).

Christie, G., *An Essay on Discretion*, 1986 DUKE L. J. 747 (1986).

Christie, G., *Judicial Review of Findings of Fact*, 87 NW. U. L. REV. 14 (1992).

Christie, G., JURISPRUDENCE: TEXT AND READINGS ON THE PHILOSOPHY OF
    LAW (1973).

Christie, G., LAW, NORMS AND AUTHORITY (1982).

Christie, G., *The Model of Principles*, 1968 DUKE L. J. 649 (1968).

Christie, G., *The Notion of Validity in Modern Jurisprudence*, 48 MINN. L.
    REV. (1964).

Christie, G., *Objectivity in the Law*, 78 YALE L .J. 1311 (1969)

Christie, G., *On the Moral Obligation to Obey the Law*, 1990 DUKE L. J. 1311 (1990).

Coleman, J., RISKS AND WRONGS (1992).

Costa, M., *Another Trip on the Trolley*, 25 S. J. PHIL. 461 (1987).

Costa, M., *The Trolley Problem Revisited*, 24 S. J. PHIL. 437 (1986).

Cover, R., JUSTICE ACCUSED (1975).

Dabin, J., GENERAL THEORY OF LAW (1944).

Damaška, M., *On Circumstances Favoring Codification*, 52 REVISTA JURIDICA DE LA UNIVERSIDAD DE PUERTO RICO 355 (1983).

Damaška, M., THE FACES OF JUSTICE AND STATE AUTHORITY (1986).

David, R. and Brierly, J., MAJOR LEGAL SYSTEMS IN THE WORLD TODAY (3d Eng. ed. 1985).

Dunne, F., MR. DOOLEY'S OPINIONS (1901).

Dworkin, R., FREEDOM'S LAW (1996).

Dworkin, R., *Hard Cases*, 88 HARV. L. REV. 1057 (1972).

Dworkin, R., *Law as Interpretation*, 60 TEX. L. REV. 527 (1982).

Dworkin, R., A MATTER OF PRINCIPLE (1985).

Dworkin, R., *The Model of Rules*, 35 U. CHI L. REV. 14 (1967).

Dworkin, R., *No Right Answer?*, 53 N. Y. U. L. REV. 1 (1978).

Dworkin, R., *The Original Position*, 40 U. CHI. L. REV. 500 (1973).

Dworkin, R., TAKING RIGHTS SERIOUSLY (1977).

Emerson, R., SELF RELIANCE, IN ESSAYS: FIRST SERIES (Random House ed. 1944).

Enker, A., *Duress, Self-Defence and Necessity in Israeli Law*, 30 ISRAELI L. REV. 188 (1996).

Fairman, C., RECONSTRUCTION AND REUNION 1864-88 (1971).

Feinberg, J., *Voluntary Euthanasia and the Right to Life*, 7 PHIL & PUB. AFF. 93 (1978).

Finnis, J., NATURAL LAW AND NATURAL RIGHTS (1980).

Fiss, O., LIBERALISM DIVIDED (1996).

Fletcher, G., *Comparative Law as a Subversive Discipline*, 46 AM. J. COMP. L. 683 (1998).

Fletcher, G., RETHINKING CRIMINAL LAW (1978).

Fletcher, G., *The Right and the Reasonable*, 98 HARV. L. REV. 949 (1985).

Foot, P., *The Problem of Abortion and the Doctrine of the Double Effect*, 5 OXFORD REV. 5 (1967).

Frank, J., LAW AND THE MODERN MIND (1930).

Fuller, L., THE MORALITY OF LAW (1964).

Gény, F., Methode o'Interprétation et Sources en Droit Privé Positif (1899).

Gert, B., *Transplants and Trolleys*, 53 Phil. & Phenom. Res. 173 (1993).

Geuss, R., The Idea of a Critical Theory (1981).

Greenawalt, K., *Discretion and Judicial Decision*, 75 Colum. L. Rev. 359 (1975).

Greenawalt, K., *The Perplexing Borders Between Justification and Excuse*, 84 Colum. L. Rev. 1897 (1984).

Greenawalt, K., Policy, Rights and Judicial Decisions (1977).

Golding, M., *Liberal Theory and Jewish Politics*, in Tikkun Olam: Social Responsibilty in Jewish Thought and Law (D. Shatz ed. 1997).

Goodhart, A., *Appeals of Questions of Fact*, 71 Law Q. Rev. 402 (1955).

Gunter, G., Learned Hand: The Man and the Judge (1994).

Guttmann, A. and Thompson, D., Democracy and Disagreement (1996).

Habermas, J., Between Facts and Norms (1997).

Habermas, J., Moral Consciousness and Communicative Action (C. Lenhardt and S. Nicholson transl. 1990).

Habermas, J., Theory and Practice (J. Viertel transl. 1973).

Hägerström, A., Inquiries into the Nature of Law and Morals (C. D. Broad transl. 1953).

Hallborg, R., Jr., *Comparing Harms: the Lesser Evil Defense and the Trolley Problem*, 3 Legal Theory 291 (1997).

Harper, F. et al., The Law of Torts (3d ed. by O. Gray 1996).

Harris, J., *The Survival Lottery*," 50 Phil 81 (1975).

Hart, H.L.A., The Concept of Law (1961).

Hart, H.L.A., *Scandinavian Realism*, [1959] Camb. L. J. 233.

Hart, H.L.A., *Book Review*, 78 Harv. L. Rev. 1281 (1965).

Herrnstein Smith, B., Belief and Resistance: Dynamics of Contemporary Controversy (1997).

Higgenbotham, A. L., Jr., *An Open Letter to Justice Clarence Thomas from a Federal Judicial Colleague*," 140 U. Pa. L. Rev. 1005 (1992).

Hobbes, T., Leviathan (European ed. 1914).

Holmes, O. W., Jr., *The Path of the Law*," 10 Harv. L. Rev. 457 (1897).

Hume, D., A Treatise of Human Nature (L. Selby-Biggs ed. 1888).

The Life and Selected Writings of Thomas Jefferson (Mod. Lib. ed. A. Koch & W. Peden 1944).

Jhering, R. von., Law as a Means to an End (I. Husik transl. 1924).

Kalman, L., Legal Realism at Yale, 1927-1960 (1986).

Kamm, F., *Harming Some to Save Others*, 57 PHIL. STUD. 227 (1989).

Kant, I., FOUNDATIONS OF THE METAPHYSICS OF MORALS (L. White transl. 1969) (1785).

Kant, I., THE METAPHYSICAL ELEMENTS OF JUSTICE (J. Ladd transl. 1965) (1797).

Katz, L., ILL-GOTTEN GAINS (1996).

Keeton, W. P. et al., PROSSER AND KEETON ON THE LAW OF TORTS (5th ed. 1984).

Keeton, R., *Conditional Fault in the Law of Torts*, 72 HARV. L. REV. 401 (1959).

Kelsen, H., GENERAL THEORY OF LAW AND STATE (A. Wedberg transl. 1945).

Kelsen, H., THE PURE THEORY OF LAW (2d ed. M. Knight transl. 1987).

Kuhn, T., THE STRUCTURE OF SCIENTIFIC REVOLUTIONS (1962).

La Vo, C., BACK FROM THE DEEP (1994).

Lewellyn, K., THE COMMON LAW TRADITION (1960).

Lewellyn, K., *A Realistic Jurisprudence—The Next Step*, 30 COLUM. L. REV. 431 (1930).

Malone, D., JEFFERSON AND THE ORDEAL OF LIBERTY (1962).

Markesinis, B., *Privacy, Freedom of Expression, and the Horizontal Effect of the Human Rights Bill: Lessons from Germany*, 115 LAW. Q. REV. 47 (1999).

Mead, G. H., MIND SELF, & SOCIETY (1934).

Meikeljohn, A., FREE SPEECH AND ITS RELATION TO SELF-GOVERNMENT (1948).

Michelman, F., *The Supreme Court 1968 Term-Foreword: On Protecting the Poor through the Fourteenth Amendment*, 83 HARV. L. REV. 7 (1969).

Miller, N., WAR AT SEA (1995).

Montesquieu, (Charles Louis de Secondat), THE SPIRIT OF THE LAWS (transl. A. Cohler et al. 1989).

Moore, M., PLACING BLAME (1997).

New Mayer, R. K., SUPREME COURT JUSTICE STORY (1985).

Oakeshott, M., RATIONALISM IN POLITICS AND OTHER ESSAYS (1991).

Oliphant, H., *A Return to Stare Decisis*, 14 AM. BAR ASS'N J. 71 (1928).

Olivecrona, K., LAW AS FACT (1939).

Olivecrona, K., LAW AS FACT (2d ed. 1971).

Otsuka, M., *Killing the Innocent in Self Defense*, 27 PHIL & PUB. AFF. 74 (1994).

Perelman, Ch. and Olbrechts-Tyteca, L., THE NEW RHETORIC: A TREATISE OF ARGUMENTATION (J. Wilkinson and P. Weaver transl. 1969).

Pierson, H., JEFFERSON AT MONTICELLO: THE PRIVATE LIFE OF THOMAS JEFFERSON (1862).

Popkin, W., *The Collaborative Model of Statutory Interpretation*, 61 SO. CAL. L. REV. 541 (1988).

Pound, R., *Hierarchy of Sources in Different Systems of Law*, 7 TUL. L. REV. 475 (1933).

Pound, R., *Individual Interest of Substance—-Promised Advantage*, 59 HARV. L. REV. 1 (1945).

Pound, R., *Interests of Personality*, 28 HARV. L. REV. 343 (1915).

Pound, R., *Mechanical Jurisprudence*, 8 COLUM L. REV. 605 (1908).

Prosser, W., HANDBOOK OF THE LAW OF TORTS (4th ed. 1971).

Prosser, W., *Privacy*, 48 CAL. L. REV. 383 (1960).

Puchta, G., OUTLINES OF JURISPRUDENCE AS THE SCIENCE OF RIGHT (W. Hastie transl. 1887).

Rakes, P., *Casualties on the Homefront: Scotts Run Mining Disasters During World War II*," 53 W. VA. HIST. REV. 95 (1994).

Rakowski, E., *Taking and Saving Lives*, 93 COLUM. L. REV. 1063 (1993).

Rawls, J., *The Idea of Public Reason Revisited*, 64 U. CHI. L. REV. 765 (1997).

Rawls, J., POLITICAL LIBERALISM (1993).

Rawls, J., A THEORY OF JUSTICE (1971).

Raz, J., PRACTICAL REASON AND NORMS (1975).

Raz, J., *The Relevance of Coherence*, 72 BOSTON UNIV. L. REV 273 (1992).

Rhoden, N., *The Judge in the Delivery Room: The Emergence of Court-Ordered Caesareans*, 74 CAL. L. REV.1951 (1986).

Robinson, G., HANDBOOK OF ADMIRALTY LAW IN THE UNITED STATES (1939).

Rosenberg, M., *Judicial Discretion of the Trial Court, Viewed from Above*, 22 SYRACUSE L. REV. 635 (1971).

Ross, A., ON LAW AND JUSTICE (1958).

Rubenfeld, J., *Affirmative Action*, 107 YALE L. J. 427 (1997).

Salzburg, S. and Powers, M., *Peremptory Challenges and Clash Between Impartiality and Group Representation*, 41 MD. L. REV. 337 (1982).

Sandel, M., DEMOCRACY'S DISCONTENT (1996).

Savigny, G. F. von., VON BERUF UNSERER ZEIT FÜR GESETZGEBUNG UND RECHTSWISSENSCHAFT (1814).

Sen, A., *Positional Objectivity*, 22 PHIL. & PUB. AFF. 126 (1993).

Skrentny, J., THE IRONICS OF AFFIRMATIVE ACTION (1996).

Stephani, G. et al., DROIT PÉNAL GÉNÉRAL (15th ed. 1995).

Sterne, L., THE LIFE AND OPINIONS OF TRISTAM SHANDY (World Classics ed. 1951).

Summers, R., INSTRUMENTALISM AND AMERICAN LEGAL THEORY (1982).

Sunstein, C., AFTER THE RIGHTS REVOLUTION (1990).

Sunstein, C., FREE MARKETS AND SOCIAL JUSTICE (1997).

Taylor, C., THE ETHICS OF AUTHENTICITY (1992).

Taylor, C., SOURCES OF THE SELF (1989).

Teichman, J., *Substitutes for Truth*, THE NEW CRITERION, Dec. 1997, at 71.

Thomas, H., THE SLAVE TRADE: THE HISTORY OF THE ATLANTIC SLAVE TRADE 1440-1870 (1998).

Thomson, J., THE REALM OF RIGHTS (1990).

Thomson, J., RIGHTS, RESTITUTION, AND RISK (1986).

Thucydides, *The Peloponnesian War*, THE LANDMARK THUCYDIDES (1996).

Twinning, W., KARL LLWELLYN AND THE REALIST MOVEMENT (1973).

Van Alstyne, W., *Congressional Power and Free Speech: Levy's Legacy Revisited*, 99 HARV. L. REV. 1089 (1986).

Warren, S. and Brandeis, L., *The Right to Privacy*, 4 HARV. L. REV. 193 (1880).

Wechsler, H., *Toward Neutral Principles of Constitutional Law*, 73 HARV. L. REV. 1 (1959).

Weinberg, G., A WORLD AT ARMS (1994).

Westen, P., The Meaning of Equality in Law, Science, Math and Morals: A Reply, 81 MICH. L. REV. 604 (1983).

White, W., THEY WERE EXPENDABLE (1942).

Williams, B., ETHICS AND THE LIMITS OF PHILOSOPHY (1985).

Williams, G., *The Foundations of Tortious Liability*, 1939 CAMB. L. J. 111 (1939).

Law and Philosophy Library

1. E. Bulygin, J.-L. Gardies and I. Niiniluoto (eds.): *Man, Law and Modern Forms of Life*. With an Introduction by M.D. Bayles. 1985
ISBN 90-277-1869-5

2. W. Sadurski: *Giving Desert Its Due*. Social Justice and Legal Theory. 1985
ISBN 90-277-1941-1

3. N. MacCormick and O. Weinberger: *An Institutional Theory of Law*. New Approaches to Legal Positivism. 1986
ISBN 90-277-2079-7

4. A. Aarnio: *The Rational as Reasonable*. A Treatise on Legal Justification. 1987
ISBN 90-277-2276-5

5. M.D. Bayles: *Principles of Law*. A Normative Analysis. 1987
ISBN 90-277-2412-1; Pb: 90-277-2413-X

6. A. Soeteman: *Logic in Law*. Remarks on Logic and Rationality in Normative Reasoning, Especially in Law. 1989
ISBN 0-7923-0042-4

7. C.T. Sistare: *Responsibility and Criminal Liability*. 1989
ISBN 0-7923-0396-2

8. A. Peczenik: *On Law and Reason*. 1989
ISBN 0-7923-0444-6

9. W. Sadurski: *Moral Pluralism and Legal Neutrality*. 1990
ISBN 0-7923-0565-5

10. M.D. Bayles: *Procedural Justice*. Allocating to Individuals. 1990
ISBN 0-7923-0567-1

11. P. Nerhot (ed.): *Law, Interpretation and Reality*. Essays in Epistemology, Hermeneutics and Jurisprudence. 1990
ISBN 0-7923-0593-0

12. A.W. Norrie: *Law, Ideology and Punishment*. Retrieval and Critique of the Liberal Ideal of Criminal Justice. 1991
ISBN 0-7923-1013-6

13. P. Nerhot (ed.): *Legal Knowledge and Analogy*. Fragments of Legal Epistemology, Hermeneutics and Linguistics. 1991
ISBN 0-7923-1065-9

14. O. Weinberger: *Law, Institution and Legal Politics*. Fundamental Problems of Legal Theory and Social Philosophy. 1991
ISBN 0-7923-1143-4

15. J. Wróblewski: *The Judicial Application of Law*. Edited by Z. Bańkowski and N. MacCormick. 1992
ISBN 0-7923-1569-3

16. T. Wilhelmsson: *Critical Studies in Private Law*. A Treatise on Need-Rational Principles in Modern Law. 1992
ISBN 0-7923-1659-2

17. M.D. Bayles: *Hart's Legal Philosophy*. An Examination. 1992
ISBN 0-7923-1981-8

18. D.W.P. Ruiter: *Institutional Legal Facts*. Legal Powers and their Effects. 1993
ISBN 0-7923-2441-2

19. J. Schonsheck: *On Criminalization*. An Essay in the Philosophy of the Criminal Law. 1994
ISBN 0-7923-2663-6

20. R.P. Malloy and J. Evensky (eds.): *Adam Smith and the Philosophy of Law and Economics*. 1994
ISBN 0-7923-2796-9

21. Z. Bańkowski, I. White and U. Hahn (eds.): *Informatics and the Foundations of Legal Reasoning*. 1995
ISBN 0-7923-3455-8

Law and Philosophy Library

22. E. Lagerspetz: *The Opposite Mirrors*. An Essay on the Conventionalist Theory of Institutions. 1995   ISBN 0-7923-3325-X

23. M. van Hees: *Rights and Decisions*. Formal Models of Law and Liberalism. 1995
                        ISBN 0-7923-3754-9

24. B. Anderson: *"Discovery" in Legal Decision-Making*. 1996   ISBN 0-7923-3981-9

25. S. Urbina: *Reason, Democracy, Society*. A Study on the Basis of Legal Thinking. 1996
                        ISBN 0-7923-4262-3

26. E. Attwooll: *The Tapestry of the Law*. Scotland, Legal Culture and Legal Theory. 1997
                        ISBN 0-7923-4310-7

27. J.C. Hage: *Reasoning with Rules*. An Essay on Legal Reasoning and Its Underlying Logic. 1997   ISBN 0-7923-4325-5

28. R.A. Hillman: *The Richness of Contract Law*. An Analysis and Critique of Contemporary Theories of Contract Law. 1997   ISBN 0-7923-4336-0; 0-7923-5063-4 (Pb)

29. C. Wellman: *An Approach to Rights*. Studies in the Philosophy of Law and Morals. 1997
                        ISBN 0-7923-4467-7

30. B. van Roermund: *Law, Narrative and Reality*. An Essay in Intercepting Politics. 1997
                        ISBN 0-7923-4621-1

31. I. Ward: *Kantianism, Postmodernism and Critical Legal Thought*. 1997
                        ISBN 0-7923-4745-5

32. H. Prakken: *Logical Tools for Modelling Legal Argument*. A Study of Defeasible Reasoning in Law. 1997   ISBN 0-7923-4776-5

33. T. May: *Autonomy, Authority and Moral Responsibility*. 1998   ISBN 0-7923-4851-6

34. M. Atienza and J.R. Manero: *A Theory of Legal Sentences*. 1998   ISBN 0-7923-4856-7

35. E.A. Christodoulidis: *Law and Reflexive Politics*. 1998   ISBN 0-7923-4954-7

36. L.M.M. Royakkers: *Extending Deontic Logic for the Formalisation of Legal Rules*. 1998
                        ISBN 0-7923-4982-2

37. J.J. Moreso: *Legal Indeterminacy and Constitutional Interpretation*. 1998
                        ISBN 0-7923-5156-8

38. W. Sadurski: *Freedom of Speech and Its Limits*. 1999   ISBN 0-7923-5523-7

39. J. Wolenski (ed.): *Kazimierz Opalek Selected Papers in Legal Philosophy*. 1999
                        ISBN 0-7923-5732-9

40. H.P. Visser 't Hooft: *Justice to Future Generations and the Environment*. 1999
                        ISBN 0-7923-5756-6

41. L.J. Wintgens (ed.): *The Law in Philosophical Perspectives*. My Philosophy of Law. 1999
    ISBN 0-7923-5796-5

42. A.R. Lodder: *DiaLaw*. On Legal Justification and Dialogical Models of Argumentation. 1999
                        ISBN 0-7923-5830-9

43. C. Redondo: *Reasons for Action and the Law*. 1999   ISBN 0-7923-5912-7

Law and Philosophy Library

KLUWER ACADEMIC PUBLISHERS – DORDRECHT / BOSTON / LONDON